THE STATE
OF FOOD
AND
AGRICULTURE

FOOD AND AGRICULTURE ORGANIZATION OF THE UNITED NATIONS
Rome, 2009

Produced by the
Electronic Publishing Policy and Support Branch
Communication Division
FAO

The designations employed and the presentation of material in this
information product do not imply the expression of any opinion whatsoever
on the part of the Food and Agriculture Organization of the United Nations (FAO)
concerning the legal or development status of any country, territory,
city or area or of its authorities, or concerning the delimitation of its frontiers
or boundaries. The mention of specific companies or products
of manufacturers, whether or not these have been patented, does not imply
that these have been endorsed or recommended by FAO in preference
to others of a similar nature that are not mentioned.
The views expressed in this information product are those of the author(s)
and do not necessarily reflect the views of FAO.

The designations employed and the presentation of material in the map does not imply
the expression of any opinion whatsoever on the part of FAO concerning the legal or
constitutional status of any country, territory or sea area, or concerning the delimitation
of frontiers.

ISBN 978-92-5-106215-9

Note:
Unless otherwise stated, data for China refer to China mainland.

Contents

Foreword vi
Acknowledgements viii
Abbreviations and acronyms x

**PART I
Livestock in the balance** 1

1. **Livestock in the balance** 3
   Livestock sector change 5
   Structure of the report and key messages 7
2. **Change in the livestock sector** 9
   Consumption trends and drivers 9
   Production trends and drivers 13
   Trade trends and drivers 19
   Outlook for consumption, production and trade 22
   Livestock sector diversity 25
   Transformation of livestock systems 27
   Challenges from continued livestock sector growth 30
   Key messages of the chapter 31
3. **Livestock, food security and poverty reduction** 32
   Livestock and livelihoods 33
   Livestock and food security 38
   Livestock sector transformation and the poor 42
   Livestock and poverty alleviation 43
   Competitiveness and the livestock sector 46
   Livestock policies for sector transition 50
   Key messages of the chapter 52
4. **Livestock and the environment** 53
   Livestock production systems and ecosystems 53
   Livestock and climate change 63
   Improving natural-resource use by livestock production 66
   Dealing with climate change and livestock 70
   Key messages of the chapter 74
5. **Livestock and human and animal health** 75
   Economic and human-health threats related to livestock disease 76
   Disease control and risk management 86
   Key messages of the chapter 93
6. **Conclusions: balancing society's objectives for livestock** 94
   Balancing opportunities against risks 94
   Balancing the needs of different smallholders 94
   Balancing food security and nutrition 95
   Balancing the trade-offs among systems, species, goals and impacts 96
   Balancing objectives in different societies 96
   The way forward: towards an agenda for action for the livestock sector 97
   Key messages of the report 98

**PART II
World food and agriculture in review** 101

Trends in global food security 104
Agricultural price developments – high variability of basic food prices 105

Domestic food prices in developing countries 107
Medium-term prospects for international agricultural commodity prices 107
Agricultural production 109
Agricultural trade 111
Policy responses to higher food prices and their impact on agricultural markets 113
Impact of policy responses on global markets 118
Conclusions 119

PART III
Statistical annex   123

Table A1   Production of livestock products, 1995–2007 125
Table A2   Production of main categories of meat, 1995–2007 130
Table A3   Per capita consumption of livestock products, 1995–2005 135
Table A4   Per capita calorie intake from livestock products, 1995–2005 140
Table A5   Per capita protein intake from livestock products, 1995–2005 145
Table A6   Trade in livestock products, 1995–2006 150

References 157
Special chapters of *The State of Food and Agriculture* 165

TABLES

1. Per capita consumption of livestock products by region, country group and country, 1980 and 2005 11
2. Urbanization: levels and growth rates 13
3. Production of livestock products by region, 1980 and 2007 15
4. Production of main categories of meat by region, 1987 and 2007 16
5. Global trade in livestock products, 1980 and 2006 21
6. Meat consumption by region, 2000 and 2050 (projected) 24
7. Global livestock population and production, by production system, average 2001–2003 26
8. Use of feed concentrate by region, 1980 and 2005 29
9. Use of feed concentrate by commodity group, 2005 30
10. Number and location of poor livestock keepers by category and agro-ecological zone 33
11. Percentage of rural households owning livestock, share of income from livestock and number of livestock per household, by country 34
12. Land use by region and country group, 1961, 1991 and 2007 55
13. Major environmental impacts of different production systems 62
14. Direct and indirect impacts of climate change on livestock production systems 66
15. Some estimated costs of disease in developed and developing countries 78
16. Some estimated costs of food-borne illness in developed countries 79

BOXES

1. Measuring productivity growth in the livestock sector 18
2. Technological progress in the poultry industry 20
3. Coordination in livestock value chains 28
4. Food versus feed: do livestock reduce availability of food for human consumption? 39
5. The Dairy Goat Development Project in Ethiopia 41

6. Sector transition – poultry in China 44
7. Sector transition – dairy in India and Kenya 46
8. The livestock sector – why supply-side factors matter 48
9. Kuroiler™ chickens – linking backyard poultry systems to the private sector 50
10. Expansion of biofuels production 54
11. Conserving animal genetic resources 58
12. Assessing the contribution of livestock to GHG emissions 64
13. The European Union – integrating environmental protection requirements
into the Common Agricultural Policy 68
14. Reducing nitrate pollution in Denmark 70
15. Tapping the climate change mitigation potential of improved land management
in livestock systems 72
16. Animal health and welfare 80
17. Global Rinderpest Eradication Programme (GREP) – elements of a success 88
18. One World, One Health 91
19. Food emergencies 105
20. Domestic food prices in developing countries remain high 110
21. A return to high agricultural commodity prices? 112

FIGURES

1. Per capita consumption of major food items in developing countries, 1961–2005 9
2. Per capita intake of energy derived from livestock products by region, 1961–2005 10
3. Per capita GDP and meat consumption by country, 2005 12
4 Production of meat, eggs and milk by developing country region, 1961–2007 14
5. World production of main categories of meat, 1961–2007 16
6. Sources of growth in livestock production: average annual growth in number
of animals and in output per animal, 1980–2007 17
7. Value of livestock products as a share of global agricultural export value,
1961–2006 21
8. Net exports of meat and dairy products from developed and developing
countries, 1961–2006 22
9. Meat consumption and share of net imports in consumption, least-developed
countries, 1961–2005 23
10. Classification of livestock production systems 25
11. Percentage of rural households owning livestock, by expenditure quintile 35
12. Share of income from livestock activity in rural households, by expenditure
quintile 36
13. Number of livestock held by rural households, by expenditure quintile 37
14. Percentage of households' total livestock production that is sold, by expenditure
quintile 38
15. Impacts of animal diseases on human well-being 76
16. Balancing policy objectives 97
17. FAO estimates of number of undernourished people in 2009, by region 104
18. Indices of agricultural prices 106
19. Consumer food price inflation 2007–2009, selected countries 108
20. Real cereal prices 109
21. Growth in agricultural production, by region 114
22. Long-term trends in agricultural production, by region 115
23. Changes in global real food commodity exports 115
24. Changes in real food commodity net trade, by region 116
25. Estimated impact of production, consumption, stock and border measures
on rice and wheat markets 120

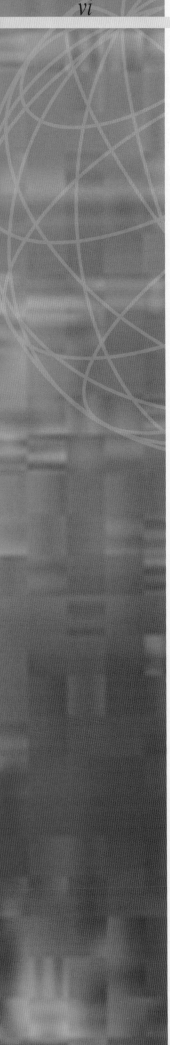

Foreword

This year's report of *The State of Food and Agriculture* is being published at a crucial point in time. The world is going through a financial turbulence that has led to a serious economic setback. But this must not mask the global food crisis that has shaken the international agricultural economy and proven the fragility of the global agricultural system.

Unfortunately, today increasing hunger is a global phenomenon and no part of the world is immune. Our estimates show that the number of those suffering from chronic hunger in the world has topped one billion in 2009 – one billion and 20 million to be more precise. The challenge that lies ahead is to secure the food security of these one billion hungry people and also to double food production in order to feed a population projected to reach 9.2 billion by 2050.

At the global level, recognition has been growing that agricultural development is crucial if we are to reverse this trend and start making significant and sustainable progress towards lifting millions of people out of poverty and food insecurity. This recognition is increasingly finding expression at the highest political levels.

However, the global food and agriculture sector is facing several challenges, including demographic and dietary changes, climate change, bioenergy development and natural-resource constraints. These and related forces are also driving structural changes in the livestock sector, which has developed as one of the most dynamic parts of the agricultural economy.

The global livestock sector has been undergoing change at an unprecedented pace over the past few decades, a process that has been termed the "livestock revolution". Booming demand in the world's most rapidly growing economies for food derived from animals has led to large increases in livestock production, supported by major technological innovations and structural changes in the sector. This surging demand has been mostly met by commercial livestock production and associated food chains. At the same time, millions of rural people still keep livestock in traditional production systems, where they support livelihoods and household food security.

The rapid transition of the livestock sector has been taking place in an institutional void. The speed of change has often significantly outpaced the capacity of governments and societies to provide the necessary policy and regulatory framework to ensure an appropriate balance between the provision of private and public goods. A number of issues are confronting the sector:

- There is increasing pressure on ecosystems and natural resources – land, water and biodiversity. The livestock sector is only one of many sectors and human activities contributing to the pressure. In some cases its impact on ecosystems is out of proportion with the economic significance of the sector. At the same time, the sector is increasingly facing natural-resource constraints and growing competition with other sectors for a number of resources. Awareness is also increasing of the interactions between livestock and climate change, with the livestock sector both contributing to it and suffering from its impacts. Conversely, it is also being recognized that the sector can play a key role in mitigating climate change through adoption of improved technologies.
- The globalization of food systems has meant an increasing flow of technology, capital, people and goods, including live animals and products of animal origin, around the world. Increased trade flows, along with the growing concentration of animals, often in proximity to large human populations, have contributed to increased risks of spreading of animal diseases and to a rise in animal-related human health risks globally. At the same time, inadequate access to veterinary services jeopardizes the livelihoods

and development prospects of many poor livestock holders throughout the developing world.

- A final critical issue relates to the social implications of the structural changes in the sector and the role of poor people in the process. How can the livestock sector contribute more effectively to alleviating poverty and ensuring food security for all? Has the rapid development of the sector in many countries benefited smallholders, or are they being increasingly marginalized? If so, is this inevitable, or can the poor be brought into the process of livestock development?

Within each of these three areas, the report discusses the most critical challenges and opportunities facing the sector. It highlights systemic risks and failures resulting from a process of growth and transformation that has outpaced the capacity and willingness of governments and societies to control and regulate. It tries to identify issues that require solutions at various levels to allow the livestock sector to meet society's expectations in the future in terms of provision of both private and public goods. The issue of governance is central. Identifying and defining the appropriate role of government, in its broadest sense, is the cornerstone on which future development of the livestock sector must build.

The challenges posed by the livestock sector cannot be solved by a single string of actions or by individual actors alone. They require integrated efforts by a wide range of stakeholders. Such efforts need to tackle the root causes in areas where the social, environmental and health impacts of the livestock sector and its rapid development are negative. They must also be realistic and equitable. By focusing our attention constructively, we can move towards a more responsible livestock sector, allowing it to meet the multiple, often competing, objectives of society. It is my hope that this report can contribute towards the first important steps in this direction.

Jacques Diouf
FAO DIRECTOR-GENERAL

Acknowledgements

The State of Food and Agriculture 2009 was prepared by a core team led by Terri Raney and comprising Stefano Gerosa, Yasmeen Khwaja and Jakob Skoet, all of the FAO Agricultural Development Economics Division; Henning Steinfeld, Anni McLeod and Carolyn Opio all of the FAO Animal Production and Health Division; and Merritt Cluff of the FAO Trade and Markets Division. Liliana Maldonado and Paola Di Santo provided secretarial and administrative support.

Overall guidance on the preparation of the report was provided by Hafez Ghanem, Assistant Director-General of the Economic and Social Development Department of FAO; as well as Kostas Stamoulis, Director, and Keith Wiebe, Deputy Director, of the FAO Agricultural Development Economics Division. Additional guidance and support for the preparation of Part I of the report was provided by James Butler, Deputy Director-General; Modibo Traoré, Assistant Director-General of the FAO Agriculture and Consumer Protection Department; and Samuel Jutzi, Director of the FAO Animal Production and Health Division.

Part I of the report, *Livestock in the balance*, was co-edited by Terri Raney, Jakob Skoet and Henning Steinfeld. Drafting was also undertaken by Stefano Gerosa and Yasmeen Khwaja, of the FAO Agricultural Development Economics Division; Jeroen Dijkman, Pierre Gerber, Nigel Key, Anni McLeod, Carolyn Opio and Henning Steinfeld, all of the FAO Animal Production and Health Division. Additional contributions were provided by Daniela Battaglia, Katinka de Balogh, Joseph Domenech, Irene Hoffmann, Simon Mack and Jan Slingenbergh, all of the FAO Animal Production and Health Division; Bernadete Neves, Luca Tasciotti and Alberto Zezza, all of the FAO Agricultural and Development Economics Division; Renata Clarke, Sandra Honour and Ellen Muehlhoff, all of the FAO Nutrition and Consumer Protection Division; Nancy Morgan of the FAO Investment Centre Division; and Patricia Colbert, Eve Crowley and Ilaria Sisto, all of the FAO Gender, Equity and Rural Employment Division.

Part I of the report drew on two forthcoming volumes entitled *Livestock in a Changing Landscape*, to be published in late 2009 by Island Press, and prepared with the support of several organizations, including FAO, the International Livestock Research Institute (ILRI), FAO Livestock, Environment and Development Initiative (LEAD), the Scientific Committee on Problems of the Environment (SCOPE), Bern University of Applied Sciences, the Swiss College of Agriculture (SHL), the Centre de coopération internationale en recherche agronomique pour le développement (CIRAD), and the Woods Institute for the Environment at Stanford University.

It also drew on research papers prepared under the Pro-Poor Livestock Policy Initiative (PPLPI), funded by the Government of the United Kingdom, and the LEAD, funded by the European Union and the Governments of Denmark, France and Switzerland.

Background papers for Part I of the report were prepared by Klaas Dietze (FAO); Jeroen Dijkman (FAO) and Keith Sones (Keith Sones Associates); Klaus Frohberg (University of Bonn); Jørgen Henriksen (Henriksen Advice, Copenhagen); Brian Perry (University of Oxford) and Keith Sones (Keith Sones Associates); Robert Pym (University of Queensland); Prakash Shetty (University of Southampton); Farzad Taheripour, Thomas W. Hertel and Wallace E. Tyner (Purdue University); Philip Thornton (International Livestock Research Institute) and Pierre Gerber (FAO); and Ray Trewin (Australian National University).

Part I of the report benefited greatly from two external workshops, made possible with financial support from the World Bank. The first workshop, held in November 2008, had participation of the following authors of background papers: Jeroen Dijkman, Pierre Gerber, Jørgen Henriksen, Brian Perry, Robert Pym, Keith Sones and Ray Trewin, in addition to Jimmy Smith (World Bank) and FAO staff from the Agricultural

Development Economics Division, the Animal Production and Health Division and the Nutrition and Consumer Protection Division. The second workshop, held in April 2009, had external participation of: Vinod Ahuja (Indian Institute of Management), Peter Bazeley (Peter Bazeley Development Consulting), Harold Mooney (University of Stanford), Clare Narrod (International Food Policy Research Institute), Oene Oenema (University of Wageningen), Fritz Schneider (Swiss College of Agriculture), Jimmy Smith (World Bank), Steve Staal (International Livestock Research Institute), and Laping Wu (China Agricultural University).

Part II of the report, *World food and agriculture in review*, was prepared by Jakob Skoet and Merritt Cluff, based on inputs from the Commodity Policy and Projections Team of the FAO Trade and Markets Division, with specific contributions from Merritt Cluff, Cheng Fang, Holger Matthey, Grégoire Tallard and Koji Yanagishima.

Part III of the report, *Statistical annex*, was prepared by Stefano Gerosa.

The expert contributions of the editors, designers, layout artists and reproduction specialists of the FAO Electronic Publishing and Support Branch are also gratefully acknowledged.

Abbreviations and acronyms

BSE	bovine spongiform encephalopathy
CBPP	contagious bovine pleuropneumonia
CIS	Commonwealth of Independent States
CSF	classical swine fever
EU	European Union
FMD	foot-and-mouth disease
GDP	gross domestic product
GHG	greenhouse gas
GIEWS	Global Information and Early Warning System
HPAI	highly pathogenic avian influenza
IFPRI	International Food Policy Research Institute
IMF	International Monetary Fund
IPCC	Intergovernmental Panel on Climate Change
ISFP	Initiative on Soaring Food Prices
LDC	least-developed country
OECD	Organisation for Economic Co-operation and Development
OIE	World Organisation for Animal Health
PPR	peste des petits ruminants
RIGA	Rural Income Generating Activities
WHO	World Health Organization

Part I

LIVESTOCK
IN THE BALANCE

Part I

1. Livestock in the balance

Livestock contribute 40 percent of the global value of agricultural output and support the livelihoods and food security of almost a billion people. The livestock sector is one of the fastest growing parts of the agricultural economy, driven by income growth and supported by technological and structural change. The growth and transformation of the sector offer opportunities for agricultural development, poverty reduction and food security gains, but the rapid pace of change risks marginalizing smallholders, and systemic risks to the environment and human health must be addressed to ensure sustainability.

In many developing countries, livestock keeping is a multifunctional activity. Beyond their direct role in generating food and income, livestock are a valuable asset, serving as a store of wealth, collateral for credit and an essential safety net during times of crisis. Livestock are also central to mixed farming systems. They consume waste products from crop and food production, help control insects and weeds, produce manure for fertilizing and conditioning fields and provide draught power for ploughing and transport. In some areas, livestock perform a public sanitation function by consuming waste products that would otherwise pose a serious pollution and public health problem.

At the global level, livestock contribute 15 percent of total food energy and 25 percent of dietary protein. Products from livestock provide essential micronutrients that are not easily obtained from plant-based foods.

Almost 80 percent of the world's undernourished people live in rural areas (UN Millennium Project, 2004) and most depend on agriculture, including livestock, for their livelihoods. Data from the FAO database on Rural Income Generating Activities (RIGA) show that, in a sample of 14 countries, 60 percent of rural households keep livestock (FAO, 2009a). A significant share of the livestock outputs of rural households is sold, making a sizeable contribution to household cash income. In some countries, the poorest rural households are more likely to hold livestock than wealthier ones; although the average number of livestock per household is quite small, this makes livestock an important entry point for poverty alleviation efforts.

Women and men typically face different livelihood opportunities and constraints in managing livestock. Small livestock keepers, particularly women, face many challenges, including: poor access to markets, goods, services and technical information; periodic drought and disease; competing resource uses; policies that favour larger-scale producers or external markets; and weak institutions. Knowledge about, and responsibilities for, various aspects of animal husbandry and livestock production commonly differ between women and men and between age groups. For example, a woman might be responsible for preventing or treating illness in the household's livestock, a man for milking or marketing, boys for grazing or watering, and girls for providing fodder to stall-fed animals.

Rural women are as likely as men to keep livestock, although the number of animals they keep tends to be lower and they are more likely to own poultry and small ruminants than large animals.

Evidence suggests that poor people, especially young children and their mothers in developing countries, are not consuming enough animal-based food (IFPRI, 2004), while other people, particularly in developed countries, are consuming too much (PAHO, 2006). However, high rates of undernourishment and micronutrient deficiency among the rural poor suggest that, despite often keeping livestock, the rural poor consume very little animal-based food. About 4–5 billion people in the world are deficient in iron, which is essential especially for the health of pregnant and lactating women and for the physical and cognitive development of young children (SCN, 2004). This and other important nutrients are more readily available in meat, milk and eggs than in plant-based foods (Neumann et al., 2003). Increasing access to affordable animal-based foods could thus significantly improve nutritional status and health for many poor people. However, excessive consumption of livestock products is associated with increased risk of obesity, heart disease and other non-communicable diseases (WHO/FAO, 2003). Furthermore, the rapid growth of the livestock sector means that competition for land and other productive resources puts upward pressure on prices for staple grains as well as negative pressures on the natural-resource base, potentially reducing food security.

Powerful forces of economic change are transforming the livestock sector in many rapidly growing developing countries. Production of livestock, especially pigs and poultry, is becoming more intensive, geographically concentrated, vertically integrated and linked with global supply chains. Higher animal-health and food-safety standards are improving public health, but are also widening the gap between small livestock keepers and large commercial producers. The "livestock ladder" – by which smallholders climb up the scale of production and out of poverty – is missing several rungs (Sones and Dijkman, 2008).

Case studies show that small commercial livestock producers can be competitive,

even in a rapidly changing sector, if they have appropriate institutional support and the opportunity cost of their labour remains low (Delgado, Narrod and Tiongco, 2008). Historical experience from member countries of the Organisation for Economic Co-operation and Development (OECD) shows that policy support in the form of subsidies and trade protection is very costly and has limited success in preventing the exit of smallholders from livestock production. Policy interventions aimed at improving smallholder productivity, reducing transaction costs and overcoming technical market barriers can be very helpful, but direct subsidies and protection could be counterproductive.

As economies grow and employment opportunities increase, the concomitant rising opportunity costs for labour often induce smallholders to abandon livestock keeping in favour of more-productive, less-onerous work in other sectors. This is an integral part of the economic development process and should not be viewed as a negative trend. Concerns arise when the pace of change in the livestock sector exceeds the capacity of the rest of the economy to provide alternative employment opportunities. Appropriate policy responses in this situation involve measures to ease the transition out of the sector, including the provision of social safety nets, and broader rural development policies, such as investments in education, infrastructure and growth-oriented institutional reforms. Smallholder agriculture should be the starting point for development, not the end-point.

Some livestock keepers are simply too poor, and their operations too small, to be able to overcome the economic and technical barriers that prevent their expansion into commercial production. Women typically face greater challenges than men, as they have poorer access to and control over livestock and other resources such as land, credit, labour, technology and services necessary to take advantage of growth opportunities. Most of the very poor depend on livestock as a safety net rather than using them as the basis of a commercial enterprise. Better access to animal-health services and a greater voice in livestock disease-control measures would improve their situation in the short run, but they would also benefit more from the creation of alternative social safety nets that protect livelihoods from external shocks. The vulnerabilities and constraints facing the poorest livestock keepers, and the important safety-net function livestock play for them, should be borne in mind. Indeed, the multiple roles of livestock in the livelihoods of people living in poverty should be considered in any policy decisions that affect them.

The agriculture sector is the world's largest user and steward of natural resources and, like any productive activity, livestock production exacts an environmental cost. The livestock sector is also often associated with policy distortions and market failures, and therefore places burdens on the environment that are often out of proportion to its economic importance. For example, livestock contribute less than 2 percent of global gross domestic product (GDP) but produce 18 percent of global greenhouse gas (GHG) emissions (Steinfeld *et al.*, 2006); it should be noted, however, that GDP underestimates the economic and social contribution of livestock as it does not capture the value of the numerous multifunctional contributions of livestock to livelihoods. There is thus an urgent need to improve the resource-use efficiency of livestock production and to reduce the negative environmental externalities produced by the sector.

Livestock grazing occupies 26 percent of the earth's ice-free land surface (Table 12, page 55), and the production of livestock feed uses 33 percent of agricultural cropland (Steinfeld *et al.*, 2006). The expansion of land used for livestock development can contribute to deforestation in some countries, while intensification of livestock production can cause overgrazing in others. The increasing geographic concentration of livestock production means that the manure produced by animals often exceeds the absorptive capacity of the local area. Manure thus becomes a waste product rather than being the valuable resource it is in less-concentrated, mixed production systems. These wastes can become valuable resources again if proper incentives, regulations and technology, such as anaerobic digestion, are applied. More generally, the negative impacts of livestock on the environment can be mitigated, but appropriate policies must be implemented.

The concentration of animal production in close proximity to human population centres poses increasing risks for human health arising from livestock diseases. Livestock diseases have always interacted with human populations. Most strains of influenza, for example, are believed to have originated in animals. Furthermore, livestock pathogens have always posed a production challenge because, at the biological level, they compete with humans for the productive output of animals. Livestock diseases impose a heavy burden on the poor because poor livestock keepers live in closer proximity to their animals, they have less access to veterinary services, and the measures used to control certain disease outbreaks can threaten the basis of their livelihoods and the safety net they rely on in emergencies. Improving the management of livestock with a view to controlling diseases can provide significant economic, social and human-health benefits for poor people and society more broadly. This may require relocating livestock production away from human population centres in order to minimize the risk of disease transmission.

Livestock sector change

The State of Food and Agriculture last provided a comprehensive review of the livestock sector in 1982. Since then, the livestock sector has developed and changed rapidly in response to shifts in the global economy, rising incomes in many developing countries and changing societal expectations. The sector is increasingly expected to provide safe and plentiful food for growing urban populations as well as public goods related to poverty reduction and food security, environmental sustainability and public health. These trends and the challenges they entail were identified a decade ago by Delgado *et al.* (1999), who coined the term the "livestock revolution" to describe the process that is transforming the sector:

> *A revolution is taking place in global agriculture that has profound implications for human health, livelihoods, and the environment. Population growth, urbanization, and income growth in developing countries are fueling a massive increase in demand for food of animal*

origin. These changes in the diets of billions of people could significantly improve the well-being of many rural poor. Governments and industry must prepare for this continuing revolution with long-run policies and investments that will satisfy consumer demand, improve nutrition, direct income growth opportunities to those who need them most, and alleviate environmental and public health stress.

(Delgado *et al.,* 1999)

Rapid income growth and urbanization over the past three decades, combined with underlying population growth, are driving growth in demand for meat and other animal products in many developing countries. Supply-side factors, such as the globalization of supply chains for feed, genetic stock and other technology, are further transforming the structure of the sector. The sector is complex and differs according to location and species. A growing divide is emerging; large-scale industrial producers serve dynamic growing markets whereas traditional pastoralists and smallholders, while often continuing to support local livelihoods and provide food security, risk marginalization.

In many parts of the world, the transformation of the livestock sector is occurring in the absence of strong governance, resulting in market failures related to natural-resource use and public health. Interventions to correct market failures have been largely absent; in some cases, government actions have created market distortions. While the livestock sector is not alone in this regard, institutional and policy failures have led to opportunities presented by growth in the livestock sector being missed. As a result, the sector has not contributed as much as it might have to poverty alleviation and food security. Nor has growth in the sector been adequately managed to deal with the increasing pressures on natural resources or to provide control and management of animal disease. Correcting market failures is thus an important underlying rationale for public policy intervention.

Meeting society's expectations

The livestock sector, like much of agriculture, plays a complex economic, social and environmental role. Society expects the sector to continue to meet rising world demand for animal products cheaply, quickly and safely. It must do so in an environmentally sustainable way, while managing the incidence and consequences of animal diseases and providing opportunities for rural development, poverty reduction and food security. Given the large number of people who depend on livestock for their food security and livelihoods and the high environmental and human-health costs often associated with the sector, the challenge for policy-makers is to strike a fine balance among competing goals.

The livestock sector is one among many human activities contributing to the increasing pressure on ecosystems and natural resources: land, air, water and biodiversity. At the same time, the sector is increasingly constrained by this pressure on natural resources and the growing competition with other sectors for resources. There is also increasing awareness that climate change is creating a new set of conditions in which the sector must operate as well as imposing additional constraints on it. Climate change will alter what men and women do, exposing them to different risks and opportunities. For example, men may migrate for work while women and youth will take on new responsibilities. Women tend to be more vulnerable to external shocks owing to unequal access to resources, lower level of education, increased work burden and poorer health.

Growing international trade in livestock and livestock products and the increasing concentration of livestock production in close proximity to large human populations have increased the risks of animal disease outbreaks and the emergence of new animal-related human-health threats. At the same time, inadequate access to veterinary services jeopardizes the livelihoods and development prospects of many livestock holders throughout the developing world.

Livestock can provide a pathway out of poverty for some smallholders, and policy-makers need to consider the different roles that livestock play in supporting livelihoods. For those smallholders who have the potential to compete as commercial enterprises, judicious policy and institutional support is needed to help them access technology, information and markets to improve their productivity. At the same time, the forces of economic change (to be discussed in Chapter 2) mean that some smallholders will need assistance to make the transition out of the sector. For others, especially the very poor, livestock primarily provide a safety-net function. The livestock sector requires renewed attention and investments from the agricultural research and development community and robust institutional and governance mechanisms that reflect the diversity within the sector. The livestock sector can contribute more effectively to improving food security and reducing poverty, but policy measures are required to ensure that it does so in ways that are environmentally sustainable and safe for human health.

This edition of *The State of Food and Agriculture* argues that the livestock sector could contribute more positively to society's goals, but significant policy and institutional changes are required. The rapid growth of the sector, in a setting of weak institutions and governance, has given rise to systemic risks that may have serious implications for livelihoods, human and animal health and the environment. Investments are required to improve livestock productivity and resource-use efficiency, both to meet growing consumer demand and to mitigate environmental and health concerns. Policies, institutions and technologies must consider the particular needs of poor smallholders, especially during times of crisis and change.

Structure of the report and key messages

Chapter 2 discusses trends in livestock, the underlying economic and social drivers, technological changes and consequent structural transformation of the sector, highlighting their impact on poverty and food security, the environment and human health. The social implications of the trends in the livestock sector, and the role of livestock in economic development, poverty alleviation and food security are the themes of Chapter 3. Chapter 4 focuses on the interrelationship of livestock with natural resources and ecosystems, including its role in climate change. Chapter 5 discusses the multiple challenges posed by animal diseases

and their management. The final chapter addresses the policy and institutional reforms that are needed to improve the performance of the livestock sector in supporting food security and poverty reduction while ensuring environmental sustainability and protection of human health.

Key messages of the report

- The livestock sector is one of the most dynamic parts of the agricultural economy. The sector has expanded rapidly in recent decades and demand for livestock products is expected to continue growing strongly through the middle of this century, driven by population growth, rising affluence and urbanization. Decisive action is required if the sector is to satisfy this growth in ways that support society's goals for poverty reduction and food security, environmental sustainability and improved human health.
- The livestock sector makes important contributions to food security and poverty reduction. It, however, could do more given judicious policy and institutional reforms and significant public and private investments aimed at: (i) enhancing the ability of smallholders to take advantage of the opportunities offered by growth in the sector; (ii) protecting the poorest households for whom livestock serve as a crucial safety net; and (iii) enacting broader rural development policies to ease the transition of some livestock keepers out of the sector.
- Governance of the livestock sector should be strengthened to ensure that its development is environmentally sustainable. Livestock production is placing increasing pressures on land, air, water and biodiversity. Corrective action is needed to encourage the provision of public goods, such as valuable ecosystem services and environmental protection. This will involve addressing policy and market failures and developing and applying appropriate incentives and penalties. Livestock contribute to and are a victim of climate change. The sector can play a key role in mitigating climate change. For example, adoption

of improved technologies, encouraged by appropriate economic incentives, can lead to reduced emissions of GHGs by livestock.

- Some animal-health services are public goods in that they protect human and animal public health and thus benefit society as a whole. Animal diseases reduce production and productivity, disrupt local and national economies, threaten human health and exacerbate poverty, but producers face a range of risks and differ in the incentives they are offered and their capacities to respond. Animal-health systems have been neglected in many parts of the world, leading to institutional weaknesses and information gaps as well as inadequate investments in animal-health-related public goods. Producers at every level, including poor livestock keepers, must be engaged in the development of animal-disease and food-safety programmes.

2. Change in the livestock sector

Rapid growth and technological innovation have led to profound structural changes in the livestock sector, including: a move from smallholder mixed farms towards large-scale specialized industrial production systems; a shift in the geographic locus of demand and supply to the developing world; and an increasing emphasis on global sourcing and marketing. These changes have implications for the ability of the livestock sector to expand production sustainably in ways that promote food security, poverty reduction and public health. This chapter reviews trends in and the outlook for consumption, production and trade of livestock products and accompanying technological and structural changes in the sector. It discusses the structure and diversity of the livestock sector and factors that will shape the sector over the coming decades. Challenges facing efforts to improve livelihoods, alleviate poverty and food insecurity, reduce pressures on natural resources and manage human and animal diseases are highlighted.

Consumption trends and drivers[1]

Trends in consumption

Consumption of livestock products has increased rapidly in developing countries over the past decades, particularly from the 1980s onwards. Growth in consumption of livestock products per capita has markedly outpaced growth in consumption of other major food commodity groups (Figure 1). Since the early 1960s, consumption of milk per capita in the developing countries has almost doubled, meat consumption more than tripled and egg consumption increased by a factor of five.

---

[1] More detailed information about the most recent trends in consumption, production and trade, by country, can be found in the Statistical annex at the end of this report. The analysis and data presented in this and the following sections cover consumption, production and trade of livestock products. Animal-source food of other origins – such as fish and bushmeat – are not included.

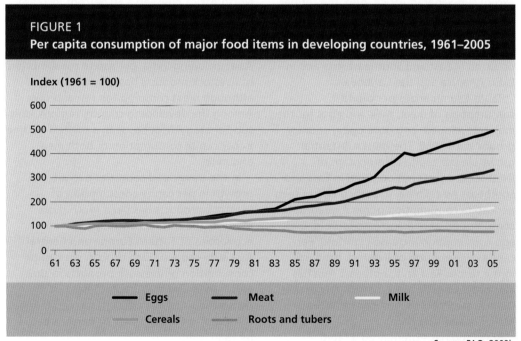

FIGURE 1
Per capita consumption of major food items in developing countries, 1961–2005

Index (1961 = 100)

Eggs   Meat   Milk

Cereals   Roots and tubers

Source: FAO, 2009b.

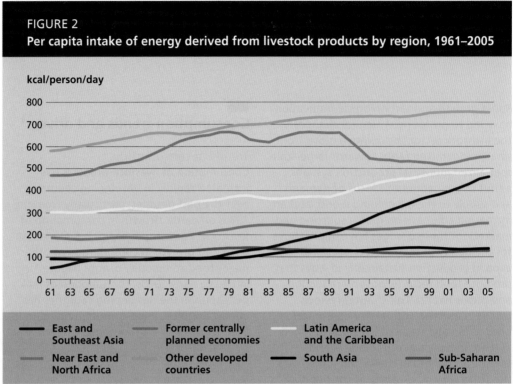

FIGURE 2

Per capita intake of energy derived from livestock products by region, 1961–2005

kcal/person/day

Note: Livestock products include meat, eggs and milk and dairy products (excluding butter).   Source: FAO, 2009b.

This has translated into considerable growth in global per capita intake of energy derived from livestock products, but with significant regional differences (Figure 2). Consumption has increased in all regions except sub-Saharan Africa. Also, the former centrally planned economies of Eastern Europe and Central Asia saw major declines around 1990. The greatest increases have occurred in East and Southeast Asia and in Latin America and the Caribbean.

Table 1 summarizes per capita consumption of meat, milk and eggs for the major developed- and developing-country groups since 1980. The most substantial growth in per capita consumption of livestock products has occurred in East and Southeast Asia. China, in particular, has seen per capita consumption of meat quadruple, consumption of milk increase tenfold, and egg consumption increase eightfold. Per capita consumption of livestock products in the rest of East and Southeast Asia has also grown significantly, particularly in the Democratic People's Republic of Korea, Malaysia and Viet Nam.

Brazil too has experienced a rapid expansion in the consumption of livestock products – per capita consumption of meat

has almost doubled, while that of milk has increased by 40 percent. In the rest of Latin America and the Caribbean, increases in consumption have been more modest, with some exceptions. The Near East and North Africa has seen a 50 percent increase in consumption of meat and a 70 percent increase in egg consumption, although milk consumption has declined slightly. In South Asia, including India, per capita consumption of livestock products has grown steadily, although meat consumption remains low. Among the developing-country regions, only sub-Saharan Africa has seen a modest decline in per capita consumption of both meat and milk.

In the developed countries overall, growth in per capita consumption of livestock products has been much more modest. The former centrally planned economies of Eastern Europe and Central Asia suffered a sudden drop in per capita consumption of livestock products in the early 1990s and consumption has not recovered since – as a result, per capita meat consumption in 2005 was 20 percent below its 1980 level.

Consumption of livestock products per capita in developing regions is still substantially lower than in the developed world, even though some rapidly developing countries are narrowing the gap (Table 1). There is significant potential for increasing per capita consumption of livestock products in many developing countries. The extent to which this potential will translate into increasing demand depends on future income growth and its distribution among countries and regions. Rising incomes are more likely to generate additional demand for livestock products in low-income countries than in middle- and high-income countries.

Drivers of consumption growth

The growing demand for livestock products in a number of developing countries has been driven by economic growth, rising per capita incomes and urbanization. In recent decades, the global economy has experienced an unparalleled expansion, with per capita incomes rising rapidly. The relationship between per capita income and

meat consumption for 2005 is illustrated in Figure 3. The figure shows a strongly positive effect of increased incomes on livestock consumption at lower income levels but a less positive, or even negative, effect at high levels of GDP per capita.

Demographic factors also underlie changing consumption patterns of livestock products. An important factor has been urbanization. The share of total population living in urban areas is larger in the developed countries than in developing countries (73 percent compared with an average of 42 percent). However, urbanization is increasing faster in developing countries than in developed countries. In the period 1980–2003, the urban population in developing countries grew at average annual rates ranging from 4.9 percent in sub-Saharan Africa to 2.6 percent in Latin America, compared with an average of only 0.8 percent in developed countries (Table 2).

TABLE 1

Per capita consumption of livestock products by region, country group and country, 1980 and 2005

REGION/COUNTRY GROUP/ COUNTRY	MEAT		MILK		EGGS	
	1980	2005	1980	2005	1980	2005
	(kg/capita/year)		(kg/capita/year)		(kg/capita/year)	
DEVELOPED COUNTRIES	76.3	82.1	197.6	207.7	14.3	13.0
Former centrally planned economies	63.1	51.5	181.2	176.0	13.2	11.4
Other developed countries	82.4	95.8	205.3	221.8	14.8	13.8
DEVELOPING COUNTRIES	14.1	30.9	33.9	50.5	2.5	8.0
East and Southeast Asia	12.8	48.2	4.5	21.0	2.7	15.4
China	13.7	59.5	2.3	23.2	2.5	20.2
Rest of East and Southeast Asia	10.7	24.1	9.9	16.4	3.3	5.1
Latin America and the Caribbean	41.1	61.9	101.1	109.7	6.2	8.6
Brazil	41.0	80.8	85.9	120.8	5.6	6.8
Rest of Latin America and the Caribbean	41.1	52.4	109.0	104.1	6.5	9.4
South Asia	4.2	5.8	41.5	69.5	0.8	1.7
India	3.7	5.1	38.5	65.2	0.7	1.8
Rest of South Asia	5.7	8.0	52.0	83.1	0.9	1.5
Near East and North Africa	17.9	27.3	86.1	81.6	3.7	6.3
Sub-Saharan Africa	14.4	13.3	33.6	30.1	1.6	1.6
WORLD	30.0	41.2	75.7	82.1	5.5	9.0

Source: FAO, 2009b.

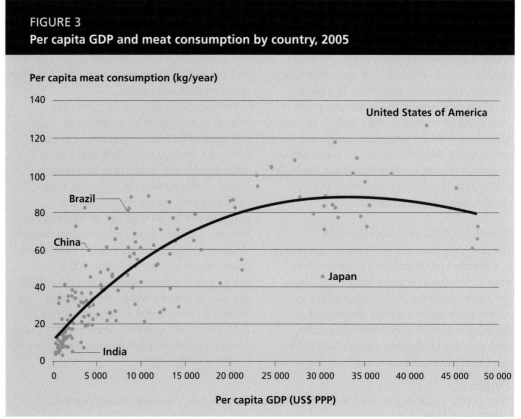

FIGURE 3
Per capita GDP and meat consumption by country, 2005

Note: GDP per capita is measured at purchasing power parity (PPP) in constant 2005 international US dollars.
Source: Based on data from FAOSTAT (FAO, 2009b) for per capita meat consumption and the World Bank for per capita GDP.

Urbanization alters patterns of food consumption, which may influence demand for livestock products. People in cities typically consume more food away from home and larger amounts of pre-cooked, fast and convenience foods than do people in rural areas (Schmidhuber and Shetty, 2005; King, Tietyen and Vickner, 2000; Rae, 1998). Urbanization influences the position and the shape of consumption functions – the relationship between income and consumption – for food products. Estimating consumption functions for total animal-derived products in a sample of East Asian economies, Rae (1998) found urbanization to have a significant effect on the consumption of animal products, independently of income levels. Another implication of urbanization in many parts of the world is the growing concentration of animals in cities, in close proximity to humans, as people tend to move livestock activities to urban areas.

Social and cultural factors and natural-resource endowments can also significantly influence local demand and shape future demand trends. For example, Brazil and Thailand have similar levels of income per capita and urbanization, but livestock product consumption is roughly twice as high in Brazil as in Thailand. The influence of natural-resource endowments can be seen in the case of Japan, which has considerably lower levels of consumption of livestock products than other countries with comparable income levels, but compensates with higher levels of fish consumption. Natural-resource endowment affects the relative costs of different food commodities. Access to marine resources favours consumption of fish while access to natural resources for livestock production favours consumption of livestock products. Cultural reasons further influence consumption habits. In South Asia, for example, consumption of meat per capita is lower than income alone would seem to explain.

TABLE 2
Urbanization: levels and growth rates

REGION/COUNTRY GROUP/ COUNTRY	URBAN SHARE OF TOTAL POPULATION	GROWTH IN TOTAL POPULATION	GROWTH IN URBAN POPULATION
	2003	1980–2003	1980–2003
	(Percentage)	(Annual percentage growth)	
DEVELOPED COUNTRIES	**73**	**0.5**	**0.8**
Former centrally planned economies	63	0.3	0.6
Other developed countries	77	0.6	0.9
DEVELOPING COUNTRIES	**42**	**1.9**	**3.7**
East and Southeast Asia	41	1.3	4.0
China	39	1.1	4.1
Latin America and the Caribbean	77	1.8	2.6
Brazil	83	1.7	2.7
Near East and North Africa	60	2.4	3.4
South Asia	28	2.0	3.1
India	28	1.9	2.8
Sub-Saharan Africa	35	2.7	4.9
WORLD	**48**	**1.5**	**3.0**

Source: FAO, 2009b.

Production trends and drivers

Trends in production
Developing countries have responded to growing demand for livestock products by rapidly increasing production (Figure 4). Between 1961 and 2007, the greatest growth in meat production occurred in East and Southeast Asia, followed by Latin America and the Caribbean. Most of the expansion in egg production was in East and Southeast Asia, while South Asia dominated milk production.

By 2007, developing countries had overtaken developed countries in terms of production of meat and eggs and were closing the gap for milk production (Table 3). Trends in production growth largely mirror those for consumption. China and Brazil show the greatest growth, especially for meat. Between 1980 and 2007, China increased its production of meat more than sixfold; today, it accounts for nearly 50 percent of meat production in developing countries and 31 percent of world production. Brazil expanded meat

production by a factor of almost four and now contributes 11 percent of developing-country meat production and 7 percent of global production.

In the remaining parts of the developing world, growth in meat output – as well as production levels – was lower, with the highest growth rates being in the rest of East and Southeast Asia and the Near East and North Africa. In spite of more than doubling meat production between 1980 and 2007, India's overall meat production levels remain low in a global context. However, after more than tripling milk production between 1980 and 2007, India now produces some 15 percent of the world's milk. Production of meat, milk and eggs also increased in sub-Saharan Africa but more slowly than in other regions.

Most of the increase in meat production has been from monogastrics; poultry meat production has been the fastest-growing subsector, followed by pig meat production. Increases from large and small ruminants have been much more modest (Figure 5). The result has been major changes in the composition of meat output globally, with

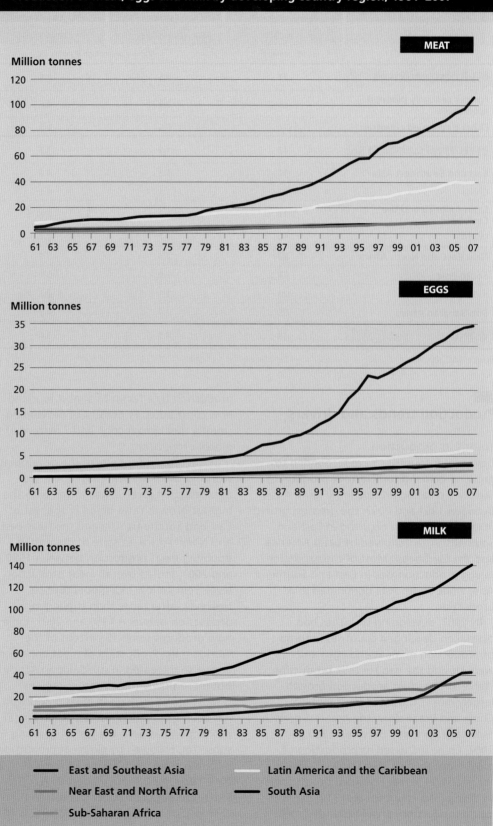

FIGURE 4
Production of meat, eggs and milk by developing country region, 1961–2007

Source: FAO, 2009b.

TABLE 3

Production of livestock products by region, 1980 and 2007

REGION/COUNTRY GROUP/ COUNTRY	MEAT		MILK		EGGS	
	1980	2007	1980	2007	1980	2007
	(Million tonnes)		*(Million tonnes)*		*(Million tonnes)*	
DEVELOPED COUNTRIES	88.6	110.2	350.6	357.8	17.9	18.9
Former centrally planned economies	24.6	19.0	127.3	101.5	5.6	5.1
Other developed countries	64.0	91.3	223.3	256.3	12.4	13.8
DEVELOPING COUNTRIES	48.1	175.5	114.9	313.5	9.5	48.9
East and Southeast Asia	19.4	106.2	4.4	42.9	4.5	34.6
China	13.6	88.7	2.9	36.8	2.8	30.1
Rest of East and Southeast Asia	5.6	17.5	1.5	6.1	1.7	4.5
Latin America and the Caribbean	15.7	40.3	35.0	68.7	2.6	6.3
Brazil	5.3	20.1	12.1	25.5	0.8	1.8
Rest of Latin America and the Caribbean	10.4	20.2	22.9	43.3	1.8	4.6
South Asia	3.7	9.4	42.7	140.6	0.8	3.4
India	2.6	6.3	31.6	102.9	0.6	2.7
Rest of South Asia	1.1	3.0	11.2	37.7	0.2	0.7
Near East and North Africa	3.4	9.7	19.3	36.4	0.9	3.0
Sub-Saharan Africa	5.5	9.3	12.9	24.3	0.7	1.5
WORLD	136.7	285.7	465.5	671.3	27.4	67.8

Note: Totals for developing countries and the world include a few countries not included in the regional aggregates.
Source: FAO, 2009b.

significant differences between regions and countries (Table 4).

Pig meat accounts for over 40 percent of global meat supplies, in part because of high levels of production and rapid growth in China, where more than half of world production takes place. The expansion of poultry meat production, which in 2007 accounted for 26 percent of global meat supplies, has been more widely distributed among both developed and developing countries, but again with China experiencing very high rates of growth. Globally, cattle production has increased much less and only in the developing countries. China and Brazil, in particular, have expanded production considerably and are each now responsible for around 12–13 percent of global cattle meat production. Meat from small ruminants remains of minor importance at the global level, but accounts for a significant portion of meat produced in the Near East and North Africa, sub-Saharan Africa and South Asia.

Drivers of production growth

Supply-side factors have enabled expansion in livestock production. Cheap inputs, technological change and scale efficiency gains in recent decades have resulted in declining prices for livestock products. This has improved access to animal-based foods even for those consumers whose incomes have not risen. Favourable long-run trends in input prices (e.g. feedgrain and fuel) have played an important role. Declining grain prices have contributed to increased use of grains as feed and downward trends in transportation costs have facilitated the movement not only of livestock products but also of feed. Recent increases in grain and energy prices may signal the end of the era of cheap inputs.

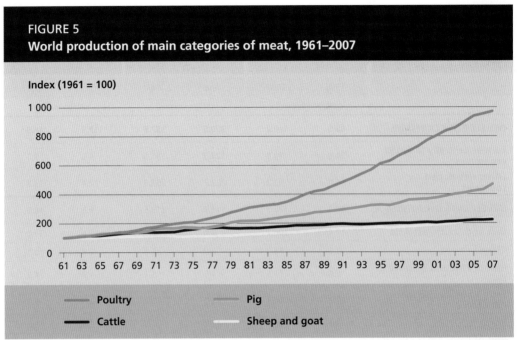

FIGURE 5
World production of main categories of meat, 1961–2007

Index (1961 = 100)

Poultry   Pig
Cattle   Sheep and goat

Source: FAO, 2009b.

TABLE 4
Production of main categories of meat by region, 1987 and 2007

REGION/COUNTRY GROUP/ COUNTRY	PIG		POULTRY		CATTLE		SHEEP AND GOAT	
	1987	2007	1987	2007	1987	2007	1987	2007
	(Million tonnes)		(Million tonnes)		(Million tonnes)		(Million tonnes)	
DEVELOPED COUNTRIES	37.1	39.5	22.9	37.0	34.1	29.4	3.7	3.2
Former centrally planned economies	12.0	7.7	5.1	5.1	10.2	5.1	1.2	0.8
Other developed countries	25.0	31.7	17.8	31.8	23.8	24.3	2.5	2.5
DEVELOPING COUNTRIES	26.6	76.0	13.0	49.8	16.9	32.5	5.0	10.8
East and Southeast Asia	22.4	68.4	4.8	22.2	1.7	8.8	1.0	5.2
China	18.3	60.0	2.2	15.3	0.6	7.3	0.7	4.9
Rest of East and Southeast Asia	4.0	8.3	2.5	6.8	1.0	1.5	0.2	0.4
Latin America and the Caribbean	3.2	6.1	4.5	17.2	9.8	15.8	0.4	0.5
Brazil	1.2	3.1	1.9	8.9	3.7	7.9	0.1	0.1
Rest of Latin America and the Caribbean	2.0	3.0	2.7	8.3	6.1	7.9	0.3	0.3
South Asia	0.4	0.5	0.5	3.0	1.5	2.1	1.1	1.5
India	0.4	0.5	0.2	2.3	1.0	1.3	0.6	0.8
Rest of South Asia	0.0	0.0	0.2	0.7	0.5	0.8	0.5	0.8
Near East and North Africa	0.0	0.1	2.1	5.3	1.1	1.8	1.5	2.0
Sub-Saharan Africa	0.5	0.8	1.0	2.0	2.7	4.0	1.0	1.6
WORLD	63.6	115.5	35.9	86.8	50.9	61.9	8.6	14.0

Note: Totals for developing countries and the world include a few countries not included in the regional aggregates.
Source: FAO, 2009b.

Increases in livestock production occur in two ways, or in a combination of the two:

- an increase in the number of animals slaughtered (in the case of meat) or producing (in the case of milk and eggs);
- increased output per animal (or yield).

Between 1980 and 2007, livestock numbers generally increased faster than yields (Figure 6). However, there are differences across regions and species.

Change in yield per animal is an important productivity indicator but it provides only a partial measure of productivity increases. It does not account for gains in terms of

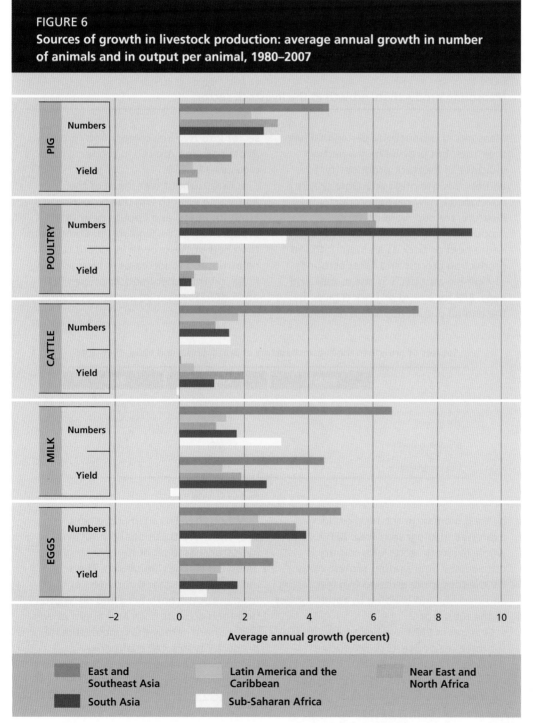

FIGURE 6

Sources of growth in livestock production: average annual growth in number of animals and in output per animal, 1980–2007

Legend:
- East and Southeast Asia
- South Asia
- Latin America and the Caribbean
- Sub-Saharan Africa
- Near East and North Africa

Source: Calculations based on data from FAO (2009b).

the rate at which animals grow and gain weight or any improved efficiency in input use or production factors. Other productivity indicators, although still imperfect, may contribute to providing a more complete picture of trends in livestock productivity (see Box 1).

Technological change in livestock production
Technological change is the single most important factor in expanding supply of cheap livestock products. At the same time,

it has affected the structure of the sector in many parts of the world.

Technological change refers to developments and innovations in all aspects of livestock production from breeding, feeding and housing to disease control, processing, transportation and marketing. Technological change in the livestock sector has mostly been the result of private research and development efforts aimed at commercial producers, in contrast with the publicly funded efforts aimed specifically

---

BOX 1
Measuring productivity growth in the livestock sector

Measures of productivity per animal have their uses, but provide only a partial indicator of livestock productivity. To address this, Steinfeld and Opio (2009) developed a new partial productivity measure, termed biomass–food productivity (BFP). BFP considers the entire herd or flock as an input into the production process and takes account of multiple outputs, e.g. meat, milk and eggs. BFP for a herd or flock is given by the annual output in protein divided

sector into two key components: growth in biomass and growth in productivity as measured by BFP.

In Brazil, about two-thirds of the aggregate growth was due to increased input (biomass) and about one-third to productivity gains. Similarly, in China more than half of the growth in output can be attributed to increases in biomass. In India, on the other hand, improved BFP accounted for over 80 percent of output growth.

Sources of growth in the livestock sectors of Brazil, China and India, 1965–2005

	BRAZIL	CHINA	INDIA
	Average annual growth (percent)		
BFP growth	1.6	2.8	3.7
Biomass growth	3.2	3.8	0.8
Output growth	4.8	6.5	4.5

by total biomass in the herd or flock, expressed in kilograms. Total BFP for the whole livestock sector of a country is obtained by aggregating protein output for the subsectors assessed (e.g. cattle, pig and chicken) and dividing by total biomass of the subsectors.

Changes in BFP have been estimated for three major livestock-producing developing countries, Brazil, China and India, over the period 1965–2005. The table separates average annual growth rates in total output of the livestock

Although BFP is an improvement over the more traditional productivity indicators based on output per single animal, it still has limitations. These include the fact that it considers only food outputs from a herd and disregards non-food outputs, such as draught power and manure. It may thus underestimate productivity in some traditional production systems where such outputs are important.

_____

Source: Steinfeld and Opio, 2009.

at developing technological innovations that could be applied by smallholders that led to the green revolution in wheat and rice. As a result, technological innovations in the livestock sector have been relatively less widely available and applicable to smallholders. Little emphasis has been given to research on the public goods aspects of technology development for livestock, such as impacts on poor people or externalities related to the environment or public health.

The application of advanced breeding and feeding technology has spurred significant productivity growth, especially in broiler and egg production and the pork and dairy sectors. Technological advances, and thus productivity growth, have been less pronounced for beef and meat from small ruminants. The use of hybridization and artificial insemination has accelerated the process of genetic improvement. The speed and precision with which breeding goals can be achieved has increased considerably over recent decades. Genetic advances are much faster in short-cycle animals, such as poultry and pigs, than in species with a longer generation interval, such as cattle. In all species, feed conversion and related parameters, such as growth rate, milk yield and reproductive efficiency, have been major targets for breeding efforts, while features corresponding to consumer demands, such as fat content, are increasing in importance. While impressive advances have been made in breeds developed for temperate regions, results have been limited in development of breeds of dairy cows, pigs and poultry that perform well in tropical low-input environments.

Improvements in feed technology include balanced feeding, precision feeding, optimal addition of amino acids and mineral micronutrients, and development of improved pasture species and animal husbandry systems such as zero-grazing.

Animal-health improvements, including the increasing use of vaccines and antibiotics, have also contributed to raising productivity. These technologies have spread widely in recent years in a number of developing countries, particularly in industrial production systems close to major consumption centres.

Technological innovations in processing, transportation, distribution and marketing of livestock products have also significantly altered the way food is delivered to consumers (cold chains, longer shelf-life, etc.).

Box 2 shows how all these different technological advances have contributed to increased production in the commercial poultry industry.

Trade trends and drivers

Growth in livestock trade has been facilitated by increasing consumption of livestock products and economic liberalization. Developments in transportation, such as long-distance cold-chain shipments (refrigerated transport) and large-scale and faster shipments, have made it possible to trade and transport animals, products and feedstuffs over long distances. This has allowed production to move away from the loci of both consumption and production of feed resources. Increasing trade flows also have implications for the management of animal diseases and a number of food-safety issues.

Livestock products represent a growing proportion of agricultural exports. Their share of agricultural export value globally rose from 11 percent to 17 percent between 1961 and 2006 (Figure 7). However, trade in crops – including feed crops – still dwarfs that of livestock products.

Between 1980 and 2006, the volume of total meat exports increased more than threefold. Exports of dairy more than doubled and exports of eggs almost doubled (Table 5). The share of production entering international trade increased, except for sheep meat and eggs, reflecting the sector's increasing degree of openness to trade. The degree of trade openness has been particularly high for monogastrics.

Although the bulk of livestock produce is consumed within the country of production and does not enter international trade, livestock exports are important for a few countries. Since mid-2002, developing countries as a whole have been net exporters of meat (Figure 8). However, this masks large disparities between countries. Developing-country meat exports are dominated by the contribution of Brazil, the world's largest meat exporter. If exports from Brazil, China, India and Thailand are excluded, all developing regions are net importers of meat. Thailand has emerged as a major force in the global market for poultry, with net exports of almost half a million tonnes in 2006. All developing regions are increasingly dependent on imports of dairy products (Figure 8).

Brazil's performance in export for livestock products is particularly noteworthy. Over the

---

BOX 2
Technological progress in the poultry industry

No other livestock industry has applied technological improvements as rapidly or effectively as the commercial poultry industry. Poultry respond well to technological change because of their high reproductive rates and short generation intervals. Moreover, the vertically integrated structure of commercial poultry production has permitted widespread application of new technologies to large numbers of birds, often across thousands of farms.

Since the early 1960s, broiler growth rates have doubled and feed conversion ratios have halved. Modern commercial layers typically produce about 330 eggs per year with a feed conversion ratio of 2 kg of feed per kilogram of eggs produced. Modern broilers weigh about 2.5 kg at 39 days, with a feed conversion ratio of 1.6 kg of feed per kilogram of body-weight gain.

The gains in the production of poultry meat and eggs from individual birds in commercial flocks are largely due to genetic selection in the nucleus breeding flocks and the rapid transfer of these gains to the commercial crossbred progeny (McKay, 2008; Hunton, 1990). Breeding advances have largely been based on the application of quantitative genetic selection, without recourse to molecular technologies. The impressive annual gain in the productivity of commercial broiler flocks is a reflection of a complex and coordinated approach by the breeders to maximize performance (McKay, 2008; Pym, 1993).

Bird health, robustness and product quality and safety have improved commensurately with gains in productivity as a result of the application of breeding, feeding, disease control, housing and processing technologies.

Disease challenges can have a major impact on efficiency, but improvements in vaccination, nutrition and biosecurity have contributed to reducing their impact. Breeding for improved disease resistance, particularly through the adoption of molecular technologies, will be an important component of future genetic programmes. Future advances in the industry depend upon the application of new molecular tools to the development of improved diagnostic techniques for poultry disease surveillance programmes and surveillance for food-borne pathogens. Past experience has demonstrated the need for rapidly addressing problems of food-borne pathogens in poultry meat and eggs, if consumer confidence in the safety of poultry products is to be maintained.

Unfortunately, technologies developed for industrial production systems with strict biosecurity controls have little applicability in small-scale mixed farming systems. The poorest farmers tend to be the least technologically advanced, operating with indigenous birds, semi-scavenging feeding systems, minimal disease control and basic housing. However, the application of some relatively simple technologies (e.g. short-term confinement rearing and creep-feeding of chicks with suitable diets, vaccination against Newcastle disease, and overnight secure housing of all birds) can yield profound improvements in smallholder profitability, household food security and the empowerment of women as poultry keepers.

_____

Source: Pym _et al._, 2008.

last decade, the country has increased the quantity of poultry meat exports fivefold, and exports of pig and bovine meat have risen by a factor of 8 and 10, respectively. In nominal value, Brazil's net exports of livestock products went from US$435 million in 1995 to US$7 280 million in 2006. In 2006, Brazil's net exports accounted for 6 percent of global exports of pig meat, 20 percent of bovine meat and 28 percent of poultry meat. Brazil has increasingly taken advantage of low feed production costs for its livestock industry and is poised to remain an important producer of feedstuffs. The combination of abundant land and recent infrastructure developments has turned previously remote areas, such as Mato Grosso and the Cerrado region of central Brazil, into feed baskets. These two regions have the lowest production costs for maize

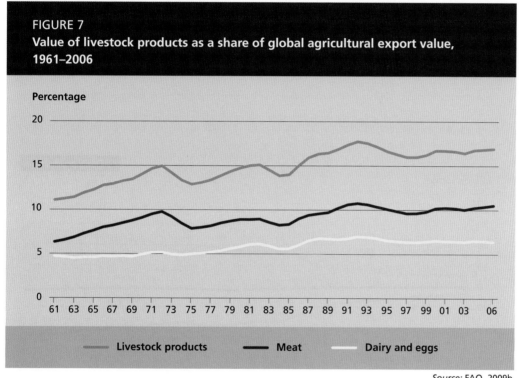

FIGURE 7
Value of livestock products as a share of global agricultural export value, 1961–2006

Percentage

Legend: Livestock products — Meat — Dairy and eggs

Source: FAO, 2009b.

TABLE 5
Global trade in livestock products, 1980 and 2006

PRODUCT	WORLD EXPORTS		SHARE OF TOTAL PRODUCTION	
	1980	2006	1980	2006
	(Million tonnes)		(Percentage)	
Total meat[1]	9.6	32.1	7.0	11.7
Pig	2.6	10.4	4.9	9.8
Poultry	1.5	11.1	5.9	13.0
Bovine	4.3	9.2	9.1	14.2
Ovine	0.8	1.1	10.6	7.7
Dairy[2]	42.8	90.2	8.7	12.7
Eggs	0.8	1.5	3.1	2.2

[1] Includes other types of meat than those listed below.
[2] Milk equivalent.
Source: FAO, 2009b.

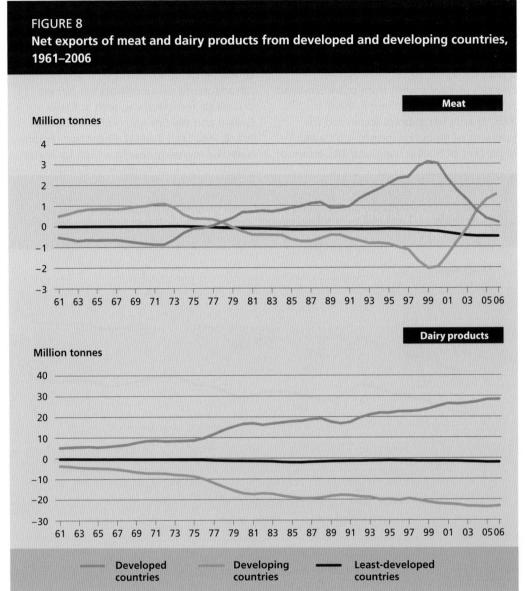

FIGURE 8
Net exports of meat and dairy products from developed and developing countries, 1961–2006

Source: FAO, 2009b.

and soybeans anywhere in the world. Since the early 1990s, Brazilian producers have actively taken strategic advantage of their position and have started to convert their feed into exportable surpluses of livestock commodities (FAO, 2006).

A particular source of concern is the net trade position in livestock products of the least-developed countries (LDCs). These countries are increasingly dependent on imports of livestock products – indeed, food commodities in general – to meet growing demand (Figure 9). The proportion of consumption met by imports has increased rapidly since 1996. As part of wider efforts to boost agricultural growth,

expanding domestic supply could potentially contribute to economic growth, rural development and an improved external trade position.

Outlook for consumption, production and trade

The factors that have encouraged growth in demand in developing countries – rising incomes, population growth and urbanization – will continue to be important over the coming decades, although the effects of some may weaken. Population growth, although slowing, will continue.

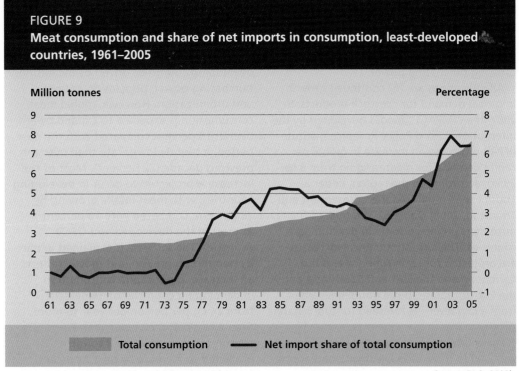

FIGURE 9
Meat consumption and share of net imports in consumption, least-developed countries, 1961–2005

Million tonnes   Percentage

Total consumption   —— Net import share of total consumption

Source: FAO, 2009b.

While projections of the future growth in the world's population vary, a recent estimate suggests the world's population will exceed 9 billion in 2050 (UN, 2008).

Trends towards increasing urbanization are considered unstoppable. By the end of 2008, it is believed that, for the first time, more than half the world's population was living in towns and cities. By 2050, around seven out of every ten people are expected to be urban dwellers; by then, there will be 600 million fewer rural residents than now (UN, 2007).

Income growth is generally considered to be the strongest driver of increased consumption of livestock products. Although short-term prospects are poor, with the global economy in a severe recession, medium-term prospects do suggest a recovery, albeit slow. In April 2009, the International Monetary Fund (IMF) projected a decline in global GDP of 1.3 percent in 2009, followed by growth of 1.9 percent in 2010, rising to 4.8 percent by 2014 (IMF, 2009). According to the IMF, the exceptional uncertainty of the growth outlook means that the transition period will be characterized by slower growth than seen in the recent past.

The effect of economic growth on demand for livestock products depends on the rate of growth and where it occurs. Demand

for livestock products is more responsive to income growth in low-income countries than in higher-income countries. Increasing saturation in per capita consumption in countries that have reached relatively high levels of consumption, notably Brazil and China, could lead to some slowing in demand. An important question is whether other major developing countries with low current levels of meat consumption will emerge as new growth poles, thus sustaining large increases in global demand. India, with its large population and low levels of per capita consumption of livestock products, has the potential to be a major source of new demand. However, opinions differ on the likely future contribution of India to global demand for livestock products (see Bruinsma, 2003).

A further question is to what extent continuing high food prices will dampen consumer demand, as consumers across the globe alter their eating habits. While it is difficult to forecast future feed and food price trends accurately, most analysts and observers agree that in the short to medium term, prices will remain higher than in the recent past, but that increased volatility of prices will become the norm (IFPRI, 2008; OECD–FAO, 2008; World Bank, 2008a).

Overall, the potential for expanding per capita consumption of livestock products remains vast in large parts of the developing world as rising incomes translate into growing purchasing power.

All indications are for continued growth in global demand for livestock products. In 2007, the "IMPACT" model developed by the International Food Policy Research Institute (IFPRI) projected an increase in global per capita demand for meat ranging from 6 to 23 kg, according to the region, under a "business-as-usual scenario" (Rosegrant and Thornton, 2008) (Table 6). The bulk of the increase is projected to be in developing countries. The largest numerical increases are projected for Latin America and the Caribbean and the East and South Asia and the Pacific regions, but a doubling – albeit from a low level – is foreseen for sub-Saharan Africa.

The model projects that growing demand will lead to increasing livestock populations, with the global population of cattle increasing from 1.5 billion to 2.6 billion and that of goats and sheep from 1.7 billion to 2.7 billion between 2000 and 2050. Demand for coarse grains for animal feed is also projected to increase over the period by 553 million tonnes, corresponding to approximately half of the total increase in demand.

The *OECD–FAO Agricultural Outlook, 2009–2018* (OECD–FAO, 2009) presents projections for the coming decade. Although methodological and measurement differences between the two prevent direct comparison of precise figures, the OECD–FAO projections nevertheless confirm the trends indicated by the longer-term IFPRI projections. In spite of low economic growth in the first part of the projection period, OECD–FAO expect demand to continue growing, especially in the developing countries, driven by increasing purchasing power, population growth and urbanization. However, global meat consumption is expected to expand by an overall 19 percent compared with the base period, a slightly lower rate than over the previous decade (22 percent). Most of the increase is projected to occur in developing countries, with meat intake growing by 28 percent, compared with 10 percent at most in the developed and OECD countries. The increase is explained in part by population growth, but mostly reflects an increase in per capita consumption in developing countries of 14 percent – from 24 kg per person per year to more than 27 kg per person per year. Per capita consumption in developed countries is projected to increase by only 7 percent, from 65 kg to 69 kg. The smallest increase, of only around 3.5 percent, is projected for the OECD countries. Globally, demand for poultry is expected to continue to show the strongest growth.

According to the OECD–FAO projections from 2009 to 2018, 87 percent of global growth in meat production will occur outside the OECD area. For the developing countries, an overall increase in meat production of 32 percent is foreseen over the projection period.

The OECD–FAO projections for dairy suggest that demand, both per capita and overall, will continue to grow. The most rapid growth will occur in developing countries, where per capita demand is expected to

TABLE 6
Meat consumption by region, 2000 and 2050 (projected)

	PER CAPITA CONSUMPTION OF MEAT	
	2000	2050
	(kg/person/year)	
Central and West Asia and North Africa	20	33
East and South Asia and the Pacific	28	51
Latin America and the Caribbean	58	77
North America and Europe	83	89
Sub-Saharan Africa	11	22

Source: Rosegrant and Thornton, 2008.

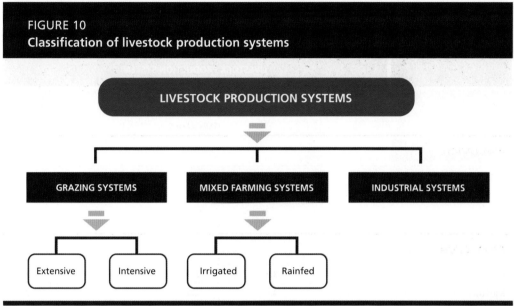

FIGURE 10
Classification of livestock production systems

LIVESTOCK PRODUCTION SYSTEMS

GRAZING SYSTEMS   MIXED FARMING SYSTEMS   INDUSTRIAL SYSTEMS

Extensive   Intensive   Irrigated   Rainfed

Source: FAO.

increase at an annual rate of 1.2 percent. Overall production growth is projected at 1.7 percent per year from 2009 to 2018, with much of the increase coming from developing countries.

Feed demand is also projected to continue increasing. Use of coarse grains as feed is expected to grow by 1.2 percent a year. The total increase will amount to 79 million tonnes, to a total of 716 million tonnes, with most of the increase in developing countries. The projection excludes distiller dried grain (DDG), a by-product from ethanol production (see Box 10, page 54). Higher feed prices may lead to slower demand growth in the developing countries. Use of wheat as feed is also projected to increase slightly. Demand for oilseed meal is projected to grow by an annual rate of 3.8 percent in the non-OECD countries and 0.7 percent in the OECD countries. This, however, is only half the rate of growth seen in the previous decade.

Livestock sector diversity

The rapid growth of the livestock sector and projections for continued expansion are affecting the sector's structure. The livestock sector is characterized by large variations in the scale and intensity of production and in the nature and degree of linkages with the broader agricultural and rural economy. Further variation is found by species, location, agro-ecological conditions, technology and level of economic development. No single classification system can capture all of this diversity. This report uses a simplified classification that distinguishes between grazing, mixed farming and industrial production systems (Figure 10). Estimates of livestock numbers and production from different production systems are given in Table 7.

Looser terms such as "modern" and "traditional" are also used in this report to distinguish between parts of the livestock sector that have undergone greater or lesser degrees of economic and technological transformation in recent decades. Industrial systems are generally described as modern, although some grazing and mixed systems also use modern techniques such as breed selection and herd management. These terms are used to facilitate a comparative discussion of the costs, benefits and trade-offs implied by different systems for food security and livelihoods, environmental sustainability and human health, not to suggest that one is preferable to the other.

Grazing systems
Grazing systems cover the largest land area and are currently estimated to occupy some 26 percent of the earth's ice-free land surface (Steinfeld *et al.*, 2006).

TABLE 7
Global livestock population and production, by production system,
average 2001–2003

	LIVESTOCK PRODUCTION SYSTEM				
	Grazing	Rainfed mixed	Irrigated mixed	Landless/ industrial	Total
	(Million head)				
POPULATION					
Cattle and buffaloes	406	641	450	29	1 526
Sheep and goats	590	632	546	9	1 777
	(Million tonnes)				
PRODUCTION					
Beef	14.6	29.3	12.9	3.9	60.7
Mutton	3.8	4.0	4.0	0.1	11.9
Pork	0.8	12.5	29.1	52.8	95.2
Poultry meat	1.2	8.0	11.7	52.8	73.7
Milk	71.5	319.2	203.7	–	594.4
Eggs	0.5	5.6	17.1	35.7	58.9

Source: Steinfeld *et al.*, 2006, p. 53.

- *Extensive grazing systems* cover most of the dry areas of the world that are marginal for crop production. Such areas tend to be sparsely populated and include, for example, the dry tropics and continental climates of southern Africa, central, eastern and western Asia, Australia and western North America. These systems are characterized by ruminants (e.g. cattle, sheep, goats and camels) grazing mainly grasses and other herbaceous plants, often on communal or open-access areas and often in a mobile fashion. The main products of these systems include about 7 percent of global beef production, about 12 percent of sheep and goat meat production and 5 percent of global milk supply.
- *Intensive grazing systems* are found in temperate zones where high-quality grassland and fodder production can support larger numbers of animals. These areas tend to have medium to high human population density and include most of Europe, North America, South America, parts of Oceania and some parts of the humid tropics. These

systems are characterized by cattle (dairy and beef) and are based mostly on individual landownership. They contribute about 17 percent of global beef and veal supply, about the same share of the sheep and goat meat supply and 7 percent of global milk supply as their main outputs.

Mixed farming systems
In mixed farming systems, cropping and livestock rearing are linked activities. Mixed farming systems are defined as those systems in which more than 10 percent of the dry matter fed to animals comes from crop by-products or stubble or where more than 10 percent of the total value of production comes from non-livestock farming activities.

- *Rainfed mixed farming systems* are found in temperate regions of Europe and the Americas and subhumid regions of tropical Africa and Latin America. They are characterized by individual ownership, often with more than one species of livestock. Globally, around 48 percent of global beef production, 53 percent of milk production and 33 percent of mutton production originates from this type of production system.

- *Irrigated mixed farming systems* prevail in East and South Asia, mostly in areas with high population density. They are an important contributor to most animal products, providing about one-third of the world's pork, mutton and milk and one-fifth of its beef.

Industrial production systems

Industrial systems are defined as those systems that purchase at least 90 percent of their feed from other enterprises. Such systems are mostly intensive and are often found near large urban centres. Industrial systems are common in Europe and North America and in parts of East and Southeast Asia, Latin America and the Near East. They often consist of a single species (beef cattle, pigs or poultry) fed on feed (grain and industrial by-products purchased from outside the farm). They contribute slightly more than two-thirds of global production of poultry meat, slightly less than two-thirds of egg production and more than half of world output of pork, but are less significant in terms of ruminant production. These systems are sometimes described as "landless" because the animals are physically separated from the land that supports them. However, about 33 percent of global agricultural cropland is used to produce animal feed (Steinfeld *et al.*, 2006), so the term "landless" is somewhat misleading.

Transformation of livestock systems

Growing demand for livestock products and technological change have led to widespread changes in livestock production systems. This has radically affected the structure of the most advanced parts of the livestock production sector in both developed countries and parts of the developing world. There has been a rapid growth in the average size of primary production units and a shift towards fewer and larger firms in many parts of the world. One major reason for this is that larger operations are better placed to benefit from technical advances and economies of scale, such as those embodied in improved genetics, compound

feeds or greater organization, especially in poultry and pig production.

Worldwide, much of the response to growing livestock demand has been through industrialized production. Large production units have a clear comparative advantage over smaller units in moving towards a global commercial market. There are a number of reasons for this. Concentration in the input and processing sector combined with vertical integration leads to increasing farm size because larger integrators prefer to deal with larger production units. In the short term, contract farming may benefit smallholders, but over the long term, integrators prefer to deal with a few large producers rather than a large number of small producers. This is most evident in pig and poultry production, where processors demand large quantities of supply at a consistent standard (Sones and Dijkman, 2008). Box 3 discusses the impact of coordination in value chains on livestock production systems.

Different commodities and different steps in the production process offer different potential for economies of scale. The potential tends to be high in post-harvest sectors, e.g. for facilities such as slaughterhouses and dairy processing plants. Poultry production is the most easily mechanized livestock production enterprise, and industrial forms of poultry production have emerged in even the LDCs. In contrast, dairy production offers fewer economies of scale because of its typically high labour requirement. For dairy and small ruminant production, farm-level production costs at the smallholder level are often comparable with those of large-scale enterprises, usually because of the cost advantages of providing family labour at well below the minimum wage.

The organization of livestock production has implications for the way the sector interacts with the natural-resource base and for the management of animal diseases and human-health risks. Structural transformation of the sector can have an impact on livelihoods, especially in rural areas. The degree to which smallholders can take advantage of the growing demand for livestock products, and the extent to which they have done so, is an important factor that must be taken into account in livestock development efforts.

BOX 3
Coordination in livestock value chains

Value chains for livestock products, especially meat, are very complex. This complexity begins at the production level, which depends on a feed supply chain that must ensure a timely supply of safe inputs. It continues through processing and retailing; these involve many steps and food items of animal origin are often more perishable than crop-based foods. The resulting interdependence among the companies in the food supply chain for animal products exerts substantial pressure for coordination beyond that provided by cash market transactions.

Companies in a food supply chain may put in place vertical coordinating mechanisms such as contracts, licences and strategic alliances to manage relationships with suppliers and customers. Firms operating at the same stage within the value chain may establish horizontal relationships in the form of cooperative groups for dealing with down- and up-stream business partners and for ensuring product quality.

Contracts are the most common mechanism for vertical coordination. For primary producers, contracts allow the establishment of more secure relationships with business partners, both to guarantee a price prior to selling or buying, thereby reducing market risks regarding price, and to specify quantity and quality. From the point of view of the contractor/buyer, contracts provide for much closer linkages with farmers and may offer them greater control over production decisions of the farmers. Selling contracts may be entered into with down-stream processors such as packing companies, while up-stream agreements may be in place between, for instance, the feed industry and animal producers.

Vertical integration entails a closer degree of coordination and occurs when two or more successive stages of the food supply chain are controlled and carried out by a single firm. In the extreme, the entire chain can be integrated. Examples of such vertical integration include companies that link farms and buying entities. Meat packers often own pig farms and cattle feedlots and dairy farmers may produce their own feed instead of buying it. In the case of vertically integrated firms, product transfers are determined by internal decisions rather than through market prices.

Horizontal coordination may also be necessary for a well-functioning supply chain. Processors can reduce transaction costs by dealing with one farm organization, such as a cooperative, instead of many small-scale farms. Cooperative organization can bring three main types of benefits to farmers: arranging for the selling of farmers' produce to down-stream business; exchange of information with partners in the food supply chain and its dissemination among the farmers; and providing advice to farmers on how to achieve the required levels of quality of the raw product. In many of the least-developed countries, cooperatives are crucial for small-scale farms to remain in business and, perhaps, to keep farmers out of poverty.

Source: Based on Frohberg, 2009.

From smallholder mixed systems to large-scale commodity-specific systems
The modern livestock sector is characterized by large-scale operations with intensive use of inputs, technology and capital and increased specialization of production units focusing on single-product operations. This is accompanied by the progressive substitution of non-traded inputs in favour of purchased inputs. Feed inputs are sourced off-farm, either domestically or internationally. Mechanical technologies substitute for human labour, with labour being used as a source of technical knowledge and for management. The move towards modern production systems has implied a decline in

TABLE 8
Use of feed concentrate by region, 1980 and 2005

REGION/COUNTRY GROUP/COUNTRY	TOTAL FEED CONCENTRATE	
	1980	2005
	(Million tonnes)	
DEVELOPED COUNTRIES	668.7	647.4
Former centrally planned economies	296.5	171.9
Other developed countries	372.2	475.4
DEVELOPING COUNTRIES	239.6	602.7
East and Southeast Asia	113.7	321.0
China	86.0	241.4
Rest of East and Southeast Asia	27.7	79.6
Latin America and the Caribbean	64.3	114.1
Brazil	33.4	54.9
Rest of Latin America and the Caribbean	30.9	59.3
South Asia	20.9	49.7
India	15.5	37.1
Rest of South Asia	5.4	12.6
Near East and North Africa	25.8	70.1
Sub-Saharan Africa	15.0	47.6
WORLD	908.4	1 250.1

Source: FAO, 2009b.

integrated mixed farming systems and their replacement by specialized enterprises. In this process, the livestock sector changes from being multifunctional to commodity-specific. There is a decline in the importance of traditionally important livestock functions, such as provision of draught power and manure, acting as assets and insurance, and serving sociocultural functions. Livestock production is thus no longer part of integrated production systems, based on local resources with non-food outputs serving as inputs in other production activities within the system.

From roughages to concentrate feeds
As livestock production grows and intensifies, it depends less and less on locally available feed and increasingly on feed concentrates that are traded domestically and internationally. There is a shift from the use of low-quality roughages (crop residues and natural pasture) towards high-quality agro-industrial by-products and concentrates. Use of feed concentrate in developing countries

more than doubled between 1980 and 2005 (Table 8). In 2005, a total of 742 million tonnes of cereals were fed to livestock, representing roughly one-third of the global cereal harvest and an even larger share of coarse grains (Table 9).

The dominance of concentrate feeds has meant that livestock production is no longer constrained by local availability of feed and the natural resources needed to provide it. As a result, the impact of production on natural resources is partly removed from the location of livestock production and transferred to where the feed is produced.

Increased use of concentrate feed explains the rapid growth in production of monogastrics, especially poultry. When livestock are no longer reliant on local resources or waste from other activities as feed, the rate at which feed is converted into livestock outputs becomes a critical factor in the economic efficiency of production. In this respect, monogastrics, with their better feed conversion ratios, have a distinct advantage over ruminants.

TABLE 9

Use of feed concentrate by commodity group, 2005

COMMODITY GROUP	FEED CONCENTRATE USE IN 2005		
	Developing countries	Developed countries	World
	(Million tonnes)		
Cereals	284.2	457.7	741.9
Brans	71.2	34.5	105.7
Pulses	6.8	7.3	14.2
Oilcrops	13.4	14.3	27.6
Oilcake	113.2	101.7	214.9
Roots and tubers	111.2	30.8	142.0
Fishmeal	2.7	1.1	3.8
Total	602.7	647.4	1 250.1

Source: FAO, 2009b.

From dispersed to concentrated production

The consolidation of livestock production activities, principally those associated with monogastrics, has affected the geography of animal populations and production.

When livestock production was based on locally available feed resources, such as natural pasture and crop residues, the distribution of ruminants was almost completely determined by the availability of such resources. The distribution of pigs and poultry followed closely that of humans, because of their role in converting agricultural and household wastes. With the increasing use of bought-in feed, especially concentrates, the importance of agro-ecological conditions as a determinant of location is replaced by factors such as opportunity cost of land and access to output and input markets.

Large-scale operators emerge as soon as urbanization, economic growth and rising incomes translate into "bulk" demand for foods of animal origin. Initially, these are located close to towns and cities. Livestock products are among the most perishable foods, and their conservation without chilling and processing poses serious quality and human-health risks. Therefore, livestock have to be kept close to the location of demand. At a later stage, following development of infrastructure and technology for transporting inputs and products and for processing and preserving outputs, livestock production may shift away

from demand centres. Factors such as lower land and labour prices, easier access to feed sources, lower environmental standards, fewer disease problems and tax incentives facilitate this shift.

As a result of such processes, livestock production has become more geographically clustered, with production units and associated processing centres and supporting infrastructure located close together. In parallel with changes in the structure of production, slaughterhouses and processing plants have increased in size and are increasingly located in the area of production.

In traditional mixed or pastoral production systems, non-food outputs such as manure are important inputs in other production activities. Concentration has meant that these outputs are often seen as wastes that must be disposed of. In addition, increasing concentration of animals, often in close proximity to major centres of human population, may exacerbate problems of animal diseases and related human-health risks.

Challenges from continued livestock sector growth

Continued growth in demand for and production of livestock products clearly has significant long-term implications in three areas that require attention. It implies increasing pressures on the world's natural resources as feed demand grows and livestock production is increasingly decoupled from the local natural-resource base. It has implications for both animal and human health as the number and concentration of people and animals increases, because some disease agents pass easily between species. Finally, the social implications for smallholders, whose opportunities to supply new markets are constrained, pose serious policy challenges.

The likely continuing rapid expansion of the livestock sector highlights the critical issues for the future of the sector that require the attention of national governments and the international community. These include harnessing the potential for growing livestock demand to contribute to poverty alleviation and improved food security, increasing the sustainability of natural-resource use and improving efforts to manage animal diseases.

Key messages of the chapter

- The livestock sector is large and growing rapidly in a number of developing countries, driven by growth in incomes, population and urbanization. The potential for increasing demand for livestock products is substantial and implies challenges in terms of efficient use of natural resources, managing animal- and human-health risks, alleviating poverty and ensuring food security.
- Growing demand for livestock products and the implementation of technological changes along the food chain have spurred major changes in livestock production systems. Small-scale mixed production systems are facing increased competition from large-scale specialized production units based on purchased inputs. These trends present major competitive challenges for smallholders and have implications for the ability of the sector to promote poverty reduction.
- The shift from small-scale mixed production systems, based on locally available resources, to large-scale industrial systems has also changed the location of livestock production units. As the constraint of locally available

natural resources is removed, the spatial distribution of livestock production facilities is becoming more clustered to exploit linkages along the supply chain. This has increased the efficiency of production but has implications for natural-resource use.
- The increasing concentration of production and growth in trade are leading to new challenges in the management of animal diseases.

3. Livestock, food security and poverty reduction

The livestock sector is one of the fastest-growing segments of the agricultural economy, particularly in the developing world. As demand for meat and dairy products in the developing world continues to increase, questions arise as to how this demand will be met and by whom. Parts of the sector, particularly poultry and pig production, have followed a trend similar to that in developed countries, where large-scale production units dominate output. The expansion of such trends across the whole livestock sector will have major implications for poverty reduction and food security. To date, the transformation of the livestock sector has occurred largely in the absence of sector-specific policies; this gap needs to be addressed to ensure that the livestock sector contributes to equitable and sustainable development.

Despite rapid structural change in parts of the sector, smallholders still dominate production in many developing countries. Livestock can provide income, quality food, fuel, draught power, building material and fertilizer, thus contributing to household livelihood, food security and nutrition. Strong demand for animal-based foods and increasingly complex processing and marketing systems offer significant opportunities for growth and poverty reduction at every stage in the value chain. These new market opportunities and livelihood options face rapidly changing patterns of competition, consumer preferences and market standards; these may undermine the ability of smallholders to remain competitive. They should also be carefully managed to ensure that women and men have the same prospects in this rapidly changing sector. Policy reforms, institutional support and public and private investments are urgently needed (i) to assist those smallholders who can compete in the new markets, (ii) to ease the transition

of those who will exit the sector, and (iii) to protect the crucial safety-net function performed by livestock for the most vulnerable households.

Productivity growth in agriculture is central to economic growth, poverty reduction and food security. Decades of economic research have confirmed that agricultural productivity growth has positive effects for the poor in three areas: lower food prices for consumers; higher incomes for producers; and growth multiplier effects through the rest of the economy as demand for other goods and services increases (Alston et al., 2000). Agricultural growth reduces poverty more strongly than growth in other sectors (Thirtle et al., 2001; Datt and Ravallion, 1998; Gallup, Radelet and Warner, 1997; Timmer, 1988). Recent research suggests that livestock sector growth can also promote broader economic growth (Pica, Pica-Ciamarra and Otte, 2008) and that smallholders can contribute to this (Delgado, Narrod and Tiongco, 2008). However, serious questions and policy challenges must be addressed if the potential of the livestock sector to promote growth and reduce poverty is to be met in a sustainable way.

This chapter explores the role of livestock in food security and in the livelihoods of men and women living in poverty. It also examines the potential for livestock to serve as an engine of growth, poverty reduction and long-term food security for these most vulnerable people. The chapter discusses the conditions under which smallholders may be able to use livestock as a pathway out of poverty. Livestock sector policies must take into account producers' differing capacities to participate in modern industrialized value chains (capacities that are often dictated by sociocultural and gender issues) and the crucial safety-net function served by livestock for many smallholders.

Livestock and livelihoods

Livestock are central to the livelihoods of the poor. They form an integral part of mixed farming systems, where they help raise whole-farm productivity and provide a steady stream of food and revenues for households. However, livestock's role and contribution to livelihoods in developing countries extends well beyond what is produced for the market or for direct consumption.

Livestock play many other important roles, including: as a provider of employment to the farmer and family members (Sansoucy, 1995); as a store of wealth (CAST, 2001); as a form of insurance (Fafchamps and Gavian, 1997); contributing to gender equality by generating opportunities for women; recycling waste products and residues from cropping or agro-industries (Ke, 1998; Steinfeld, 1998); improving the structure and fertility of soil (de Wit, van de Meer and Nell, 1997); and controlling insects and weeds (Pelant *et al.*, 1999). Livestock residues can also serve as an energy source for cooking, contributing to food security. Livestock also have a cultural significance – livestock ownership may form the basis for the observation of religious custom (Horowitz, 2001; Ashdown, 1992; Harris, 1978) or for establishing the status of the farmer (Birner, 1999). The non-tradable roles played by livestock commonly vary between different parts of a country, and almost certainly among countries. They are also likely to

change over time as economic conditions of livestock owners evolve.

The number of poor people who depend on livestock for their livelihoods is not known with certainty, but the most commonly cited estimate is 987 million (Livestock in Development, 1999) or about 70 percent of the world's 1.4 billion "extreme poor".[2] Table 10 shows this estimate broken down by agro-ecological zone and type of farming system. Data in the FAO RIGA database (FAO, 2009a), which compiles information from nationally representative household surveys from 14 countries, indicate that 60 percent of rural households keep livestock (Table 11).

Data from the 14 RIGA countries are shown by expenditure quintile in Figures 11–14. Livestock keeping is pervasive among all income brackets of rural households (Figure 11). In about one-third of the countries in the sample, poorer households are more likely to be engaged in livestock activities than are wealthier households. While there is no clear relationship between income level and engagement in livestock activities, it is clear that, in all the countries, even the poorest households commonly keep livestock.

The extent to which livestock contribute to income varies across countries and income levels (Figure 12). The share of household income derived from livestock ranges from less than 5 percent for many households to

[2] Defined as those with consumption of less than US$1.25 per person per day, measured in constant 2005 purchasing power.

TABLE 10

Number and location of poor livestock keepers by category and agro-ecological zone

AGRO-ECOLOGICAL ZONE	CATEGORY OF LIVESTOCK KEEPER		
	Extensive graziers	Poor rainfed mixed farmers	Landless livestock keepers[1]
	(Millions)		
Arid or semi-arid	87	336	ns
Temperate (including tropical highlands)	107	158	107
Humid, subhumid and subtropical	ns	192	ns

[1] People in landless households keeping livestock; not industrial landless production systems.
Note: ns = not significant.
Source: Livestock in Development, 1999.

TABLE 11
Percentage of rural households owning livestock, share of income from livestock and number of livestock per household, by country

COUNTRY AND YEAR	SHARE OF RURAL HOUSEHOLDS OWNING LIVESTOCK	SHARE OF INCOME FROM LIVESTOCK[1]	SHARE OF LIVESTOCK PRODUCTION SOLD	NUMBER OF LIVESTOCK HELD PER RURAL HOUSEHOLD[1]
	(Percentage)			*(TLU[2])*
Africa				
Ghana (1998)	50	4	23	0.7
Madagascar (1993)	77	13	47	1.6
Malawi (2004)	63	9	9	0.3
Nigeria (2004)	46	4	27	0.7
Asia				
Bangladesh (2000)	62	7	28	0.5
Nepal (1996)	88	18	41	1.7
Pakistan (2001)	47	11	na	na
Viet Nam (1998)	82	15	62	1.1
Eastern Europe				
Albania (2005)	84	23	59	1.5
Bulgaria (2001)	72	12	4	0.5
Latin America				
Ecuador (1995)	84	3	27	2.8
Guatemala (2000)	70	3	18	0.9
Nicaragua (2001)	55	14	14	2.1
Panama (2003)	61	2	17	2.0
Average of above[3]	60	10	35	0.8

[1] Including all rural households in the samples, whether they hold livestock or not.
[2] The number of livestock is computed using the tropical livestock unit (TLU), which is equivalent to a 250 kg animal. The scale varies by region. For example, in South America, the scale is: 1 bovine = 0.7 TLU, 1 pig = 0.2, 1 sheep = 0.1 and 1 chicken = 0.01.
[3] The total weighted average by rural population.
Note: na = not available.
Source: FAO, 2009a.

over 45 percent for middle-income households in Malawi. Although there is no systematic pattern, in several instances poor people earn a larger share of their income from livestock than do the wealthier households.

While the majority of rural households in the RIGA sample keep livestock, the average livestock holdings tend to be small, ranging from 0.3 tropical livestock units (TLUs) in Malawi to 2.8 TLUs in Ecuador. Holdings tend to be smaller in the African and Asian countries and larger in the Latin American countries (Figure 13). Also, although the proportion of households keeping livestock does not seem to be clearly associated with income level, average holdings tend to increase with wealth in 8 out of the 14 countries.

The proportion of livestock production sold, in terms of value, differs widely among countries in the sample, but not among expenditure quintiles (Figure 14). There seems to be no clear relationship between income levels and the share of livestock production that is sold. In several cases, the share of livestock production sold is less for the lowest-expenditure quintiles than for higher-expenditure quintiles, indicating that livestock are kept more for own consumption by the less well-endowed households, while they are kept as a source of cash income by better-off households. However, the pattern

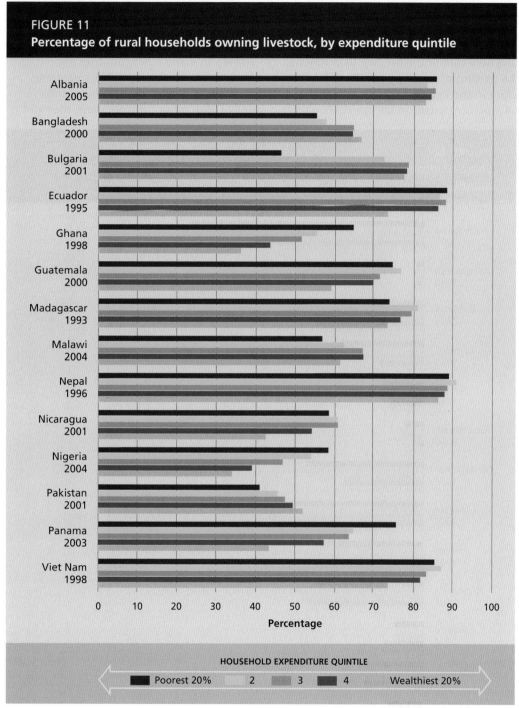

FIGURE 11
Percentage of rural households owning livestock, by expenditure quintile

Percentage

HOUSEHOLD EXPENDITURE QUINTILE

Poorest 20%   2   3   4   Wealthiest 20%

Source: FAO, 2009a.

is not similar across the countries, with several countries revealing differences.

In all the countries considered, more men than women own livestock, and households headed by men have larger livestock holdings than households headed by women. This is particularly true in the case of large animals (cattle and buffalo). Inequality in livestock holdings is particularly acute in Bangladesh, Ghana, Madagascar and Nigeria, where male-headed households keep more than three times as many livestock as do female-headed households (Anriquez, forthcoming). However, in the case of small livestock, particularly poultry, women play a much larger role. A large percentage of poultry production in Asia takes place in backyards, and it is mostly women who own and take care of the poultry. In Indonesia, 3.5 percent of poultry production takes place in the industrial sector, whereas 64.3 percent occurs in backyards. Poultry production in backyards by women is also substantial in Cambodia, the Lao People's Democratic Republic and Viet Nam (FAO, 2004b). In many other countries and regions, women own poultry, sometimes in numbers greater than do men, and, unlike with other livestock, have the right

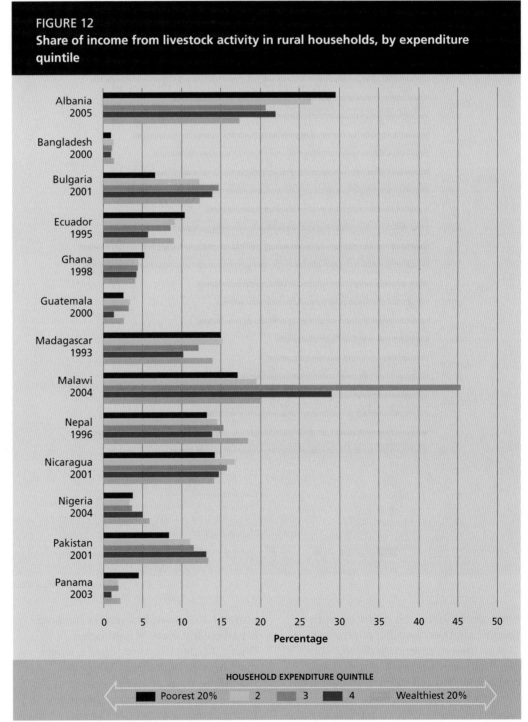

FIGURE 12

Share of income from livestock activity in rural households, by expenditure quintile

HOUSEHOLD EXPENDITURE QUINTILE

Poorest 20%   2   3   4   Wealthiest 20%

Source: FAO, 2009a.

to dispose of the poultry they raise without consulting men. The fact that women are responsible for poultry production in these areas has implications also for programmes to combat avian influenza.

The evidence from the RIGA database is generally consistent with the earlier findings. For example, Delgado *et al.* (1999) studied 16 different countries to compare the dependence on income from livestock of "very poor" and "not so poor" households. They found that most poor rural households are dependent on livestock to some extent, but the "not so poor" are likely to be much

FIGURE 13
Number of livestock held by rural households, by expenditure quintile

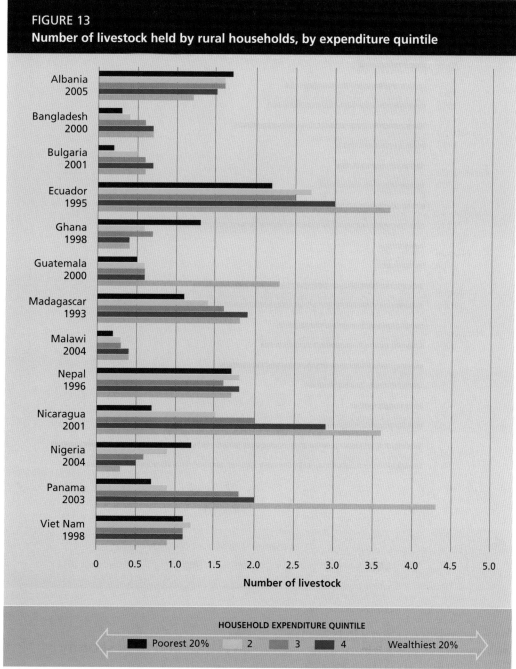

Number of livestock

HOUSEHOLD EXPENDITURE QUINTILE

Poorest 20%   2   3   4   Wealthiest 20%

Note: The number of livestock is computed using the tropical livestock unit (TLU), which is equivalent to a 250 kg animal. The scale varies by region. For example, in South America, the scale is: 1 bovine = 0.7 TLU, 1 pig = 0.2, 1 sheep = 0.1 and 1 chicken = 0.1.

Source: FAO, 2009a.

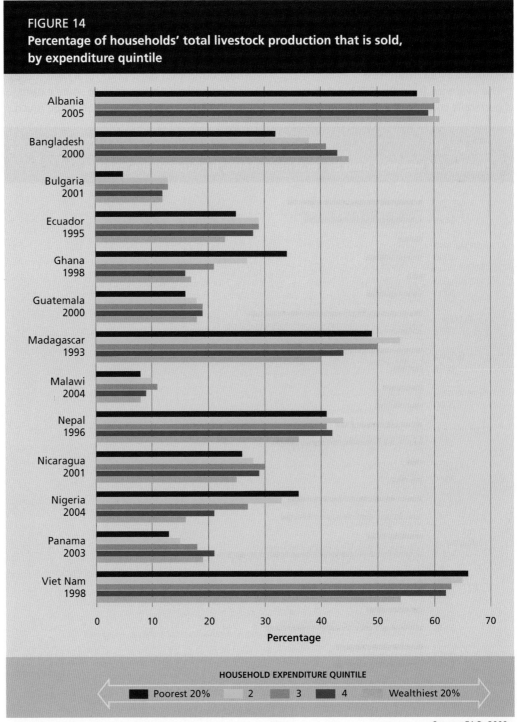

FIGURE 14
Percentage of households' total livestock production that is sold, by expenditure quintile

HOUSEHOLD EXPENDITURE QUINTILE

■ Poorest 20%   □ 2   ▨ 3   ■ 4   Wealthiest 20%

Source: FAO, 2009a.

more dependent on income from animals than are the "very poor". In contrast, Quisumbing *et al.* (1995) found that, in many instances, the poor earn a larger share of their income from livestock than do the wealthy because they can exploit common property resources for grazing, so keeping production costs low.

Livestock and food security

Undernutrition remains a persistent problem in many developing countries. The latest FAO figures (FAO, 2009c) indicate that nearly one billion people in the world are undernourished. Food security exists

BOX 4
Food versus feed: do livestock reduce availability of food for human consumption?

It is often assumed that lack of food for the poor and hungry could be remedied by reducing demand for feed. In reality, the relationship between feed demand and food security is complex, involving both physical and economic dimensions.

Each year livestock consume 77 million tonnes of protein from feed that is potentially suitable for human consumption, whereas only 58 million tonnes of protein are contained in food products supplied by livestock (Steinfeld *et al.*, 2006). In terms of dietary energy, the proportionate loss is much greater. This loss is a result of the recent trend towards more concentrate-based diets for livestock. However, this simple picture does not tell the whole story. It obscures the fact that proteins contained in animal products are of higher quality for human nutrition than those in the feed provided to the animals.

Also, from an economic perspective, it is important to remember that hunger and food insecurity are, in most cases, not a supply problem but a demand problem, caused by lack of purchasing power. In the hypothetical case in which the livestock

sector did not compete with humans for food, the surplus grain would not simply become available as food; rather, the reduced demand would mean that most of it would not be produced. However, while livestock may not directly take food from those who currently go hungry, they do contribute to raising overall demand, and thus prices, for crops and agricultural inputs. This tends to favour net producers but puts net consumers (in both urban and rural areas) at a disadvantage.

An important aspect that is often not considered is that livestock and their feed also make a contribution to food security objectives by providing a buffer in national and international markets that can be drawn upon in case of food shortages. In the previous world food crises of 1974/75 and 1981/82, overall grain supplies fell significantly. The livestock sector provided an important buffer function by contracting or switching to alternative feed supplies, thus contributing to lowering demand for grains. A similar buffer function has also been observed in the most recent food crisis in 2007 and 2008.

when all people at all times have access to adequate levels of safe, nutritious food for an active and healthy life. The livestock sector is central to food security, not only for rural smallholders who rely directly on livestock for food, incomes and services, but also for urban consumers, who benefit from affordable high-quality animal-based food. Livestock play an important role in all four main dimensions of food security: availability, access, stability and utilization.

Availability refers to the physical availability of adequate levels of food in a particular location. Food is made available through home production, local markets or imports. **Access** refers to the ability of people to acquire food. Even if food is physically present in an area, it may not be accessible if prices are very high or people lack purchasing power. Backyard and extensive grazing systems that rely

on waste products and land that cannot be cultivated contribute unambiguously to the availability of food. The intensive livestock systems described in Chapter 2 are an important source of affordable animal-based foods for urban consumers. By making efficient use of resources, they provide abundant low-cost food, contributing to the availability of and access to food. This role will become increasingly important as demand for livestock products continues to grow in coming years. At the same time, rapid growth in demand for livestock products means that, as noted earlier, one-third of all cropland is now used to produce livestock feed. Other things being equal, this competition for land traditionally reserved for the cultivation of other crops puts upward pressure on prices of staple foods and may undermine people's access to food. This is discussed in Box 4.

Most rural households, including the very poor, keep livestock. Livestock contribute directly to food availability and access for smallholders, often in complex ways. Smallholders sometimes consume their home production directly, but they often choose to sell high-value eggs or milk in order to buy lower-cost staple foods. The indirect role of livestock in supporting food security through income growth and poverty reduction is crucial to overall development efforts. When calculating the economic contribution of livestock to individual households, it is also essential to recognize that men and women typically face different livelihood opportunities and constraints in managing livestock. Selling livestock allows resource-poor families to earn more income, but this may not always translate into improved nutrition, depending on whether it is men or women who have control over the income generated. The extent to which nutrition is improved depends on whether increases in income create more diverse diets. In the long run, there is an established connection between income growth and improved nutrition. However, in the short run, policy interventions may be necessary to promote increased consumption of foods of animal origin in the diets of the poor.

Stability is the third dimension of food security. Livestock contribute to the stability of food security of rural households by serving as an asset, a store of value and a safety net. Livestock can be used as collateral for credit, sold for income or consumed directly in times of crisis, thus buffering external shocks to the household such as an injury or illness of productive family members. Livestock also provide draught power, fertilizer and pest control in mixed farming systems, contributing to total farm productivity and hence to food security.

The fourth dimension of food security – **utilization** – is particularly relevant in the case of livestock and animal-based foods. Research shows that livestock products are an excellent source of high-quality protein and essential micronutrients such as vitamin B and highly bioavailable[3] trace elements such as iron and zinc. This "bioavailability" is particularly important for mothers and small children, who find it difficult to obtain adequate levels of micronutrients in a plant-based diet. Small quantities of animal-based foods can provide essential nutrients for maternal health and the physical and mental development of small children.

Livestock and nutrition

The impact of poor nutrition on child growth and mental development is well documented and includes stunted growth and increased risk of infectious disease morbidity and mortality. Over the long term, undernutrition impairs cognitive development and school performance. Undernutrition is morally unacceptable, but it also comes at a high economic price. It reduces work performance and productivity in adults, lowers human capital development and constrains the potential for economic growth of countries (FAO, 2004a). Undernutrition can also make women, men and children more vulnerable to diseases such as malaria, tuberculosis and HIV/AIDS.

Foods of animal origin can provide high-quality protein and a variety of micronutrients that are difficult to obtain in adequate quantities from foods of plant origin alone. Although essential minerals such as iron and zinc are also present in cereal staples, they have lower bioavailability in plant-based foods owing to their form and the presence of inhibitors of absorption such as phytates; they are more readily bioavailable in foods of animal origin.

Six nutritive elements that can be lower in primarily vegetarian diets and that are provided by animal-based foods include vitamin A, vitamin B_{12}, riboflavin, calcium, iron and zinc. Health problems associated with inadequate intake of these nutrients include anaemia, poor growth, impaired vision and blindness, rickets, impaired cognitive performance and increased risk of infectious disease morbidity and mortality, especially in infants and children. Animal-origin foods are particularly rich sources of all six of these nutrients, and relatively small amounts of these foods, added to a plant-based diet, can substantially enhance nutritional adequacy.

The high nutrient density of animal foods has a further advantage in food-based interventions targeting vulnerable groups such as infants, children and people living

---

[3] Bioavailability refers to the degree to which nutrients are absorbed and utilized by the organism.

with HIV/AIDS, who may have difficulty consuming the large volumes of food needed to meet their nutritional requirements.

Available evidence indicates that in the poorest countries, where micronutrient deficiencies are most common, a moderate intake of foods of animal origin will improve the nutritional adequacy of diets and improve health outcomes. The Nutrition Collaborative Research Support Program reported strong associations between the intake of foods of animal origin and better growth, cognitive function and physical activity in children, better pregnancy outcomes and reduced morbidity resulting from illness in three parallel longitudinal observational studies in disparate ecological and cultural parts of the world, i.e. Egypt, Kenya and Mexico (Neumann *et al.*, 2003). These associations remained positive even after controlling for factors such as socio-

economic status, morbidity, parental literacy and nutritional status.

Better access to foods of animal origin through the promotion of livestock together with nutrition education can thus be considered a strategic intervention for avoiding the poverty–micronutrient–malnutrition trap (Demment, Young and Sensenig, 2003). Reviews of livestock interventions and their role in nutrition improvement and poverty reduction, although limited, show that livestock can play an important role in human nutrition and health and in poverty reduction in developing countries (Randolph *et al.*, 2007). Such interventions should be gender-specific to ensure that they effectively target food-insecure and vulnerable groups. Box 5 presents the example of a dairy-goat development project in Ethiopia, which significantly

---

BOX 5
The Dairy Goat Development Project in Ethiopia

Food and Agricultural Research Management (FARM)-Africa is an international non-governmental organization working to reduce poverty by enabling African farmers and herders to make sustainable improvements to their well-being, through more effective management of their renewable natural resources. The Dairy Goat Development Project was initiated in Ethiopia to improve family welfare by increasing income and milk consumption. It did so by improving the productivity of local goats managed by women, through a combination of better management techniques and genetic improvement.

Before the Dairy Goat Development Project, 21 percent of the households involved in the project had no access to milk; 67 percent made occasional purchases of milk for about one-quarter of the year. Forty-two percent of the households surveyed consumed meat, with an annual average consumption of 1.3 kg of meat per person. The remaining 58 percent of households consumed no meat at all. Following the project, each participating household was milking

its lactating goats twice a day and was obtaining an average of 75 litres of goat milk per household per year. Average per capita milk consumption was 15 litres/person per year. Further, each household sold an estimated 50–100 kg less cereal grain, which used to be sold to buy milk.

A similar intervention by FARM-Africa in another location in Ethiopia increased the per capita availability of milk by 109 percent, energy from animal sources by 39 percent, protein by 39 percent, and fat by 63 percent. The proportion of animal protein reached 20 percent. During the 3-year study, 67 households (63 percent) slaughtered 77 goats. This provided an average of 575 g of meat/person per year. The study concluded that developing the capacity of poor rural households to own and manage small livestock, such as dairy goats, had a direct impact on a family's ability to challenge the vicious cycle of poverty and undernutrition and could significantly improve their access to and consumption of foods of animal origin.

Source: Ayele and Peacock, 2003.

increased poor households' access to foods of animal origin.

While there are strong arguments for promoting livestock in developing countries to improve nutrition and health, it is important to recognize that excessive consumption of foods of animal origin may have adverse health effects, such as obesity and associated chronic diseases, including heart disease and diabetes (WHO/FAO, 2003). In a recent major review of the evidence on food, nutrition, physical activity and cancer undertaken by the World Cancer Research Fund and the American Institute for Cancer Research, the panel of international experts involved in the review judged the evidence that red meats and processed meats are causes of colorectal cancer as "convincing" (red meats referring to beef, pork, lamb and goat from domesticated animals). There was considered to be limited evidence that fish and foods containing vitamin D (found mostly in fortified foods and animal foods) decrease the risk of colorectal cancer. But the Panel judged that milk probably protects against colorectal cancer. The Panel also noted limited evidence suggesting that red meats and processed meats are causes of other cancers (WCRF/AICR, 2007, pp. 116, 129).

A "nutrition transition" is occurring in rapidly growing economies in the developing world (Popkin, 1994). Rapid changes in diet and decreasing levels of physical activity are leading to one form of malnutrition (obesity) replacing another (undernutrition). Growing consumption of high-fat animal products is one of several contributing factors. Using data on Chinese adults, for example, Popkin and Du (2003) have shown linkages between increased fat intake from animal-origin foods and a change in disease patterns. Sometimes these dietary shifts occur so rapidly that the two forms of malnutrition coexist in the same population. This has been referred to as the "double burden of malnutrition" (Kennedy, Nantel and Shetty, 2004). Globally, by 2000, roughly equal numbers of people were overweight and underweight (Gardner and Halwell, 2000). The World Health Organization (WHO) estimates that more than 1.6 billion people are overweight, a number that is projected to increase to 2.3 billion by 2015 (WHO, 2006).

The costs for developing countries that have to face this double burden of malnutrition are large. The human and financial costs of prevention and treatment of obesity and non-communicable diseases are high and place huge strains on existing health care systems. In the European Union (EU), the cost of obesity to society has been estimated at about 1 percent of GDP (WHO, 2006). In China, the economic cost of diet-related chronic diseases has already surpassed that of undernutrition – a loss of more than 2 percent of GDP (IFPRI, 2004; World Bank, 2006a). In Latin America and the Caribbean, such costs have been estimated at 1 percent of GDP of the region (PAHO, 2006).

Such diet-related concerns are often considered lifestyle choices over which governments have little control. Governments can and do attempt to influence consumption patterns, however, through education, incentives and broader agricultural and food policies (Schmidhuber, 2007). Pacific island countries, which have the highest obesity rates in the world (International Obesity Taskforce, 2009), have taken drastic measures to address diet-related health concerns. The Government of Fiji, concerned about the high fat content of sheep meat (mutton flaps) and turkey tails and the health consequences of importing such products, imposed an import ban on mutton flaps and instituted a ban on the sale (whether imported or locally produced) of these high-fat foods (Nugent and Knaul, 2006; Clarke and McKenzie, 2007). Following the lead of Fiji, the Government of Tonga imposed an outright ban on the importation of mutton flaps. In 2007, the Government of Samoa also banned the importation of turkey tail meat in support of measures aimed at curbing the rapidly expanding problem of obesity and diet-related non-communicable diseases.

Livestock sector transformation and the poor

The transformation of the livestock sector described in Chapter 2 is occurring most rapidly in developed countries and in developing countries that are experiencing strong economic growth. Livestock production remains largely unchanged in the poorest countries, where consumption and production of meat and milk have increased little, if at all, over recent decades. Livestock are kept under traditional management systems by poor, small-scale farmers, for whom they are an important safety net, providing both high-quality food and cash in times of need. Non-tradable livestock products and functions remain important in these systems. Livestock products are processed and marketed largely through informal systems. Nevertheless, even in the poorest countries, an emerging urban middle class has stimulated a fledgling, albeit small, formal market that supplies certified, processed and packaged products.

Wherever rural poverty persists and non-farm employment options are limited, small-scale mixed crop–livestock systems persist. Globally, it is estimated that 90 percent of milk and 70 percent of ruminant meat is produced in mixed systems, as are more than one-third of pig and poultry meat and eggs. In these mixed systems, livestock typically generate up to one-third of farm income. Mixed crop–livestock systems thus make important contributions to the livelihoods, incomes and food and nutritional security of the rural poor (Costales, Pica-Ciamarra and Otte, 2007).

In poor countries with pastoralist populations, traditional herders support subsistence livelihoods and sell live animals through local markets. In some countries in the Horn of Africa and the Sahel, pastoralists also supply cattle, sheep, goats and camels to traders who export live animals to traditional trading partners, mostly in the Near East and the growing coastal urban centres in West Africa. However, increasingly stringent sanitary standards threaten this trade. Pastoralism is under threat worldwide as mobility and access to traditional grazing areas become ever more restricted through border controls and the expansion of cultivation or, especially in parts of Africa, conservation-oriented activities. In addition, climate change appears to be making arid and semi-arid areas even drier and extreme weather events, including drought and floods, more common. Traditional coping mechanisms tend to fail in these situations and pastoralists are abandoning livestock production, voluntarily or involuntarily, in increasing numbers (Thornton *et al.*, 2002).

In those developing countries where income growth and the rise of an urban middle class have stimulated demand for livestock products, smallholder livestock keepers continue to operate in rural areas, but larger-scale, more-intensive and technologically sophisticated commercial operators begin to appear in peri-urban areas, especially in the poultry sector. Integrated operations also become established, in which large companies or cooperatives supply inputs and provide markets for small and medium-sized contract growers.

With economic growth, non-farm employment opportunities increase, rural wages rise, supermarkets extend their reach beyond urban centres and demand for livestock products increases further. Small-scale livestock keepers start to leave the sector as their need to keep a few livestock diminishes and the attractiveness and viability of the enterprise decline. The average size of holding of poultry and pigs tends to increase, although dairy herds often remain small. Even in rapidly growing markets, production and marketing of milk may still be dominated by the informal sector. Vertically integrated operators become larger and increasingly dominant, and small-scale poultry farmers find it increasingly difficult to stay in business, although small-scale pig keepers tend to be more successful in this regard.

In the most rapidly growing economies, smaller-scale livestock producers, especially of poultry and pigs, either join the ranks of subsistence farmers or leave the sector. A few may graduate to larger-scale operations. However, in many other countries "dual-track" development of the poultry sector has occurred, with backyard/village and industrial poultry existing together (see Box 6 for the example of China). This situation is likely to persist as long as rural poverty exists and local regulations permit, and has implications for human and animal diseases, which are discussed in Chapter 5. In countries that have seen little or no increase in poultry consumption, such as most African countries, the vast majority of production remains in backyard and village poultry flocks, frequently managed by women.

Livestock and poverty alleviation

Expanding markets for livestock products would appear to offer opportunities for improving the incomes of the many rural poor who depend on livestock for their livelihoods. However, while the growth and

BOX 6
Sector transition – poultry in China

Over recent decades, China has seen an enormous increase in production of poultry meat and eggs through a combination of a growing number of birds and increasing productivity per bird. Feed conversion ratios for broilers in large-scale enterprises improved markedly between 1985 and 2005 and are now comparable to those achieved in similar operations in Europe and North America. Dramatic improvements in transport infrastructure since the mid-1980s have facilitated the rapid intensification of the poultry sector. Railways are especially important for feed distribution and roads for transport of poultry products.

In 1985, production was dominated by more than 150 million small-scale poultry farmers, each keeping a few birds to supplement other farming activities. At the time, there were virtually no large-scale operations. Since then, there has been a rapid increase in intensification, with a trend towards fewer, larger, privately owned operations. Between 1996 and 2005, some 70 million small-scale poultry farmers left the sector, mostly in the more economically developed east of the country and around major cities. Over the same period, large-scale operations (with annual output of more than 10 000 birds) expanded their share of production from about one-quarter to one-half.

Today, the commercial broiler market is dominated by large, integrated companies that control the entire production and marketing chain: feed, breeding, fattening and processing. One large, integrated operation in Fujian Province, for example, produces 50 million broilers a year and employs 4 000 employees – one job for every 12 500 birds produced annually. Extrapolating this ratio to the national level suggests that the integrated broiler sector provides around 800 000 jobs (Bingsheng and Yijun, 2008). Contract rearing is the norm, with the integrator supplying feed and chicks, together with various services and advice, and buying back finished birds.

Between 1985 and 2005, the proportion of farming households that kept poultry fell from 44 percent to less than 14 percent. However, more than 34 million rural households still keep backyard poultry, and poultry remain an important source of income and food for poor households, especially in the less-developed western part of the country. However, backyard producers play a marginal role, if any, in meeting burgeoning market demand. As food marketing channels extend their reach ever further into the rural areas, and non-farm employment options increase, the need for rural households to keep poultry is declining (Bingsheng and Yijun, 2008).

In China, the livestock sector in general is becoming less important as a source of income for small-scale farmers. The contribution of this sector to incomes fell from 14 percent in 1990 to 9 percent in 2005, and in the most developed eastern provinces the share is even lower. As non-farm employment options for rural people increase and rural incomes rise, backyard livestock rearing, which is labour-intensive, becomes less attractive. In addition, rural populations are reported to be becoming less tolerant of the nuisance, such as flies and odour, caused by backyard livestock. Increasingly, the rural people work in village or town enterprises. In addition, it is estimated that up to 140 million former rural dwellers are now migrant workers in cities. The predominant trend among the young in the eastern provinces has been to leave agriculture and take up jobs in the non-farm sector (Bingsheng and Yijun, 2008), although the recent economic crisis has slowed or reversed this trend, at least temporarily.

transformation of the sector have created opportunities, the degree to which these can be harnessed by people living in poverty and in marginalized areas is not clear. The rapid changes in food demand in some parts of the developing world have required the livestock sector to produce as much as possible, as quickly as possible, as cheaply as possible and as safely as possible. This emphasis on speed, quantity, price and safety has created a bias towards large-scale intensive production, especially in some subsectors such as poultry and pigs. However, the situation in the dairy subsector appears to be different, and there are cases where smallholders have played a dominant role in satisfying growing demand (see Box 7).

The nature of the livestock sector has changed dramatically in some parts of the world, although the impacts vary among countries, species and genders. Countries where per capita consumption of livestock products has increased dramatically over recent decades, especially the rapidly emerging economies such as Brazil, China and India, are diverging from those where consumption remains static or is decreasing, such as much of sub-Saharan Africa. At the same time, within the countries in which transformation of the livestock sector has taken off, a widening gulf is opening between a small-scale traditional sector, where women play an active role, at one extreme and a growing large-scale, intensive sector, in which men tend to dominate, at the other.

As economic growth continues to drive livestock development, there is increasing pressure for parts of the sector to industrialize. Overall, while strong growth within the sector should be seen as a positive sign of economic development, the *speed* of change may put pressure on smallholders. Some livestock producers will probably find it hard to adjust quickly enough to safeguard their income and, in some cases, their food security. Experiences in OECD countries from the 1950s onwards show that changing production structures require labour markets to adjust. However, when the transition is extremely rapid, as is happening in the livestock sector in many places today, the implications for poverty and food security can be dramatic and warrant intervention.

For the past decade, researchers and policy-makers have assumed that growth in the livestock sector was primarily demand-driven (Delgado *et al.*, 1999) and that policies should aim at supporting demand growth and improving market opportunities (World Bank, 2007). Recent research however, shows that supply-side factors are also important. In many developing countries, growth in the livestock sector actually leads to GDP growth (see Box 8). This means that policies aimed directly at promoting productivity growth in the livestock sector can support broader economic growth. The complex value chains for animal-based foods – from feed and animal production through processing and marketing – mean that growth in the sector can generate strong backward and forward economic linkages and employment opportunities, with important impacts on growth that favours the poor. Creating the conditions necessary for smallholders to take advantage of these opportunities is a major policy challenge, requiring careful attention also to gender issues and environmental dimensions. Overcoming supply constraints for smallholders and increasing their productivity are important both to allow them to benefit from the demand-led gains and to allow the sector to play its role as a driver of growth.

Demand growth will continue to be a significant factor driving trends in the livestock sector in the future. However, supply-side factors, including relative competitiveness of different production systems and supply constraints faced by different producers, will also shape the sector and influence its contribution to poverty alleviation.

Reducing rural poverty through agricultural development alone is difficult. The challenge for livestock development is to foster development in rural areas in ways that benefit entire rural communities, and not only those who are engaged in livestock activities. Rural development policies can further facilitate the transformation of the sector by creating alternative opportunities for income generation and employment.

The objective of livestock sector development policies should be to enhance the competitiveness of smallholder production systems, where feasible, while mediating sector transition and protecting the poorest households, which rely on livestock as a safety net. Poor people need

BOX 7
Sector transition – dairy in India and Kenya

India, now the world's largest milk producer, witnessed a fourfold increase in milk production from cattle and buffalo between 1963 and 2003. Over the same period, the average herd size decreased. Production increases were obtained through a 40 percent increase in the number of farms engaged in milk production and an increase in the proportion of crossbred dairy cows in the national herd. In 1982, fewer than 5 percent of animals in the Indian dairy herd were crossbred. By 2003, this proportion had nearly trebled. It has been estimated that 56 percent of production growth can be accounted for by the increased number of milking animals and 37 percent by the higher productivity of the crossbred animals. Smallholder dairy production received an important impetus from the active support of government-sponsored programmes, such as Operation Flood, and a major effort to market milk in urban areas (Staal, Pratt and Jabbar, 2008a).

In 1999/2000, it was estimated that dairying in India, including production, processing and marketing, engaged around 18 million people, 5.5 percent of the national workforce. Of these jobs, 92 percent were in rural areas, 58 percent were occupied by women and 69 percent by socially and economically disadvantaged groups. Annual returns to farm-level labour in dairying are 2.5 times those for agriculture in general. For every 1 000 litres of milk produced per day, 230 jobs were generated by the smallest farms but fewer than 18 jobs by

the largest commercial farms. However, the majority of farms are small, with 80 percent of the national herd being kept on farms with eight or fewer milking animals (Staal, Pratt and Jabbar, 2008a).

Kenya has also experienced a fourfold increase in milk production over the past four decades. As in India, smallholders dominate production in Kenya, accounting for 85 percent of all milk produced. An estimated 2 million households are engaged in dairy farming in Kenya, together maintaining a national herd of some 5 million crossbred or exotic dairy cattle. The typical farm is small – 1–2.5 hectares, depending whether it is located in a high- or medium-potential area – and dairy farming is often integrated with crop farming in mixed crop–livestock systems. Use of zero- or semi-zero-grazing systems is common, and fodders are routinely cultivated for feed. Milk is predominantly marketed through informal systems, which supply mostly raw milk to consumers via small-scale market agents. Most Kenyan consumers prefer cheaper raw milk over significantly more expensive pasteurized milk. As the vast majority of people boil milk before consumption, potential health problems associated with consumption of raw milk are largely avoided. Alongside the informal marketing system, a well-organized but smaller formal sector supplies processed and packaged milk to more affluent, urban consumers (Staal, Pratt and Jabbar, 2008b). Production and marketing of milk in Kenya is a major

to be considered broadly, including their roles as consumers, market agents and employees, as well as small-scale producers and, possibly, as providers of environmental services (FAO, 2007a). All of this needs to take into account gender-related issues to ensure that the needs, priorities and constraints of women and men, both young and old, are taken into consideration in the design and implementation of livestock sector development policies.

Competitiveness and the livestock sector

A series of country case studies, focused on countries with rapidly developing economies (Brazil, India, the Philippines and Thailand), have investigated the competitiveness of smallholder livestock producers (Delgado, Narrod and Tiongco, 2008). The studies showed that relative efficiency gains varied

source of employment and small-business opportunities, both for family labour and hired employees.

Based on survey data collected between 1997 and 2000, the sector is estimated to provide 841 000 full-time jobs at the farm level, including self-employment and both permanent and casual hired labour. On average, 77 jobs are created for every 1 000 litres of milk produced per day (compared with just one job for every 2 500 litres produced in the Netherlands). The smallest farms, with up to two cows, generate twice as many jobs per 1 000 litres of milk as larger farms with six or more cows (Staal, Pratt and Jabbar, 2008b). Return to labour at the farm level is close to four times per capita GDP, suggesting that dairying provides significantly higher incomes to farmers than rural waged labour could offer. An additional 54 000 well-remunerated jobs are provided by milk marketing; average wages are three times the government minimum wage (Staal, Pratt and Jabbar, 2008b). The Kenyan example shows that a successful, growing livestock subsector can be dominated by small-scale producers and represent a significant source of employment and small-business opportunities.

However, in both India and Kenya, the development of the dairy subsector may have relied largely on specific national circumstances.

In India, the dairy sector's growth depended in large part on the use of buffalo which, unlike high-yielding dairy cattle, are well adapted to tropical climes. Today, across India, more than half of all milk is produced from buffalo. Cross-bred cattle numbers are increasing but they still account for less than 14 percent of the total cattle population. Milk and dairy products are the predominant culturally acceptable animal protein source. Although meat consumption is increasing, especially among younger, more cosmopolitan Indians, hundreds of millions of Indians remain vegetarian (*The Times of India*, 2005). The sector has received significant financial and political support for more than 50 years: modernization of the dairy sector was a government priority in the very first Five-Year Plan, while in the 1970s Operation Flood targeted cooperative development at the village level and physical and institutional infrastructure for milk procurement, processing and marketing at the district level (Staal, Pratt and Jabbar, 2008a).

In Kenya, the dairy sector built on a strong base and benefited from favourable climatic conditions in the Kenyan highlands, which are well suited to keeping exotic dairy breeds.

Globally, dairy production and trade are dominated by the temperate regions of the developed world. Heat stress in the humid tropics depresses productivity of high-yielding dairy cattle, such as Holsteins, which puts temperate regions at a comparative advantage. The majority of countries within the humid zone are, therefore, not traditional milk-producing and consuming countries.

as scale of operation increased, although not in a linear fashion: there was a significant gain in efficiency in moving from very small backyard production to smallholder commercial (e.g. from rearing 15–20 piglets a year to rearing 150–200, or from 1–2 milking cows to a herd of 15–30 head); further large efficiency gains were not then achieved until much larger increases in unit size occurred. Vertical coordination, including cooperatives and various contract farming arrangements, were also associated with increased efficiency as a result of reduction in transaction costs.

Overall, small farms were less efficient at securing a profit (a measure of efficiency of use of resources) than large farms, even when family labour was not included as a cost. The studies looked at various determinants of profit efficiency, including dealing with environmental externalities. In general, small-scale farmers made greater efforts, and therefore incurred more costs, in mitigating environmental impacts of their livestock. On larger farms, the balance of evidence showed that those farms that expended the greatest efforts on environmental mitigation were also relatively more profitable per unit of resources used. This is perhaps because those farms that prioritized environmental mitigation also adopted other types of best practice, which tended to boost productivity.

Two factors seemed to be particularly important for the relative competitiveness of smallholder producers: transaction costs and labour costs. On the one hand, economies of scale associated with input and output markets tended to favour large-scale producers, offering lower transaction costs relative to those faced by small producers. This difference was particularly significant in the poultry and pig sectors. On the other hand, small-scale producers often used family labour, which may arguably have a lower opportunity cost, at least where much of the labour is contributed by women and children and alternative employment options are limited. This represents a competitive advantage over large-scale

enterprises, which depend on labour hired at prevailing market rates, but has important social implications for school attendance of boys and girls.

Small-scale farmers typically face higher transaction costs than do large-scale enterprises. It is more difficult and costly for them to access high-quality inputs (especially feed), credit and technology. On the output side, market information is particularly important in higher-end markets, where quality is important. The impact of transaction costs differed across the countries and sectors studied (Delgado, Narrod and Tiongco, 2008). In the dairy sector, transaction costs had little impact on profit efficiency, as feed was largely forage-based, not requiring access to credit. However, transaction costs could be high in dairy distribution and processing, with the costs tending to be higher for small farms than larger ones. In some countries, this was causing smallholders to leave the sector as dairies considered it too costly to serve them. Transaction costs had a greater impact on competitiveness in the poultry and pig sectors than in the dairy sector because of

---

BOX 8
The livestock sector – why supply-side factors matter

A recent study carried out by Pica, Pica-Ciamarra and Otte (2008) found a statistically significant causal relationship between economic growth and livestock sector productivity growth in 36 out of the 66 developing countries examined. Most of the 36 countries are agricultural-based or transforming economies. In 33 of the 36 countries, livestock sector productivity appears to have been a driver of per capita GDP growth. In nine of these, causality was bidirectional: livestock sector growth stimulated economic growth and economic growth positively affected livestock sector productivity. Only in three of the 36 countries was there a unidirectional causality from growth in per capita GDP to increases in livestock sector productivity.

Overall the study indicates that the orthodox paradigm of increased agricultural productivity as a driver of

economic growth in developing countries also applies to the livestock sector. This implies that a vision of the livestock sector as primarily driven by exogenous factors may mislead policy development. Whereas policies that enable smallholders to sell profitably in high-value markets may be important, policies addressing the fundamental constraints to the development of the livestock sector may be equally important. Thus, policies aimed at improving smallholder productivity should not focus only on basic staple crops but also on livestock products, which may be basic food items and an important source of income in many rural communities in developing countries.

Source: Pica, Pica-Ciamarra and Otte, 2008.

the critical needs for credit to buy feed and stock and for access to market information.

Reducing transaction costs for small producers

High transaction costs for smallholder producers can be reduced through collective action, such as the setting up of cooperatives and various forms of contract farming. Such arrangements also have potential to incorporate smallholders in high-value supply chains from which they would otherwise be excluded. This kind of arrangement can also encourage gender equality by providing equal access to resources, including capacity building targeted equally at women and men. Contract arrangements vary and often involve the contractor supplying genetically superior breeds (particularly in poultry and pig production), feed, advice and support, and a guaranteed market for the end product.

Formal contracts are often made between integrator companies and larger-scale farmers in peri-urban locations, rather than with rural smallholders. They often demand a form of bond as collateral to mitigate the integrator company's initial risk in engaging with a new producer. The tendency of formal contracts to favour larger farmers stems from the economies of scale achieved by integrator companies in dealing with fewer suppliers that offer larger volumes, as well as avoiding the high transaction costs associated with dealing with and monitoring a large number of smallholders with different capacities to deliver (Costales and Catelo, 2008). Moreover, contract farming has not always been welcomed by small producers because it often offers them reduced margins and less independence (Harkin, 2004). In China, integrator companies have been found to honour contracts only when market prices exceeded the contract prices, providing a disincentive for farmers to enter into such contracts (Zhang *et al.*, 2004).

Smallholders are more commonly involved in informal contracts than in formal ones. Entry into such contracts requires a degree of prior social capital, such as membership of a farmers' organization or established reputation, rather than just physical collateral (Costales and Catelo, 2008). Smallholders tend to be the target of formal contracts only when they are the dominant production system and majority suppliers in locations where the integrator company operates, when they possess sufficient human capital and are receptive to training within the system, or when the integration of smallholders in a particular location in the supply chain is an explicit goal of the integrator company.

In general, smallholders do not participate in contract farming but independently produce and sell in spot markets. In a review of case studies on various types of contract, Costales and Catelo (2008) found that the "ability of contract farming in efficiently and profitably integrating rural smallholder producers in high-value markets, revealed rather mixed results, with some promising successful cases, and many failed ones." One successful example is that of dairy sector cooperatives in India. The success of the dairy sector cooperative movement in Gujarat, India, was coupled with links to the green revolution and support to agriculture in general through, for example, technology transfers (Staal, Pratt and Jabbar, 2008a). The Indian example highlights the importance of linking and integrating sector development to wider agricultural and rural development for the benefit of smallholders in livestock (see Box 9).

Analysis of the overall benefits of contract farming by smallholders has thus shown mixed results. In some cases, contract farming has been shown to be more profitable than farming independently, but in others – such as small-scale pig producers in the Philippines – independent farms were more profitable. Crucially, contract farming tends to increase the competitiveness of large farms relative to small, and there are cost and quality-control incentives for the integrators in dealing with fewer, larger producers rather than with many smaller producers.

It appears that smallholder producers can stay in business provided that the opportunity cost of family labour remains low and they can benefit from some sort of collective organization and support network to reduce transaction costs. Where alternative employment options offer higher wages, such as the more developed parts of China, the competitive advantage of smallholder producers disappears and there

BOX 9
Kuroiler™ chickens – linking backyard poultry systems to the private sector

The development community increasingly recognizes the role of backyard poultry production in sustaining and enhancing poor peoples' livelihoods in developing countries. Market-oriented backyard poultry enterprises are seen as a stepping stone for the poorest households, enabling them to take the first step towards breaking out of the vicious circle of poverty and deprivation. There is growing evidence to demonstrate that keeping poultry can enhance the food and nutrition security of the poorest households, improving livelihoods and promoting gender equity (Ahuja and Sen, 2008; Ahuja, 2004; Dolberg, 2004).

The private sector also sees business potential offered by backyard poultry. One example of private-sector involvement in backyard poultry production is the development of the Kuroiler™ breed, developed in India by Kegg Farms Private Ltd in 1993. The Kuroiler™ breed was bred for the Indian rural market and is supplied to farmers through a network of local suppliers.

In the first year, the company sold more than 1 million day-old Kuroiler™ chicks. In 2005–06, it sold 14 million – an annual growth rate of almost 22 percent sustained for more than a decade. A field study of Kuroiler™ production (Ahuja *et al.*, 2008) showed that, in the sample selected, a large proportion of those raising the birds were landless households or marginal farmers with less than one acre of land. On average, households raising Kuroilers™ generated more than five times as much from their poultry enterprise as did households that kept non-Kuroiler™ poultry.

There were, however, aspects of the operation that required attention. There was no monitoring of vaccination, mortality or the level of drug use in the chain. This has significant implications for reducing risk and containing losses in the chain. The risk-bearing ability of participating households is extremely low, and any sign of inherent risk – in the form of a disease outbreak, for example – could be destabilizing. The study suggested that addressing such issues required public or private investment in skill building in poultry management, livelihood analysis, and certification of various inputs used in the value chain.

is likely to be a mass exit from the sector as farmers are drawn into more remunerative employment. However, in a context of overall economic development, people leaving the livestock sector to take up new, better-paid waged employment cannot be considered a negative development.

Livestock policies for sector transition

Rapid growth and transformation in the livestock sector offer both challenges and opportunities for smallholders and require a difficult balancing act by policy-makers. Scarce public and donor resources should not be spent on fighting the forces of economic change; rather, they should focus on mediating change to produce more desirable outcomes for all members of society.

Growth in the livestock sector offers significant opportunities to enhance food security and reduce poverty, but concerted gender-sensitive action is required to help those smallholders who can compete to take advantage of the emerging opportunities. Without appropriate support for technological and institutional innovation, many smallholders will be unable to respond to the opportunities to supply new markets, and the divide will widen between those who can successfully negotiate change and those who cannot. Some smallholders will leave the sector as the forces of competition erode their competitiveness and as the opportunity cost of their labour rises. For many others, livestock will remain an important part of their sustenance or survival strategy. The safety-net function of livestock for these people should be recognized, but it should not be considered a development strategy in its own right.

A mix of policy change, technological and institutional innovation and investment is needed. Building locally specific capacity that can respond to change is especially important. In all cases, the imperative should be to see livestock sector management in the broader context of rural development; that is, to create a rural sector that is as dynamic as the manufacturing and service sectors and that can provide a range of alternative remunerative activities both within and outside livestock production *per se* (PPLPI, 2008).

Significant and sustained innovation in national, regional and global food and agricultural systems will be required in order to support rural development. In the case of livestock, the notion of capacity for innovation needs to be expanded to encompass the complex set of activities, players and policies involved in developing, accessing and using knowledge and technology for agriculture and food-system innovation (World Bank, 2006b). Research arrangements need to pay more attention to technology demand from users, particular poor women and men, and other key economic actors, such as entrepreneurs and industrialists, who can create new opportunities for growth and welfare (Hall and Dijkman, 2008). Innovations in livestock production, processing, utilization and distribution usually take place where different players in the sector are well networked together, allowing them to make creative use of ideas, technologies and information from different sources, including from research.

The viability of small farmers in general – not just in livestock production – continues to be an important matter of debate. In managing sector transition, a significant difficulty lies in identifying sets of policies that work in different contexts. Three categories of small-scale livestock keepers should be considered: (i) small commercial operators who are and can remain competitive given appropriate policies, institutional support and investments; (ii) backyard producers who keep livestock only because the lack of alternative

opportunities makes it feasible; and (iii) the very poor who keep livestock primarily as a form of insurance or safety net. Governments should help those smallholders who can thrive, while recognizing that some will be forced to leave the sector and will need assistance in the transition. Broader rural development policies aimed at the creation of off-farm employment, for both women and men, along the value chain within the sector or outside the sector may provide more stable long-term incomes for those who currently use livestock for survival rather than for production.

Some small commercial livestock producers are competitive and can take advantage of the growth opportunities in the sector. In rapidly growing economies where the livestock sector is in the early stages of transition, smallholders need support in order to be able to participate in the transition. Appropriate interventions include: support for technological innovations to increase productivity and to meet increasingly stringent health and food-safety standards; access to capital and credit for investment; access to input and output services and markets; and improved transportation and communication infrastructure. The capacity to respond to changing contexts and conditions is essential if smallholders are to thrive. Such capacity relates not only to financial, technical and infrastructure requirements, but also involves routines and networks that, in combination with policies, allow technology and other forms of information to be put into productive use (World Bank, 2007).

Some smallholders are unlikely to be able to compete as the livestock sector becomes increasingly concentrated and linked to modern processing and marketing channels. These producers require support as they leave the sector. Many livestock producers move out of the sector as the opportunity cost of family labour rises. The development of off-farm rural employment opportunities, through improving the quality and access to general education for girls and boys, can assist these households in finding new, more sustainable livelihoods. In these scenarios, the objective of pro-poor development policies for the livestock sector should be to mediate sector transition in which the roles of poor women, men and youths are considered broadly, including as consumers, market agents and employees, as well as small-scale producers.

The very poor, who rely on livestock primarily as a safety net, need policies and institutional arrangements that reduce their vulnerability. Livestock production may remain a pillar of livelihoods and safety nets for poor households for many years to come. As discussed in Chapters 4 and 5, there is a need to minimize risks from zoonotic and food-borne diseases and environmental hazards to these livestock keepers themselves and the wider community (Sones and Dijkman, 2008).

Key messages of the chapter

- Livestock are important to the livelihoods of a large percentage of rural women, men and children living in poverty. They play a number of different roles, from income generation and the provision of inputs into mixed cropping systems to providing a buffer against environmental and economic shocks. Policy-makers need to consider the multiple roles of livestock in the livelihoods and food security of the poor.
- Smallholders need support in order to take advantage of the opportunities provided by an expanding livestock sector and to manage the risks associated with increasing competition and closer linkages with modern value chains. This requires significant and sustained innovation in national, regional and global food and agricultural systems, and a mix of policy and institutional change, capacity building, technological innovation and investment that is gender-sensitive and responsive.
- Policy-makers need to consider the different capacities of smallholders to respond to change. Some smallholders may be unable to compete in a rapidly modernizing sector and will give up their livestock, as opportunity costs for family labour rise. Broader rural development strategies aimed at creating off-farm employment for women, men and youths can ease their transition out of the livestock sector.

- Policy-makers need to recognize and protect the safety-net function performed by livestock for the very poor. Within the livestock sector, poor people are particularly vulnerable to risks related to zoonotic diseases and environmental hazards.

4. Livestock and the environment

Policy action is required to mitigate the impact of livestock production on the environment and to ensure that the sector makes sustainable contributions to food security and poverty reduction. Livestock production, like any economic activity, can be associated with environmental damage. Unclear property rights and the lack of adequate governance of the livestock sector can contribute to the depletion and degradation of land, water and biodiversity. At the same time, the livestock sector is affected by the degradation of ecosystems and faces increasing competition for these same resources from other sectors. Climate change represents a special "feedback loop", in which livestock production both contributes to the problem and suffers from the consequences. Unless appropriate action is taken to improve the sustainability of livestock production, the livelihoods of millions of people will be at risk.

The livestock sector suffers from market and policy failures at many levels, including problems associated with open-access resources, externalities and perverse incentives that encourage damaging practices. While some countries have made progress in reducing pollution and deforestation associated with livestock production, many more require appropriate policies and enforcement capacity. Given the likely continued strong growth in global demand for livestock products and the reliance of many people on livestock for their livelihoods, there is an urgent need to enhance the efficiency of natural-resource use in the sector and to reduce the environmental footprint of livestock production. Given better management practices, the livestock sector can reduce its footprint and contribute substantially to climate change mitigation. Achieving these objectives requires action on policy, institutional and technical levels.

Livestock production systems and ecosystems

The interaction of livestock with ecosystems is complex and depends on location and management practices. Most traditional livestock production systems are resource-driven in that they make use of locally available resources with limited alternative uses or, expressed in economic terms, low opportunity costs. Examples of such resources include crop residues and extensive grazing land not suitable for cropping or other uses. At the same time, in mixed production systems, traditionally managed livestock often provide valuable inputs to crop production, ensuring a close integration between the two.

The rising demand for livestock products is changing the relationship between livestock and natural resources. Modern industrial production systems are losing the direct link to the local resource base and are based on bought-in feed. At the same time, some of the resources previously available to livestock at a low cost are becoming increasingly costly, either because of growing competition for the resources from other economic sectors and other activities (such as production of biofuels; see Box 10) or because society is placing greater value on the non-market services provided by these resources (such as water and air quality).

The separation of industrialized livestock production from the land used to produce feed also results in a large concentration of waste products, which can put pressure on the nutrient absorptive capacity of the surrounding environment. In contrast, grazing and mixed farming systems tend to be rather closed systems, in which waste products of one production activity (manure, crop residues) are used as resources or inputs to the other.

The livestock sector is also a source of gaseous emissions that pollute the atmosphere and contribute to the

BOX 10
Expansion of biofuels production

Growing use of cereals and oilseeds to produce fossil fuel substitutes – ethanol and biodiesel – represents a significant challenge for the livestock sector in terms of competition for resources. The global biofuel industry has experienced a period of extraordinary growth, driven by a combination of high oil prices, ambitious goals for use of renewable energy set by governments around the world and subsidies in many OECD countries.

This rapid growth has had important consequences for the price and availability of crops, such as maize and oilseed rape, that are used as biofuel feedstocks. Most studies to date have focused on impacts on the crop sector. However, the livestock sector has also been strongly affected. The most obvious consequence of large-scale liquid biofuel production for the livestock industry is higher crop prices, which raise feed costs. Biofuel production also increases returns to cropland, which encourages conversion of pastureland to cropland.

On the other hand, producing biofuels creates valuable by-products, such as distillers' dried grains with solubles (DDGS) and oilseed meals, that can be used as animal feed and can substitute for grain in animal rations. Production of these by-products has increased dramatically in recent years as a result of the boom in biofuel production. The prices of these by-products have fallen relative to other feedstuffs, and, as a result, they have

been increasingly used in feeds in some countries and production systems.

This suggests that biofuel by-products have helped to offset some of the adverse cost implications of the biofuels boom for the livestock industry. At the same time, biofuel by-products represent an important component of biofuel industry revenues. If the livestock industry could not absorb these by-products, their prices would fall sharply, thereby making biofuel less economically viable.

The impact of large-scale biofuel production on the livestock industry varies across regions and across livestock types. The strongest impact is being felt in those countries that are actively pursuing efforts to increase biofuel use (e.g. the United States of America and countries of the European Union), as well as those countries that are closely tied into the global agricultural economy. The impacts across different livestock sectors are also quite diverse. For example, dairy and beef producers traditionally use DDGS in their feed rations as it is palatable to cattle and well digested. They are thus better positioned to gain from increased DDGS availability than are other livestock producers, who may not be able to adjust their feed rations as readily to absorb the increased supply of DDGS.

Sources: Taheripour, Hertel and Tyner, 2008a and 2008b.

greenhouse effect. Continued growth in livestock production will exacerbate pressures on the environment and natural resources, calling for approaches that allow for increased production while lowering the environmental burden.

Livestock and land
Livestock is the world's largest user of land resources, with grazing land and cropland dedicated to the production of feed representing almost 80 percent of all agricultural land. The sector uses

3.4 billion hectares for grazing (Table 12) and 0.5 billion hectares for feed crops (Steinfeld _et al._, 2006); the latter figure corresponds to one-third of total cropland.

The total land area occupied by pasture is equivalent to 26 percent of the ice-free terrestrial surface of the planet. Much of this area is too dry or too cold for cropping, and is only sparsely inhabited. Management practices and use of pastureland vary widely, as does the productivity of livestock per hectare. In arid and semi-arid rangelands, where most of the world's grasslands

TABLE 12
Land use by region and country group, 1961, 1991 and 2007

REGION/COUNTRY GROUPING	ARABLE LAND				PASTURE				FOREST[1]		
	Area			Share of total land	Area			Share of total land	Area		Share of total land
	1961	1991	2007	2007	1961	1991	2007	2007	1991	2007	2007
	(Million ha)			(Percentage)	(Million ha)			(Percentage)	(Million ha)		(Percentage)
Baltic states and CIS[2]	235.4	224.4	198.5	9.2	302.0	326.5	362.1	16.9	848.8	849.9	39.6
Eastern Europe	48.7	45.0	39.7	34.9	20.0	20.4	16.6	14.6	34.7	35.9	31.6
Western Europe	89.0	78.6	72.8	20.4	69.7	60.7	58.9	16.5	122.5	132.9	37.2
Developing Asia	404.4	452.5	466.4	17.6	623.4	805.1	832.8	31.5	532.8	532.6	20.1
North Africa	20.4	23.0	23.1	3.8	73.4	74.4	77.3	12.9	8.1	9.1	1.5
Sub-Saharan Africa	133.8	161.3	196.1	8.3	811.8	823.8	833.7	35.3	686.8	618.2	26.2
Latin America and the Caribbean	88.7	133.6	148.8	7.3	458.4	538.5	550.1	27.1	988.3	914.6	45.1
North America	221.5	231.3	215.5	11.5	282.3	255.4	253.7	13.6	609.2	613.5	32.9
Oceania	33.4	48.5	45.6	5.4	444.5	431.4	393.0	46.3	211.9	205.5	24.2
DEVELOPED COUNTRIES	633.8	632.4	576.2	10.9	1 119.0	1 094.1	1 083.4	20.5	1 815.7	1 829.0	34.7
DEVELOPING COUNTRIES	647.6	770.9	834.9	10.8	1 967.8	2 242.6	2 294.8	29.7	2 252.6	2 108.4	27.3
WORLD	1 281.3	1 403.2	1 411.1	10.8	3 086.7	3 336.8	3 378.2	26.0	4 068.3	3 937.3	30.3

[1] Forest data available only from 1991.
[2] CIS = Commonwealth of Independent States.
Source: FAO, 2009b.

are found, intensification of pastures is frequently technically unfeasible or unprofitable. Also, in much of Africa and Asia, pastures are traditionally common-property areas. As a result of weakening traditional institutions and increased land pressure, many of these have become open-access areas. In these and other major grassland-based systems, incentives and technology to improve pasture management are lacking; thus potential productivity gains and ecosystem services are lost.

There are three major trends relating to pasturelands: valuable ecosystems are being converted to pastureland (e.g. clearing of forest); pastureland is being converted to other uses (cropland, urban areas and forest); and pastureland is degrading.

Ranching-induced deforestation is a common feature in Central and South America (Wassenaar et al., 2006). At the same time, grasslands are increasingly fragmented and encroached upon by cropland and urban areas. White, Murray and Rohweder (2000) estimate that more than 90 percent of the North American tallgrass prairie and almost 80 percent of the South America cerrado have been converted to cropland and urban uses. In contrast, the Asian Daurien steppe and the Eastern and Southern Mopane and Miombo woodlands in sub-Saharan Africa are relatively intact, with less than 30 percent converted to other uses.

About 20 percent of the world's pastures and rangeland have been degraded to some extent, and the proportion may be as high as 73 percent in dry areas (UNEP, 2004). The Millennium Ecosystem Assessment estimated that 10–20 percent of all grassland is degraded, mainly by overgrazing. Pasture degradation is generally a consequence of a mismatch between livestock density and the capacity of the pasture to recover from grazing and trampling. Ideally, the land-to-livestock ratio should be continuously adjusted to the conditions of the pasture, especially in dry climates. However, because of weakened traditional institutions, increased pressures on resources and increased obstacles to livestock movements, such adjustment is often not possible. This is particularly the case in the arid and semi-arid communal grazing areas of the Sahel and Central Asia. In these areas, increasing human population and encroachment of arable farming on grazing lands have severely restricted the mobility of the herds and limited options for their management. Among the environmental consequences of pasture degradation are soil erosion, degradation of vegetation, release of carbon from organic matter deposits, reduction in biodiversity and impaired water cycles.

Pasture degradation can be reversed to some extent, although how quickly this can occur and what methodologies are best remain matters of debate. There is little doubt, however, that current productivity is constrained by high stocking rates in parts of Africa and Asia, where grazing lands are overexploited. Grazing lands can be sustainably managed under common-property systems. However, where common-property systems have broken down, overexploitation is often observed. The economic rationale by which individual livestock holders attempt to maximize their personal benefits when common-property systems break down is clear: maximizing the number of animals per hectare allows for the harvesting of more of the resource for individual gain. This encourages overexploitation of land resources to the detriment of overall productivity.

Land dedicated to feed-crop production
Most of the world's feed-crop production occurs in OECD countries, but some developing countries are rapidly expanding their production of feed crops, notably maize and soybean in South America. Intensive feed-crop production can lead to severe land degradation, water pollution and biodiversity losses, while expanding arable land into natural ecosystems often has serious ecological consequences, including the loss of biodiversity and of ecosystem services such as water regulation and erosion control.

While increases in grain production have been mostly achieved through intensification on existing areas, much of the rapid increase in soybean production has been achieved through expansion of cropping into natural habitats. Pressure on land resources for feed inputs has been mitigated in recent decades by the shift away from ruminants towards pigs and poultry, which have better feed conversion, and high-yielding breeds and improved management practices.

Meeting future demand for livestock products will, however, require further improvements in livestock and land productivity as well as expanding feed production area, at the expense of pastureland and natural habitats.

Livestock and water
Livestock production systems differ in the amount of water used per animal and in how these requirements are met. In extensive systems, the effort expended by animals in search of feed and water increases the need for water considerably compared with intensive or industrialized systems. However, intensive production has additional service water requirements for cooling and cleaning facilities, generally resulting in much higher overall water consumption than extensive systems. Both intensive and extensive systems can contribute to water pollution through waste runoff, although the concentration of livestock associated with intensive systems exacerbates this problem. The processing of livestock products also uses large amounts of water.

The livestock sector accounts for about 8 percent of global water use, primarily for irrigation of feed crops. The growth of industrial production systems is increasing the need for water for feed-crop production. Water used directly for livestock production and processing is less than 1 percent of water use globally, but often represents a much greater percentage of water use in dry areas. For example, the water consumed directly by livestock represents 23 percent of total water use in Botswana (Steinfeld *et al.*, 2006).

The livestock sector can harm water quality through the release of nitrogen, phosphorus and other nutrients, pathogens and other substances into waterways and groundwater, mainly from manure in intensive livestock operations. Poor manure management often contributes to pollution and eutrophication of surface waters, groundwater and coastal marine ecosystems and to the accumulation of heavy metals in soils. This may lead to harm to human health and loss of biodiversity, and contribute to climate change, soil and water acidification and degradation of ecosystems.

The separation of industrialized livestock from its supporting land base interrupts the nutrient flows between land and livestock. This creates problems of depletion of nutrients at the source (land, vegetation and soil) and problems of pollution at the sink (animal wastes, increasingly disposed of into waterways instead of back on the land). The magnitude of the issue is illustrated by the fact that the total amounts of nutrients in livestock excreta are as large as or larger than the total contained in all chemical fertilizers used annually (Menzi *et al.*, 2009).

There are a number of options available to reduce the impact of the livestock sector on water resources. These include reducing water use (e.g. through more efficient irrigation methods and animal cooling systems), reducing depletion or harm to water supplies (e.g. through increased water-use efficiency and improved waste management and feed-crop fertilization practices) and greater replenishment of water resources through better land management.

Looking at manure treatment in particular, there is a wide range of proven options, including separation technologies, composting and anaerobic digestion. These offer a number of benefits, including: allowing safe application of manure on food and feed crops; improved sanitation; better odour control; production of biogas; and improved fertilizer value of the manure. Most importantly, replacing mineral fertilizer with manure would lower the environmental impact of food production (Menzi *et al.*, 2009).

The increased number of livestock needed to meet the projected growth in demand for livestock products is likely to have substantial impacts on water resources and on competition for their use. However, livestock–water interactions have been largely neglected in both water and livestock research and planning to date (Peden, Tadesse and Misra, 2007). This oversight will have to be addressed if the livestock sector is to continue to develop without causing greater harm to the environment.

Livestock and biodiversity

Biodiversity refers to the range of animal, plant and microbial species (interspecific biodiversity) on earth as well as the richness of genes within a given species (intraspecific biodiversity). It encompasses the genetic variation among individuals within the same population and among populations. Ecosystem diversity is another dimension of biodiversity.

Agricultural biodiversity is a particular case of intraspecific diversity that is an artefact of human activity. It includes domesticated animals and plants as well as non-harvested species that support food provision within agro-ecosystems. Knowledge about biodiversity is often embedded in social structures and may not be equally distributed or necessarily freely communicated between different groups of people, including ethnic groups, clans, gender or economic groups (FAO, 2004b). For example, women who process wool may have very different knowledge about breed characteristics, focusing as they do on wool, than men who herd livestock and focus on fodder and water consumption or disease resistance.

Livestock production systems affect biodiversity differently. Intensive systems rely on a limited number of crop species and animal breeds, although each may be quite rich in terms of genetic background. These systems depend on intensively managed feed crops, which are often blamed for ecosystem degradation. However, intensive land use may actually protect non-agricultural biodiversity by reducing pressure to expand crop and pasture areas. Extensive systems may host a larger number of breeds and make use of a wider variety of plant resources as feed, but their lower productivity may increase pressure to encroach more on natural habitats. In general, the effect of livestock on biodiversity depends on the magnitude of livestock impacts or the extent to which biodiversity is exposed to those impacts, how sensitive the biodiversity in question is to livestock and how it responds to the impacts (Reid *et al.*, 2009).

Many livestock breeds – a component of agricultural biodiversity – are at risk of disappearing, in large part as a result of increasing use of a narrow range of livestock breeds in intensive systems. Box 11 addresses the need to conserve domestic animal diversity.

According to the Millennium Ecosystem Assessment (MEA, 2005), the most important direct drivers of biodiversity loss and ecosystem service changes are: habitat change (such as land-use changes, physical modification of rivers or water withdrawal from them, loss of coral reefs, and damage to sea floors resulting from trawling); climate change; invasive alien species; overexploitation; and pollution. Livestock contribute directly or indirectly to all these drivers of biodiversity loss, from the local to global levels. Typically, biodiversity loss is caused by a combination of various processes

BOX 11
Conserving animal genetic resources

The livestock species contributing to today's agriculture and food production are shaped by a long history of domestication and development. Developments in the late twentieth century – including increased commercialization of livestock breeding, rising demand for animal products in the developing world, production differentials between developed and developing countries, new reproductive biotechnologies that facilitate the movement of genetic material and the feasibility to control production environments independently of the geographical location – have led to a new phase in the history of international gene flows. International transfer of genetic material occurs on a large scale, both within the developed world and from developed to developing countries. These flows are focused on a limited number of breeds. There is also some movement of genetic resources from developing to developed regions, largely for research purposes. Today, the world's most widespread cattle breed, the Holstein-Friesian, is found in at least 128 countries. Among other livestock species, Large White pigs are reported in 117 countries, Saanen goats in 81 countries, and Suffolk sheep in 40 countries.

FAO's Domestic Animal Diversity Information System (http://dad.fao.org), a global databank for animal genetic

resources, is the most comprehensive global information source on livestock genetic diversity. A total of 7 616 breeds are recorded in the Global Databank, comprising 6 536 local breeds and 1 080 transboundary breeds. Of these, 1 491 are classified as being "at risk".[1] The true figure is likely to be even higher, as population data are unavailable for 36 percent of breeds. The regions with the highest proportion of their breeds classified as at risk are Europe and the Caucasus (28 percent of mammalian breeds and 49 percent of avian breeds) and North America (20 percent of mammalian breeds and 79 percent of avian breeds). These two regions have highly specialized livestock industries, in which production is dominated by a small number of breeds. However, problems elsewhere may be obscured by the large number of breeds with unknown risk status. In Latin America and the Caribbean, for example, 68 percent of mammalian breeds and 81 percent of avian breeds are classified as being of unknown risk status. The figures for Africa are 59 percent for mammals and 60 percent for birds. This lack of data is a serious constraint to effective prioritization and planning of breed conservation efforts. There is a need for improved surveying and reporting of breed population size and structure, and of other breed-related information.

of environmental degradation. This makes it difficult to isolate the contribution of the livestock sector. A further complication is represented by the many steps in the animal food product chain at which environmental impact occurs.

Livestock-related land use and land-use change modify ecosystems that are the habitats for given species. Livestock contribute to climate change (see "Livestock and climate change", below), which in turn has an impact on ecosystems and species. The sector also directly affects biodiversity through transfer of invasive alien species

and overexploitation, for example through overgrazing of pasture plants. Water pollution and ammonia emissions, mainly from industrial livestock production, reduce biodiversity, often drastically in the case of aquatic ecosystems. Pollution from livestock enterprises, as well as overfishing to provide fishmeal for animal feed, reduces biodiversity in marine ecosystems (Reid *et al.*, 2009).

Livestock first started to affect biodiversity when animals were domesticated millennia ago and provided humans with a way to exploit new resources and territories that

The rapid spread of intensive livestock production that utilizes a narrow range of breeds has contributed to the marginalization of traditional livestock production systems and the associated animal genetic resources. Global production of meat, milk and eggs is increasingly based on a few high-output breeds – those that under current management and market conditions are the most profitable in industrialized production systems. Policy measures are necessary to minimize the loss of the global public goods embodied in animal genetic diversity.

Acute threats such as major disease epidemics and disasters of various kinds (droughts, floods, military conflicts, etc.) are also a concern – particularly in the case of small, geographically concentrated breed populations. The overall significance of these threats is difficult to quantify.

Threats of this kind cannot be eliminated, but their impacts can be mitigated. Preparedness is essential in this context, as ad hoc actions taken in an emergency will usually be far less effective. Knowledge of which breeds have characteristics that make them priorities for protection, and how they are distributed geographically and by production system, is fundamental to such plans, and more broadly to sustainable livestock diversity management. From a livelihood perspective, local knowledge

of men and women continues to be an important asset for resource-poor people, especially in terms of increased food security and health.

In September 2007, the international community adopted the first ever *Global Plan of Action for Animal Genetic Resources* (FAO, 2007b), comprising 23 strategic priorities aimed at combating the erosion of animal genetic diversity and at using genetic resources sustainably. They also adopted the *Interlaken Declaration on Animal Genetic Resources*. The Declaration recognizes that there are significant gaps and weaknesses in national and international capacities to inventory, monitor, characterize, sustainably use, develop and conserve animal genetic resources, and that these need to be addressed urgently. It also calls for mobilization of substantial financial resources and long-term support for national and international animal genetic resources programmes.

---

[1] A breed is categorized as at risk if the total number of breeding females is less than or equal to 1 000 or the total number of breeding males is less than or equal to 20, or if the overall population size is greater than 1 000 and less than or equal to 1 200 and decreasing and the percentage of females being bred to males of the same breed is below 80 percent.
Sources: FAO, 2007b and 2007c.

had previously been unavailable. Current degradation processes are superimposed on these historical changes, which continue to affect biodiversity.

Differences in impacts between species and production systems

There are significant differences in the environmental impact between species, and between the different forms of livestock production. Both intensive and extensive production systems may damage the environment, but in different ways. Pressure to expand production, either through intensification (increasing output per unit of land by increasing non-land inputs) or area expansion (increasing output by expanding land in production without changing inputs per unit of land), can have negative environmental consequences unless the value of common-property resources and the cost of negative externalities are fully recognized and accounted for.

Species
Cattle provide many products and services, including beef, milk and traction. In many mixed farming systems, cattle are usually well integrated in nutrient flows and can have a positive environmental impact (Steinfeld, de Haan and Blackburn, 1998) (see Table 13). In many developing countries, cattle and buffalo provide draught power for field operations; in some areas, particularly parts of sub-Saharan Africa, use of animal traction is increasing, substituting for fossil fuel use. Cattle manure is a good fertilizer; it presents a low risk of over-fertilization and improves soil structure. Livestock also use crop residues and agro-industrial by-products, such as molasses cake and brewers grains, some of which would otherwise be burned. However, cattle in extensive production systems in developing countries often have limited productivity. As a result, a large share of feed is spent on the animal's maintenance rather than on producing products or services useful to people. The result is inefficient use of resources and often high levels of environmental damage per unit of output, particularly in overgrazed areas.

Dairy cattle require large amounts of bulky fibrous feed in their diets. As a result, dairy herds need to be close to the source of their feed, more so than other forms of market-oriented livestock production. This provides greater opportunities for nutrient cycling, which is beneficial to the environment. However, excessive use of nitrogen fertilizer on dairy farms is one of the main causes of high nitrate levels in surface water in OECD countries (Tamminga, 2003). Manure runoff and leaching from large-scale dairy operations may also contaminate soil and water.

Beef is produced in a wide range of systems that operate at different intensities and scales. At both ends of the intensity spectrum, considerable environmental damage can occur. On the extensive side, cattle are often involved in degradation of vast grassland areas and are a contributing factor to deforestation through clearing of forest to provide pastureland (Table 13). The resulting carbon emissions, biodiversity losses and negative impacts on water flows and quality constitute major environmental impacts. On the intensive side, concentration of livestock in feedlots often results in soil and water pollution, as the amount of manure and urine produced far exceed the capacity of surrounding land to absorb nutrients. Moreover, cattle in feedlots require more concentrate feed per kilogram of output than do poultry or pigs; as a result, they have significantly higher resource requirements and hence greater environmental impact. Greenhouse gas emissions are also substantial from all livestock production systems. In extensive systems, most GHGs result from land degradation and enteric fermentation, whereas in intensive operations manure is the main source of GHGs. The higher relative productivity of animals and lower fibre content of feed rations in intensive operations reduce methane emissions from enteric fermentation when expressed per unit of animal product.

The production of sheep and goats is usually extensive, except for small pockets of feedlots in the Near East and West Asia and in North America. The capacity of small ruminants, particularly goats, to grow and reproduce under conditions that cannot support any other form of agricultural production makes them useful and very often essential to poor farmers pushed into these environments for lack of alternative livelihoods. However, sheep and goats can severely reduce land cover and the potential for forest regrowth. Under overstocked conditions, they are particularly damaging to the environment through degradation of vegetative cover and soil.

Pigs in traditional mixed systems, fed on household waste and agro-industrial by-products, turn biomass that would otherwise go to waste into high-value animal protein. Pigs also require less feed per unit of output than ruminants. As such, they have lower demand for land for feed production. However, it is estimated that pigs in mixed systems now account for only about 35 percent of global production. Pig manure can be a valuable fertilizer but crop producers generally prefer cattle and poultry waste because pig manure has a strong odour and often comes in a slurry form. It is, however, well adapted to use in biogas digestors.

Poultry production systems have undergone the most extensive structural change of any livestock subsector. In OECD countries, production is almost entirely industrial, while in many developing countries it is already predominantly industrial. Among traditional livestock species (excluding fish), poultry is the most efficient feed converter, and industrial poultry production is thus the most efficient form of livestock production, despite its dependence on feedgrains and other high-value feed material. Poultry manure has a high nutrient content, is relatively easy to manage and is widely used as fertilizer; it is also sometimes used in feed for ruminants. Other than that caused by feed-crop production, the environmental damage caused by poultry is much less than that caused by other species, although it may be locally important.

Production systems
As discussed in Chapter 2, in response to escalating demand for livestock products, the livestock sector is undergoing structural change towards more capital-intensive systems, specialized and larger production units relying on purchased inputs, higher animal productivity and greater geographical concentration. This has altered the environmental impacts of the sector. It has also offered the sector new options for mitigating such impacts, with a range of cost, socio-economic and gender implications.

The structural changes in livestock production are often detrimental to the environment but also bear opportunities for mitigation. Table 13 shows preliminary observations on the environmental impacts associated with different level of intensity in production, also discussed below. With the specialization of crop and livestock activities and in areas of animal waste concentration, nutrient cycles traditionally achieved in mixed crop–livestock systems are being broken. The cost of transporting nutrients to cropland is often prohibitive (especially for water-rich slurries), and manure is disposed of in the local environment, often exceeding its absorption capacity. This often causes severe water and soil pollution, particularly in densely populated areas. However, on the positive side, the growing scale and geographical concentration of livestock production facilitate the implementation of environmental policies by reducing enforcement costs; the higher profitability of production units attenuates costs of compliance, while the concentration of production in a smaller number of easily accessible units minimizes monitoring costs.

Longer food chains, driven by the concentration of consumers in urban centres, mean that production systems have to bridge long geographical distances between the site of feed production and the consumer. Decreasing transport costs have allowed the relocation of production and processing activities to minimize production costs. Globally, this process has helped to overcome local resource constraints and allowed people located in food-deficit areas to be fed. However, it also involves large-scale extraction and transfers of nutrients and virtual water embedded in feed and animal products, with detrimental long-term consequences for ecosystems and soil fertility.

Improved animal productivity and feed conversion efficiency have been achieved through the application of a wide range of technologies, including feeding, genetics, animal health and housing. The shift towards monogastric species, and poultry in particular, has further improved the sector's feed conversion efficiency. This has resulted in substantially less land and water being needed to produce feed to achieve the levels of production to meet current demand.

Productivity gains are, however, also associated with a number of environmental concerns. The relatively low resistance to

TABLE 13

Major environmental impacts of different production systems[1]

	RUMINANT SPECIES (CATTLE, SHEEP, ETC.)		MONOGASTRICS (PIGS, POULTRY)	
	Extensive grazing[2]	Intensive systems[3]	Traditional systems[4]	Industrial systems
GREENHOUSE GAS EMISSIONS				
CO_2 emissions from land use and land-use change for grazing and feed-crop production	- - -	-	ns	- -
CO_2 emissions from energy and input use	ns	- -	ns	- -
Carbon sequestration in rangelands	+ +	ns	ns	ns
Methane emissions from digestion	- - -	- -	ns	ns
Nitrous oxide from manure	-	- - -	ns	- -
LAND DEGRADATION				
Expansion into natural habitat	- - -	ns	ns	- -
Overgrazing (vegetation change, soil compaction)	- - -	ns	ns	ns
Intensive feed production (soil erosion)	ns	- -	ns	- -
Soil fertilization	+	+	+	+ +
WATER DEPLETION AND POLLUTION				
Alteration of water cycle	- -	-	ns	ns
Pollution with nutrients, pathogens and drug residues	ns	- -	ns	- - -
BIODIVERSITY				
Habitat destruction from feed-crop production and animal wastes	- - -	-	ns	- - -
Habitat pollution from feed-crop production and animal wastes	ns	- -	ns	- - -
Loss of domestic animal genetic diversity	ns	- -	ns	- - -
Ecosystem maintenance	+ +	ns	ns	ns

[1] Observed relationships under common management practices.
[2] Extensive grazing systems for ruminants are predominantly based on natural grasslands in marginal environments.
[3] Intensive systems for ruminants are generally based on improved grasslands (using irrigation, fertilizers, improved varieties and pesticides), with supplementary feeding or confined feeding of grain and silage.
[4] Traditional systems for monogastrics include mixed farming systems or backyard scavenging systems.
Note: ns = not significant.
Source: FAO.

diseases of highly productive breeds, the concentration of large numbers of animals in large production units and the need to avoid disease outbreaks has led producers to use substantial amounts of drugs, often as routine preventive measures. Residues from these drugs pass into the environment, harming ecosystems and public heath. In particular, the sometimes indiscriminate use of antibiotics has led to the selection of antibiotic-resistant strains of bacteria, now threatening human health in Europe and North America (Johnson *et al.*, 2009). Highly productive breeds also require a tighter control of their environment (temperature, light) than traditional breeds, thus increasing water and energy consumption.

Deforestation and land degradation are the main processes through which extensive grazing systems emit GHGs. Range management can be improved to prevent carbon losses and sequester carbon, turning extensive systems into net GHG removers. Intensification and restoration of pasture and fodder production, driven by rising land prices, generally also have other positive environmental consequences as they limit land expansion and improve feed quality. The latter, in turn, contributes to the reduction of methane emissions from enteric fermentation. Nutrient overloads in dairy production areas have generally been related more to the import of nutrients through supplementary feed and fertilizer for silage production than to deficiencies in pasture management.

Overall, the change from traditional mixed and extensive systems to more intensive systems has probably had a positive effect in improving land- and water-use efficiency but negative effects on water pollution, energy consumption and genetic diversity. Moreover, traditional and mixed systems have been unable to meet the burgeoning demand for livestock products in many developing countries, not only in terms of volume but also in terms of sanitary and other quality standards. Intensification of production appears thus indispensable, while avoiding excessive geographical concentration of animals.

The potential to improve the environmental performance of intensive systems is also greater than for traditional and extensive systems. Experience shows that when economic incentives are properly set, productivity gains associated with capital and labour intensification significantly improve the efficiency of natural-resource use; where resources and pollution are priced appropriately, intensification of production has been associated with improved environmental efficiency (less consumption of natural resources and lower emissions per unit of animal product). This is already the case for land use on a global scale, but also for water and nutrients in an increasing number of OECD countries.

Livestock and climate change

Global average surface temperatures have increased by about 0.7 °C in the last century (IPCC, 2007). Ocean temperatures have risen, there has been significant melting of snow and ice in the polar regions and sea levels are projected to rise. The Intergovernmental Panel on Climate Change (IPCC) concludes that anthropogenic GHGs, including carbon dioxide (CO_2), methane (CH_4), nitrous oxide (N_2O) and halocarbons, have been responsible for most of the observed temperature increase since the middle of the twentieth century.

Amid growing concerns over climate change, agriculture, particularly livestock, is increasingly being recognized as both a contributor to the process and a potential victim of it. Policy interventions and technical solutions are required to address both the impact of livestock production on climate change and the effects of climate change on livestock production.

The impact of livestock on climate change

Livestock contribute to climate change by emitting GHGs, either directly (e.g. from enteric fermentation) or indirectly (e.g. from feed-production activities, deforestation to create new pasture, etc.).

Greenhouse gas emissions can arise from all the main steps of the livestock production cycle. Emissions from feed-crop production and pastures are linked to the production and application of chemical fertilizer and pesticides, to soil organic-matter losses and to transport. When forest is cleared for pasture and feed crops, large amounts of carbon stored in vegetation and soil are also released into the atmosphere. In contrast, when good management practices are implemented on degraded land, pasture and cropland can turn into net carbon sinks, sequestering carbon from the atmosphere. At the farm level, methane (CH_4) and nitrous oxide (N_2O) are emitted from enteric fermentation and manure. In ruminant species (i.e. cattle, buffalo, goat and sheep), microbial fermentation in the rumen converts fibre and cellulose into products that can be digested and utilized by the animals. Methane is exhaled by these animals as a by-product of the process. Nitrous oxide is released from manure during storage and spreading, and methane is also generated when manure is stored in

anaerobic and warm conditions. Finally, the slaughtering, processing and transportation of animal products cause emissions mostly related to use of fossil fuel and infrastructure development.

The impact of climate change on livestock

Table 14 summarizes the direct and indirect impacts of climate change on grazing and non-grazing livestock production systems. It is likely that some of the greatest impacts of climate change will be felt in grazing systems in arid and semi-arid areas, particularly at low latitudes (Hoffman and Vogel, 2008). Climate change will have far-reaching consequences for animal production through its effects on forage and range productivity. Increasing temperatures and decreasing

---

BOX 12
Assessing the contribution of livestock to GHG emissions

The IPCC Fourth Assessment Report presents agreed levels of overall anthropogenic GHG emissions for defined categories representing economic sectors (e.g. industry, 19.4 percent; agriculture, 13.5 percent; forestry, 17.4 percent; transport, 13.1 percent) (Barker *et al.*, 2007). The IPPC suggests that these figures should be seen as indicative, as some uncertainty remains, particularly with regard to CH_4, N_2O and CO_2 emissions. In addition, for agriculture and forestry, the above figures are expressed as gross emissions and do not take into account the existing carbon capture that is the basis for photosynthesis. Emissions associated with animal products fall across several of these categories. Feed production causes emissions in the agriculture, forestry (through land-use change), transport and energy categories. Enteric fermentation and manure management associated with livestock rearing lead to methane and nitrous oxide emissions accounted for under agriculture. Slaughtering, processing and distribution cause emissions accounted for in the industry, energy and transport categories. Taken together in a food chain approach, livestock therefore contribute about 9 percent of total anthropogenic carbon-

dioxide emissions, 37 percent of methane and 65 percent of nitrous oxide emissions (FAO, 2006). The combined emissions expressed in CO_2 equivalents amount to about 18 percent of anthropogenic GHG emissions.

Along the animal food chain, the major sources and amounts of emissions are:

- Land use and land-use change: 2.5 gigatonnes of CO_2 equivalent. Includes CO_2 release from forest and other natural vegetation replaced by pasture and feed crop in the neotropics and carbon releases from soils, such as pasture and arable land dedicated to feed production.
- Feed production (excluding carbon released from soil and plants): 0.4 gigatonnes of CO_2 equivalent. Includes CO_2 from fossil fuel used in manufacturing chemical fertilizer for feed crops and N_2O and ammonia (NH_3) released by chemical fertilizers applied to feed crops and from leguminous feed crops.
- Animal production: 1.9 gigatonnes of CO_2 equivalent. Includes CH_4 from enteric fermentation and CO_2 from on-farm use of fossil fuel.
- Manure management: 2.2 gigatonnes of CO_2 equivalent. Includes CH_4, N_2O

LIVESTOCK IN THE BALANCE 65

rainfall reduce yields of rangelands and contribute to their degradation. Higher temperatures tend to reduce animal feed intake and lower feed conversion rates (Rowlinson, 2008). Reduced rainfall and increased frequency of drought will reduce primary productivity of rangelands, leading to overgrazing and degradation, and may result in food insecurity and conflict over scarce resources. There is also evidence that growing seasons may become shorter in many grazing lands, particularly in sub-Saharan Africa. The probability of extreme weather events is likely to increase.

In the non-grazing systems, which are characterized by the confinement of animals (often in climate-controlled buildings), the direct impacts of climate change can be expected to be limited and mostly indirect (Table 14). Reduced agricultural yields and increased competition from other sectors are predicted to result in increased prices for both grain and oilcakes, which are major sources of feed in non-grazing systems (OECD–FAO, 2008). The development of energy-saving programmes and policies promoting the use of clean energy may also result in increased energy prices. A warmer climate may also increase the costs of keeping animals cool.

Climate change will play a significant role in the spread of vector-borne diseases and animal parasites, which will have disproportionately large impacts on the most vulnerable men and women in the livestock sector. With higher temperatures and more variable precipitation, new diseases may emerge or diseases will occur in places where they formerly did not. Moreover, climate

and NH_3 mainly from manure storage, application and deposition.
- Processing and international transport: 0.03 gigatonnes of CO_2 equivalent.

Comparing species, cattle and buffalo are responsible for more of these emissions than are pigs and poultry (see table). Emissions associated with large ruminants are predominantly related to land-use changes (such as deforestation), pasture management, enteric fermentation and manure management. Cattle and buffalo are responsible for an especially large share of the livestock sector's emissions in Latin America and South Asia, where they are estimated to account for more than 85 percent of the sector's emissions, mainly in the form of methane.

Emissions of greenhouse gases along the animal food chain and estimated relative contribution from major species

STEP IN ANIMAL FOOD CHAIN	ESTIMATED EMISSIONS[1]		ESTIMATED CONTRIBUTION BY SPECIES[2]			
			Cattle and buffaloes	Pigs	Poultry	Small ruminants
	(Gigatonnes)	(Percentage of total livestock sector emissions)				
Land use and land-use change	2.50	36	■■■	■	■	ns
Feed production[3]	0.40	7	■	■■	■■	ns
Animal production[4]	1.90	25	■■■■	■	■	■■
Manure management	2.20	31	■■	■■■	ns	ns
Processing and transport	0.03	1	■	■	■■■	ns

[1] Estimated quantity of emissions expressed as CO_2 equivalent.
[2] ■ = lowest to ■■■■ = highest.
[3] Excludes changes in soil and plant carbon stocks.
[4] Includes enteric methane, machinery and buildings.
Note: ns = not significant.
Source: Adapted from Steinfeld *et al.*, 2006.

TABLE 14

Direct and indirect impacts of climate change on livestock production systems

	GRAZING SYSTEMS	NON-GRAZING SYSTEMS
DIRECT IMPACTS	• Increased frequency of extreme weather events • Increased frequency and magnitude of drought and floods • Productivity losses (physiological stress) due to temperature increase • Change in water availability (may increase or decrease, according to region)	• Change in water availability (may increase or decrease, according to region) • Increased frequency of extreme weather events (impact less acute than for extensive systems)

INDIRECT IMPACTS	• Agro-ecological changes and ecosystem shifts leading to:
	  – alteration of fodder quality and quality
	  – changes in host–pathogen interactions resulting in an increased incidence of emerging diseases
	  – disease epidemics
		• Increased resource prices, e.g. feed, water and energy
		• Disease epidemics
		• Increased cost of animal housing, e.g. cooling systems

Source: FAO.

change may result in new transmission mechanisms and new host species. All countries are likely to be subject to increased animal-disease incidence but poor countries are more vulnerable to emerging diseases because of the paucity of veterinary services.

Can climate change benefit livestock? There may be some positive outcomes for the livestock sector from warmer temperatures, but this largely depends on when and where temperature changes happen. General conclusions thus cannot be drawn. For example, higher winter temperature can reduce the cold stress experienced by livestock raised outside. Furthermore, warmer winter weather may reduce the maintenance energy requirements of animals and reduce the need for heating in animal housing.

Improving natural-resource use by livestock production

Measures need to be taken to address the impact of livestock production on ecosystems, which otherwise may worsen dramatically given the projected expansion of the livestock sector. Demand for animal products needs to be balanced with the growing demand for environmental services, such as clean air and water, and recreation areas.

Current prices of land, water and feed resources used for livestock production often do not reflect the true scarcity value of these resources. This leads to their

overuse and to major inefficiencies in the production process. Policies to protect the environment should introduce adequate market pricing for the main inputs, for example, by introducing full-cost pricing of water and grazing. Defining men's and women's property rights and access rights to scarce shared resources is also a key factor in ensuring efficient resource use and preservation of natural resources.

A host of tested and successful technical options are available to mitigate environmental impacts of agricultural activities (Steinfeld *et al.*, 2006). These can be used in resource management, in crop and livestock production, and in reduction of post-harvest losses. However, for these to be widely adopted and applied requires appropriate price signals that more closely reflect the true scarcities of production factors, and correction of the distortions that currently provide insufficient incentives for efficient resource use. The recent development of water markets and more appropriate water pricing in some countries, particularly those facing water scarcity, are steps in that direction.

Correcting for environmental externalities

Although the removal of price distortions at the input and product levels will go a long way to enhancing the technical efficiency of natural-resource use in livestock production, this often may not be sufficient to control the sector's environmental impacts more effectively. Externalities[4], both negative and positive, need to be explicitly factored into the policy framework so that the full costs of pollution and other negative environmental impacts are recognized. The application of the "provider gets – polluter pays" principle can be helpful, although the challenge for society is to decide who has the right to pollute and how much.

Correcting for externalities, both positive and negative, will lead livestock producers to make management choices that are less costly to the environment and to society at large. Livestock holders who generate positive externalities need to be compensated, either by the immediate beneficiary (such as for improved water quantity and quality for downstream users) or by the general public (such as for carbon sequestration from reversing pasture degradation).

While regulations remain an important tool in controlling negative externalities, there is a trend towards taxation of environmental damage and provision of financial incentives for environmental benefits. This may gain momentum in future, initially tackling local externalities but increasingly addressing also transboundary impacts through international treaties, underlying regulatory frameworks and market mechanisms. Government policies may be required to provide incentives for institutional innovation in this regard.

The opportunity cost for livestock to use marginal land is changing. In many regions, livestock occupy land for which there is no viable alternative use. Increasingly, other uses (e.g. biodiversity conservation, carbon sequestration, production of feedstock for biofuels) are competing with pasture in some regions. In future, next-generation ethanol production from cellulosic material may emerge as another competitor for rangeland use. Water-related services will probably be the first to grow significantly in importance, with local service provision schemes the first to be widely applied. Biodiversity-related services (e.g. species and landscape conservation) are more complex

to manage because of major methodological issues in the valuation of biodiversity, but they already find a ready uptake where they can be financed through tourism revenues. Carbon sequestration services, through adjustments in grazing management or abandonment of pastures, may also play a much larger role; given the potential of the world's vast grazing lands to sequester large amounts of carbon, mechanisms are being developed to use this potentially cost-effective avenue to address climate change.

Suggesting a shift from current extractive grazing practices to practices that enhance the provision of environmental services raises two questions of paramount importance: How should the profits from environmental services be distributed? And how can poor people who currently derive their livelihoods from extensive livestock benefit from this? *The State of Food and Agriculture 2007* discussed the concept of payments for environmental services and the implications for poverty alleviation in detail (FAO, 2007a).

Accelerating technological change
A number of technical options could lessen the impacts of intensive livestock production. Good agricultural practices can reduce pesticide and fertilizer use in feed cropping and intensive pasture management. Integration of ecological production systems and technologies can restore important soil habitats and reduce degradation. Improvements in extensive livestock production systems can also make a contribution to biodiversity conservation, including, for example, adoption of silvipastoral and flexible grazing management systems that actually increase biodiversity, quantity of forage, soil cover and soil organic matter and thus reduce water loss and drought impact and increase CO_2 sequestration. Combining such local improvements with restoration or conservation of an ecological infrastructure at the watershed level may offer a good way to reconcile the conservation of ecosystem function with the expansion of agricultural production.

In industrial and mixed production systems, there is a large gap between current levels of productivity and levels that are technically

---

[4] An externality is an unintended or undesired side-effect of an economic activity that harms (negative externality) or benefits (positive externality) another party.

attainable, indicating that considerable efficiency gains can be realized through better management. However, achieving these is more difficult in resource-poor areas, which are often also ecologically more marginal areas.

Improved and efficient production technologies exist for most production systems. However, access to relevant information and the capacity to select and implement the most appropriate technologies are constraining factors. These constraints can be reduced through interactive knowledge management, capacity building and informed decision-making at the policy, investment, rural development and producer levels. Technological improvements need to be oriented towards optimal integrated use of land, water, human, animal and feed resources.

Reducing the negative environmental impacts of intensive livestock production
The environmental problems created by industrial systems mostly derive from their geographical location and concentration. In extreme cases, size may be a problem – sometimes units are so large

---

BOX 13

The European Union – integrating environmental protection requirements into the Common Agricultural Policy

Since the Agenda 2000 reform (March 1999), the Common Agricultural Policy (CAP) of the European Union (EU) has had two pillars: a market and income policy (first pillar); and a policy to promote the sustainable development of rural areas (second pillar). A number of measures introduced with the 2003 CAP reform (effective as of January 2005) and the Rural Development Policy 2007–2013 are expected to lead to a mitigation of the environmental impact of livestock production through the following:

• **Decoupling.** The Single Farm Payment decoupled from production has replaced most of the direct payments under different Common Market Organizations. This implies reducing many of the incentives for intensive production associated with increased environmental risks, thus encouraging extensification, decreased livestock numbers, reduced fertilizer use, etc. However, Member States have been allowed to keep a part of the payments coupled, *inter alia*, the suckler cow premium (up to 100 percent), the special beef premium (up to 75 percent), the slaughter premium for cattle (up to 40 percent for adults and 100 percent for calves) and the sheep and goat premium (up to 50 percent).

• **Cross-compliance.** The full granting of income support is now conditional on the respect of: statutory management requirements (relating to the environment, animal welfare and public, animal and plant health), including those stemming from five environmental Directives; minimum standards of good agricultural and environmental conditions (GAECs); and the obligation to maintain land under permanent pasture. This is a further incentive to comply with environmental legislation such as the Nitrates Directive (reduced fertilizer use and improved practices, e.g. for manure management). The GAECs have to include, *inter alia*, provisions related to the maintenance of soil organic-matter levels (e.g. crop rotation and arable stubble management), the protection of soils against erosion and the maintenance of carbon sinks (e.g. through the requirement to maintain permanent pasture).

• **Assistance to sectors with special problems** (so-called Article 69 measures). Member States may retain by sector (e.g. livestock sector) up to 10 percent of national budget ceilings for direct payments. Payments are made to farmers in the sector (or sectors) concerned by

(hundreds of thousands of pigs, for example) that waste disposal will always be an issue, no matter where these units are located.

What is required, therefore, is to bring the amount of waste generated into line with the capacity of locally accessible land to absorb that waste. Industrial livestock must be located as much as possible where cropland within economic reach can be used to dispose of the waste, without creating problems of nutrient loading, rather than geographically concentrating production units in areas favoured by market access or feed availability, as at present. Policy options to overcome the current economic drivers of the peri-urban concentration of production units include zoning, mandatory nutrient management plans, financial incentives and facilitation of contractual agreements between livestock producers and crop farmers (see Box 14). In Thailand, high taxes were levied on poultry and pig production within a 100 km radius of Bankok, while areas further away enjoyed tax-free status. This led to many new production units being established away from the major consumption centre (Steinfeld *et al.*, 2006).

the retention. They can be spent in specific types of farming important for the protection or enhancement of the environment or improving the quality and marketing of agricultural products.

- **Modulation.** The Agenda 2000 reform introduced the possibility of shifting support from market policy to measures contributing to environmentally benign practices (the concept is referred to as "modulation"). The 2003 CAP reform made modulation a compulsory measure, with direct payments having to be reduced (by 3 percent in 2005, 4 percent in 2006 and 5 percent in the years from 2007 onwards). The funds are being shifted into rural development, increasing the possibility to stimulate the adoption of environmentally friendly production techniques.

The rural development regulation for the period 2007–2013 provides further opportunities to strengthen the contribution of the CAP to improving the environment. Three key priority areas related to the environment were defined in the Community strategic guidelines for rural development: climate change, biodiversity and water.

In 2008, the CAP underwent a so-called "Health Check" reform. The reform, in addition to eliminating or phasing out some production-constraining measures (abolition of set-aside of arable land and gradual phasing out of milk quotas), strengthened some of the aforementioned instruments. Beef and veal payments, except the suckler cow premium, are to be fully decoupled by 2012 at the latest. Cross-compliance was amplified with a new GAEC standard concerning the establishment of buffer strips along watercourses. Measures to address disadvantages for farmers in certain regions (Article 68 [ex-Article 69] measures) were made more flexible, covering farmers in the dairy, beef and sheep and goat meat sectors (and in the rice sector) in disadvantaged areas as well as economically vulnerable types of farming in these sectors. The modulation rate was increased by 5 percent, in four steps from 2009 to 2012, and an additional reduction in payments by 4 percent is applied to payments exceeding €300 000 (about US$425 000). The funds thus obtained are transferred to rural development for the financing of new operations (biodiversity, water management, renewable energies, climate change, accompanying measures for dairy production, and innovation).

Source: EU Commission Web site (ec.europa.eu/agriculture/index_en.htm).

BOX 14
Reducing nitrate pollution in Denmark

In Denmark, the intensification of agriculture during the last 50 years disturbed the natural nitrogen cycle, causing significant emissions of ammonia to the atmosphere and nitrate pollution of water. High concentrations of nitrates in groundwater and surface water impaired drinking water quality (EEA, 2003) and caused eutrophication of lakes and coastal marine areas. In the early 1980s, public concern over eutrophication of Danish coastal waters helped motivate the Danish Government to regulate nitrogen emission from the country's agriculture sector.

Beginning in 1985, Denmark adopted a series of action plans and regulatory measures that have dramatically increased nitrogen use efficiency in agriculture and reduced nitrogen pollution (Mikkelsen *et al.*, 2009). Among other things, these plans required livestock producers to increase manure slurry storage capacity, stop spreading slurry during the winter months, adopt mandatory fertilizer budgets to match plant uptake to nutrient applications, install covers on slurry tanks, and reduce stocking density in some areas. In 2001, the Ammonia Action Plan provided subsidies to encourage good manure handling in

animal housing and improved housing design, required covers on dung heaps, banned slurry application by broadcast spreader, and required slurry to be incorporated into the soil within 6 hours of application.

The main instruments of nitrogen regulation in Denmark are mandatory fertilizer and crop-rotation plans, with crop-specific limits on the amount of plant-available nitrogen that can be applied, and statutory norms for the utilization of nitrogen from animal manure. The norms reflect how much nitrogen in the manure is assumed to be plant-available. This also sets a limit on how much mineral fertilizer each farmer may apply. Each year, farmers are required to inform the Ministry of Food how much mineral nitrogen fertilizer they have purchased. The application of nitrogen from animal manure and mineral fertilizer cannot exceed the total nitrogen norm for a given farm.

The regulations have been very successful in reducing nitrogen leaching from soils. However, nitrogen leaching in some water basins is still high and further regional reduction may be needed to achieve good ecological quality in all coastal waters (Dalgaard *et al.*, 2004).

Regulations are also needed to deal with heavy-metal and drug-residue issues at the feed and waste levels, and to address other public health aspects, such as food-borne pathogens.

Both industrialized and more-extensive livestock production systems need to strive to minimize possible emissions, with waste management adapted to local conditions. In parallel, there is a need to address the environmental impacts associated with production of feedgrain and other concentrate feed. Feed is usually produced in intensive agricultural systems, and the principles and instruments that have been developed to control environmental issues there need to be widely applied.

Dealing with climate change and livestock

Livestock can play an important role in both adapting to climate change and mitigating the effects of climate change on human welfare. Efforts to mitigate the effects of livestock on climate change focus on reducing GHG emissions from livestock. Livestock can also help the poor adapt to the effects of climate change. The ability of communities to adapt to and mitigate climate change depends on their socio-economic and environmental circumstances and their access to the right information and technology.

An important question to consider is how to blend adaptation and mitigation strategies. This requires a careful analysis of the trade-offs between economic growth, equity and environmental sustainability. Dealing with climate change poses challenges for growth and development, particularly in the low-income countries, but there are also significant synergies between adaptation and mitigation actions, e.g. improved range management can both sequester carbon and improve grassland productivity.

Strategies for adaptation

There is an urgent need for effective strategies for adapting to climate change. Climate change is occurring much faster than adaptation. It can exacerbate already existing vulnerabilities and increase the impact of other stresses, such as natural disasters, poverty, unequal access to resources, food insecurity and incidence of animal diseases.

Livestock producers have traditionally adapted to environmental and climate changes. However, increased human population, urbanization, economic growth, growing consumption of foods of animal origin and commercialization have made those coping mechanisms less effective (Sidahmed, 2008). Coping and risk management strategies are urgently needed.

Livestock are key assets held by poor people, particularly in pastoral and agropastoral systems, fulfilling multiple economic, social, and risk management functions. Livestock are also a crucial coping mechanism in variable environments; as this variability increases, they will become even more important. For many poor people, the loss of livestock assets means a decline into chronic poverty with long-term effects on their livelihoods.

There are a number of ways to increase the adaptation capacity of traditional producers in extensive systems (Sidahmed, 2008). These include:

- *Production adjustments* through:
  (i) diversification, intensification, integration of pasture management, livestock and crop production, changing land use and irrigation, altering the timing of operations, conservation of nature and ecosystems; and
  (ii) introduction of mixed livestock

farming systems, i.e. stall feeding and grazing.
- *Breeding strategies*, such as: (i) strengthening local breeds, which are adapted to local climate stress and feed sources; and (ii) improving local breeds through cross-breeding with heat- and disease-tolerant breeds.
- *Market responses* through promoting interregional trade, credit schemes and market access.
- *Institutional and policy changes*, e.g. introduction of livestock early-warning systems, and other forecasting and crisis-preparedness systems.
- *Science and technology research* to provide greater understanding of the causes of climate change and its impact on livestock, to facilitate development of new breeds and genetic types, to improve animal health, and to improve water and soil management.
- *Livestock management systems* to allow efficient and affordable adaptation practices to be developed for rural poor who are generally unable to purchase expensive adaptation technologies. Systems should: (i) provide shade and water to reduce heat stress from increased temperature, a natural low-cost alternative to air-conditioning; (ii) reduce livestock numbers, using more productive animals to increase efficiency of production while reducing GHG emissions; and (iii) adjust the livestock numbers and herd composition to optimize use of feed resources.

There is reasonable information on the component pieces of livestock systems and how they may be affected by climate change. At the systems level, however, less is known about how these changes may interact to affect livelihoods. These interactions must be understood at the micro level in order to tailor adaptation strategies. At the same time, there is a need to identify vulnerable populations more clearly as a key step in assessing adaptation needs. This urgently calls for research programmes that can support the development of national and regional policies.

Strategies for mitigation

Many impacts of climate change can be avoided, reduced or delayed. It is important to stress that adaptation and mitigation efforts cannot eliminate all impacts of climate change and sometimes are in conflict. In identifying mitigation strategies, it is essential to bear in mind the cost of implementation and potential trade-offs with adaptation needs. Reforestation is considered cost-effective, but other strategies may not be easy to implement or cost-effective.

The impact of livestock on climate change is largely through their production of GHGs (see "The impact of livestock on climate change", above). Greenhouse gas emissions from the livestock sector can be reduced by changes in animal feeding management, in manure management and in management of feed-crop production:

- *Improved feeding management.* Feed composition has some effect on enteric fermentation and emission of methane from the rumen or the hindgut (Dourmad, Rigolot and van der Werf, 2008). Also, the amount of feed intake is related to the amount of waste product. A higher proportion of concentrate in the diet results in a reduction in methane emission (Lovett *et al.*, 2005).
- *Reducing methane produced during digestion.* Methane production in the digestive system of the animal (especially ruminants) can be reduced by use of feed additives, antibiotics or vaccines (UNFCCC, 2008).
- *Improved feed conversion.* Reducing the amount of feed required per unit of output (beef, milk, etc.) has the potential to both reduce the production of GHGs and to increase farm profits. Feed efficiency can be increased by developing breeds that are faster growing, and that have improved hardiness, weight gain or

---

BOX 15

Tapping the climate change mitigation potential of improved land management in livestock systems

Agricultural systems that combine improved pasture management with soil improvements (reduced soil disturbance and improved soil cover) can lock up more carbon in soils and biomass, emit less methane (CH_4) per unit product and release less nitrous oxide (N_2O) than less-well-run systems. Many of these measures can also increase productivity by enhancing the amount of fodder available and increasing the water-holding capacity of the soil. In Latin America, a project that introduced silvipastoral measures (improved feeding practices with trees and shrubs) to increase biodiversity and carbon sequestration, was shown also to increase carbon storage and reduce CH_4 and N_2O emissions (by 21 percent and 36 percent, respectively) (World Bank, 2008b). The land-use changes were also shown to raise incomes by 55.5 percent in Costa Rica and 66.9 percent in Nicaragua (World Bank, 2008b).

More widespread adoption of improved land management techniques for greenhouse gas mitigation is currently hindered, in part, by high costs faced by individual producers trying to access carbon markets. Accessing the carbon market is currently an expensive and complex process, requiring substantial upfront investment in financial and biophysical analysis before carbon credits can be sold. Concerns over permanence and additionality[1] of these sink-enhancing activities, investment risks and accounting uncertainties have prevented most land-based mitigation measures from becoming eligible for offsets under the Kyoto mechanisms. So far, only animal waste management (methane capture and combustion) and afforestation or reforestation activities are allowed as offsets in the compliance market. These offsets account for only about 1 percent of the total value of offsets issued under the Clean Development Mechanism (CDM) in 2007, or about US$140 million out of the total of some US$14 billion available under the CDM.

Land-based mitigation options play a more prominent role in voluntary carbon markets. Currently, there are two voluntary standards issuing carbon offsets for grassland management – the Voluntary

milk or egg production. Feed efficiency can also be increased by improving herd health through improved veterinary services, preventive health programmes and improved water quality.

- *Improved waste management*. Most methane emissions from manure derive from pigs, beef cattle feedlots and dairy farms, where production is concentrated in large operations and manure is stored under anaerobic conditions. Methane mitigation options involve the capture of methane by covered manure-storage facilities (biogas collectors). Captured methane can be flared or used to provide a source of energy for electric generators, heating or lighting (which can offset CO_2 emissions from fossil fuels).
- *Grazing management*. Increased use of pasture to provide feed and good pasture management through rotational

grazing are potentially the most cost-effective ways to reduce and offset GHG emissions (see Box 15). The resultant increases in vegetation cover and soil organic-matter content sequester carbon, while inclusion of high-quality forage in the animals' diet contributes to reducing methane emissions per unit of product. Improved grazing management also generally improves the profitability of production.

- *Reducing deforestation*. Deforestation to provide new pasture or land to produce feed crops releases more CO_2 than any other livestock-related activity. Intensification of pasture management and feed production can reduce the land requirements per unit of animal product produced, thus curbing land-use expansion. Intensification alone is not sufficient, however, and complementary measures are required

Carbon Standard (VCS) and the Chicago-based Climate Exchange (CCX). The VCS standard, for example, has recently issued guidelines for activities aimed at generating carbon credits for improved grassland management. The improved practices aim at enhancing soil carbon stocks by increasing below-ground inputs or slowing decomposition, enhancing nitrogen-use efficiency of targeted crops, fire management, feed improvements, improved livestock genetics and improved stocking rate management (VCS, 2008). Soil carbon credits account for about half of the credits traded by CCX, and nearly 20 percent of those traded under the voluntary carbon market overall. While the voluntary market is relatively small, it has been growing quickly – from US$97 million in 2006 to US$331 million in 2007 (Hamilton *et al.*, 2008).

The high costs faced by individual producers accessing carbon markets has led to discussions on whether the current offset generation system and its strict accounting requirements are well suited to agricultural activities. These activities

could instead be supported under mechanisms that require less stringent monitoring, for example at the sectoral or regional level. An increased awareness of the contribution of land management to control of greenhouse gas emissions and of the important economic and environmental co-benefits associated with some mitigation options is raising the profile of agriculture in the climate change debate in the lead-up to the United Nations Framework Convention on Climate Change (UNFCCC) Post-2012 Climate Agreement negotiations in Copenhagen at the end of 2009.

---

[1] Additionality refers to activities that would not have happened in the absence of the carbon finance support: (i) the proposed voluntary measure would not be implemented, or (ii) the mandatory policy/regulation would be systematically not enforced and that non-compliance with those requirements is widespread in the country/region, or (iii) the programme of activities will lead to a greater level of enforcement of the existing mandatory policy/regulation. (Adapted from UNFCCC CDM glossary, available at http://cdm.unfccc.int/Reference/Guidclarif/glos_CDM_v04.pdf.)

in order to address the other drivers of deforestation such as unclear land tenure and logging for timber.

- *Changing livestock consumption.* Shifting consumption from animal products with high associated GHG emissions (beef and sheep meat) to products with lower emissions (poultry, vegetable protein) can reduce total global GHG emissions. Increasing the consumption of livestock products by poor consumers with no or limited access to them can provide important human health benefits, but reducing high levels of consumption could help lower emissions with no adverse health effects (McMichael *et al.*, 2007).

Constraints on adaptation and mitigation

There are still many gaps in our knowledge about how climate change will affect livestock production. In particular, we need to understand better how climate affects pasture and range composition and the consequences for livestock production. It has been predicted that climate change will bring with it new animal diseases. The World Organisation for Animal Health (OIE) estimates that, to date, 70 percent of all newly emerging infectious human diseases originate in animals (OIE, 2008a). What is more uncertain is to exactly what degree heat affects the biology of animals and the promotion of new diseases. We have quite good understanding of how climate change affects broad regions but are much less certain on its impacts at local levels, on localities and poor households. The way climate change alters the fragile relationship between livelihoods and production dependent on natural resources is particularly fraught with uncertainty.

Key messages of the chapter

- There is an urgent need for governments and institutions to develop and enact appropriate policies, at the national and international levels, that focus more on and account for livestock–environment interactions. Continued growth in livestock production will otherwise exert enormous pressures on ecosystems,

biodiversity, land and forest resources and water quality, and will contribute to global warming.

- A key policy focus should be on correcting market distortions and policy failures that encourage environmental degradation. For example, subsidies that directly or indirectly promote overgrazing, land degradation, deforestation, overuse of water or GHG emissions should be reduced or eliminated. Market-based policies, such as taxes and fees for natural-resource use, should cause producers to internalize the costs of environmental damages caused by livestock production.

- Some negative environmental consequences from livestock production stem from problems associated with open-access common-property resources. Clarifying property rights and promoting mechanisms for cooperation are vital to sustainable management of common property.

- The application of technologies that improve the efficiency of land use and feed use can mitigate the negative effects of livestock production on biodiversity, ecosystems and global warming. Technologies that increase livestock efficiency include improved breeds, improved grazing-land management, improved herd-health management and silvipastoralism.

- Payments from public or private sources for environmental services can be an effective means to promote better environmental outcomes, including soil conservation, conservation of wildlife and landscapes and carbon sequestration.

- The livestock sector has enormous potential to contribute to climate change mitigation. Realizing this potential will require new and extensive initiatives at the national and international levels, including: the promotion of research on and development of new mitigation technologies; effective and enhanced means for financing livestock activities; deploying, diffusing and transferring technologies to mitigate GHG emissions; and enhanced capacities to monitor, report and verify emissions from livestock production.

5. Livestock and human and animal health

Innovative strategies and responses are required to meet the economic and human-health risks associated with livestock diseases. The most serious health threat is that of a human pandemic, recently highlighted by the outbreak of a new strain of influenza, A(H1N1), containing genetic material from human, swine and poultry viruses. The economic threats from livestock diseases and their treatment may be less dramatic, but they too may exact a high cost in terms of human welfare and can pose livelihood risks for smallholders.

Humans, animals and their pathogens have coexisted for millennia, but recent economic, institutional and environmental trends are creating new disease risks and intensifying old ones. Systemic risks are emerging owing to the combination of rapid structural change in the livestock sector, geographic clustering of intensive livestock production facilities near urban population centres and the movement of animals, people and pathogens between intensive and traditional production systems. Because these production systems rely on different disease-control strategies, the exchange of pathogens between them can create major disease outbreaks. Meanwhile, climate change is altering patterns of livestock disease incidence, as pathogens and the insects and other vectors that carry them enter new ecological zones.

Animal-health and food-safety systems are facing new and additional challenges as a result of the lengthening and increasing complexity of supply chains in the livestock sector that have been facilitated by globalization and trade liberalization. At the same time, increasingly stringent food-safety and animal-health regulations and private standards aimed at promoting consumer welfare are creating challenges for producers, especially smallholders who have less technical and financial capacity to comply with them.

Many national institutions for disease control are obliged to respond to an increasing number of crises instead of focusing on principles of prevention, progressive disease containment, or elimination of a new emerging disease before it spreads. Consequently, the economic impact of diseases and the cost of control measures are high and becoming higher. In addition, sometimes necessary control measures such as culling may greatly affect the entire production sector, and may be devastating for the poorest households for whom livestock forms a major asset and safety net.

This chapter reviews some of the major problems and controversies surrounding issues of animal health and food safety and discusses alternatives for controlling livestock diseases and mitigating their effects. It highlights the fact that interventions, investment and institutions have focused most strongly on trade and global food systems, and that too little attention has been paid to the concerns of the poor and the endemic diseases and unrecorded food-safety problems that affect their livelihoods. The challenge is to manage livestock diseases and food-borne illnesses in ways that optimize economic and human-health outcomes across the wide diversity of systems and for people everywhere.

Policy-makers should balance the needs of producers against consumers, those of smallholders against commercial operators, and routine animal-health and food-safety concerns against potentially catastrophic risks. This may involve measures to encourage the movement of intensive livestock production facilities away from urban population centres and to reduce the potential for pathogens to move between systems. Risk management of livestock disease risks should involve improving information and early-warning systems, and engaging all stakeholders, including poor people, in decision-making.

This includes enhanced local capacities, improved collaboration between national and international animal-health and food-safety authorities (including greater transparency on the occurrence of animal diseases), and investment in technologies to mitigate risk.

Economic and human-health threats related to livestock disease

Animal diseases pose two basic types of problem for humans: socio-economic and health. Figure 15 illustrates the pathways through which livestock diseases and the risk of livestock disease affect human welfare.

Economic and socio-economic threats from livestock diseases come in three broad categories: (i) losses in production, productivity and profitability caused by disease agents and the cost of their treatment; (ii) disruptions to local markets, international trade and rural economies arising from disease outbreaks and the control measures aimed at containing their spread, such as culling, quarantines and travel bans; and (iii) livelihood threats to the poor. Livelihood threats arise from the first two categories of threat. Because livestock serve multiple functions in the livelihoods of poor people, livestock diseases affect poor livestock producers differently from commercial producers. The poor face different incentives and have different capacities to respond to disease outbreaks. An economic problem for some producers can destroy the livelihoods of others.

Human-health threats from livestock come in two basic forms: (i) zoonotic diseases, and (ii) food-borne illnesses. Zoonotic diseases are those that arise in animals but can be transmitted to humans. Potentially pandemic viruses, such as influenza, are the most newsworthy, but many others exist, including rabies, brucellosis and anthrax. Food-borne illness can come from disease agents such as salmonella and *E. coli* or contaminants that enter the food chain during the production and processing of animal-based foods. These illnesses and the way they are managed create problems for everyone, but smallholders are often particularly vulnerable because they are more exposed to the risk and have less capacity to respond and recover.

Livestock disease specialists differ regarding the prevalence and impacts of diseases, owing in part to a lack of information. For example, in some areas it is not clear whether the prevalence of an animal disease is actually increasing or whether more instances are being detected

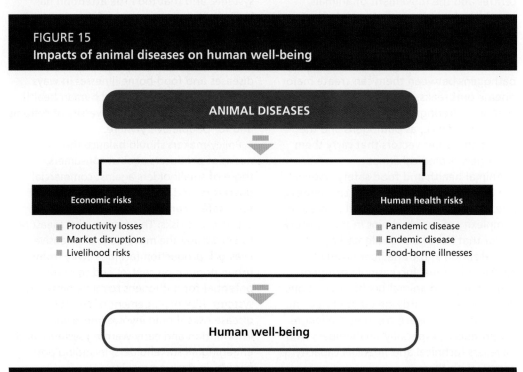

FIGURE 15
Impacts of animal diseases on human well-being

ANIMAL DISEASES

Economic risks	Human health risks
▪ Productivity losses	▪ Pandemic disease
▪ Market disruptions	▪ Endemic disease
▪ Livelihood risks	▪ Food-borne illnesses

Human well-being

Source: FAO.

because of better surveillance and diagnostic capabilities. The available evidence suggests that there has been a steady decline in the prevalence of many animal diseases in developed countries, although they still experience periodic outbreaks of some diseases and the prevalence of stress-related diseases associated with intensive production systems is increasing. In contrast, there has been very little apparent change in the prevalence of endemic livestock diseases in the developing world, particularly in many African countries. However, at the global level there is evidence to suggest that new pathogens are emerging at the human–animal–ecosystem interface.

It is inappropriate to formulate a "one-size fits all" response to disease because people and countries are affected differently depending on their economic circumstances. A disease has different impacts depending on the scale and intensity of production and the importance of commercial market outlets. Consequently, countries face different costs and incentives, just as they have varying capacities to implement control measures. Many of these differences are explained by the changing production and marketing systems, the continued coexistence of industrial and traditional systems and the resulting imbalances in national animal-health and food-safety systems. While the objective of animal disease-control measures is the protection of animal and public health, policy-makers should consider the diversity of impacts and incentives confronting different people in the sector and tailor interventions and compensation accordingly.

Strict biosafety and food-safety measures are used to restrict the emergence and spread of diseases in countries where the livestock sector is dominated by large-scale intensive production systems and complex processing and marketing operations. These production systems and their associated value chains roughly correspond to the "industrial" production systems described in previous chapters. They are typically supported by strong national animal-health and food-safety systems and by powerful consumer and public interest groups and food retailers that insist on high standards of public health, food safety and quality.

The overarching strategy of industrial systems is to control disease-causing agents by eradicating them from the food chain – from feed and animal production through food processing and retailing. Strict biosecurity measures and food-handling procedures are implemented at every step in the chain. These systems generally perform well in delivering high levels of public health and food safety, but they are vulnerable when pathogens enter an otherwise secure system. For example, an outbreak of foot-and-mouth disease (FMD) in the United Kingdom in 2001 may have cost almost UK£30 billion since then in direct costs for control measures and indirect costs (lost revenues) (Table 15). Similarly, in the United States of America, outbreaks of food-borne illnesses linked to animal sources cost more than US$8 billion per year in terms of illness, premature deaths and lost productivity (Table 16).

Many animal diseases are always present in some systems, especially where the livestock sector is dominated by "traditional" small-scale, mixed or extensive production systems. Endemic diseases are generally tolerated in countries where traditional systems dominate, even though the diseases impose economic and health burdens on producers and consumers. Such countries tend to have less robust animal-health and food-safety systems; they often focus their limited resources on the problems of the small segment of the livestock sector concerned with international trade, while neglecting the needs of poorer livestock keepers. While the small-scale systems may be less vulnerable to dramatic disease outbreaks than are industrial systems, disease nonetheless imposes large, often unmeasured, costs on producers and consumers. For example, in Africa there are several tropical parasitic livestock diseases that do not occur anywhere else, such as the tick-borne East Coast fever (*Theileria parva)* and tsetse-transmitted trypanosomosis, both with a subcontinental scale of distribution and posing a major burden on cattle farming and rural livelihoods even when there are no precise cost estimates. Contagious bovine pleuropneumonia (CBPP) is estimated to cost almost €45 million per year in lost productivity. Table 15 contrasts cost estimates for disease outbreaks in both developed and developing countries of various diseases. The variability illustrates the magnitude of

TABLE 15

Some estimated costs of disease in developed and developing countries

LOCATION	OCCURRENCE	ESTIMATED COST
United Kingdom	FMD 2001	From UK£3 billion to the public sector + UK£5 billion to the private sector to UK£25–30 billion in total (NAO, 2002; Bio-Era, 2005)
Scotland, United Kingdom	FMD 2001	Direct cost to agriculture UK£231 million. Loss of gross revenue to tourism up to UK£250 million (Royal Society of Edinburgh, 2002)
United States of America	HPAI 1983–84	US$65 million (USDA, 2005)
Netherlands	CSF 1997–98	US$2.34 billion (Meuwissen *et al.*, 1999)
North America	Lyme disease (endemic)	Approximately US$20 million annually (Maes, Lecomte and Ray, 1998)
Spain	African horse sickness 1967, 1987, 1988–90	US$20 million (Mellor and Boorman, 1995)
European Union	BSE 1990s	€92 billion long-term cost (Cunningham, 2003)
United States of America	BSE 2003	US$11 billion from export restrictions (USITC, 2008)
Africa	CBPP annually	€44.8 million (Tambi, Maina and Ndi, 2006)
India	*Theileria annulata* annually in traditional cattle	US$384.3 million annually (Minjauw and McLeod, 2003)
East, Central and southern Africa	*Theileria parva* annually in traditional cattle	US$168 million annually (Minjauw and McLeod, 2003)
Global	Ticks and tick-borne diseases in cattle	US$13.9–18.7 billion annually (de Castro, 1997)
Uruguay	FMD	US$7–9 million annually prior to FMD vaccination prior to eradication in 1997 (Leslie, Barozzi and Otte, 1997)

Notes: BSE = bovine spongiform encephalopathy; CBPP = contagious bovine pleuropneumonia; CSF = classical swine fever; FMD = foot-and-mouth disease; HPAI = high-pathogenicity avian influenza.

occurrences as well as the difficulty in comparing countries, diseases and their impact. The cost of food-borne illnesses is not known with any degree of accuracy in many developing countries because such incidents are rarely reported.

When industrial and traditional systems intersect through trade or travel, problems can erupt. Industrial systems are always vulnerable to the emergence or re-emergence of disease agents, for which countries with weak animal-health systems often act as a reservoir. At the same time, the high animal-health and food-safety standards required to protect livestock and consumers in countries with industrial livestock systems can serve as insurmountable barriers to trade for products from countries with weaker systems, limiting export opportunities from poorer countries.

Economic threats

From the point of view of producers, livestock diseases are essentially an economic problem. Diseases reduce production and productivity, disrupt trade and local and regional economies and exacerbate poverty. At the biological level, pathogens compete for the productive potential of animals and reduce the share that can be captured for human ends. A sick animal produces less meat, less milk or fewer eggs. It provides less draught power and poorer-quality food and fibre. In economic terms, output declines, costs rise and profits fall.

In traditional systems, the costs of animal diseases are considerable but are rarely calculated explicitly. Veterinary services are

TABLE 16
Some estimated costs of food-borne illness in developed countries

LOCATION	CAUSE	ESTIMATED COST
United States of America	Shiga toxin-producing *Escherichia coli* O157 (O157 STEC)	US$405 million annually (in 2003 dollars), including US$370 million for premature deaths, US$30 million for medical care, and US$5 million in lost productivity (Frenzen, Drake and Angulo, 2005)
Ohio State, United States of America	All food-borne illnesses	Between US$1.0 and US$7.1 billion annually (Scharff, McDowell and Medeiros, 2009)
United States of America	Multiple species annually	US$8.4 billion: salmonellosis US$4.0 billion; staphylococcal intoxication US$1.5 billion; toxoplasmosis US$445 million; listeriosis US$313 million; campylobacteriosis US$156 million; trichinosis US$144 million; *Clostridium perfringens* enteritis US$123 million; *E. coli* infections including hemorrhagic colitis US$223 million; botulism US$87 million (Archer and Kvenberg, 1985)
Japan	*E. coli* O157-H7 outbreak	¥82 686 000. Laboratory costs, about ¥21 204 000, Also, the cost of foodstuffs that were not purchased during the suspension of the lunch service (about 19%), personnel expenses paid to lunch service employees (about 17%), human illness costs (about 15%), and the repair costs of facilities (about 15%) (Abe, Yamamoto and Shinagawa, 2002)
Belgium	*Campylobacter*	€10.9 million annually (Gellynck *et al.*, 2008)

often not available or affordable, so the routine costs of controlling and treating disease in traditional systems are low, but the continual drain on production and productivity caused by endemic infectious and parasitic diseases reduces the ability of smallholders to lift themselves out of poverty.

Producers in industrial systems view the costs of controlling and treating animal diseases as part of the economic cost of production. The disease burden *per se* is relatively low, but the costs associated with maintaining biosecure production facilities and paying for veterinary services and medications can be significant. These costs affect the overall profit of the firm.

Production, productivity and profitability
Many diseases affect livestock productivity. Some are discussed below as transboundary and emerging diseases or as food-borne illness, but the same diseases can also persist in an endemic form, posing a constant drain on productivity. Causes of loss of productivity include death of the animal or illness leading to condemnation at slaughter, as well as reduction in weight gain, milk yield, feed conversion, reproductive capacity and work capacity for ploughing and transport.

Treatment costs, where veterinary services are available, include direct financial costs and indirect costs of time taken up by seeking or providing treatment. The

increase in production costs is expected to be compensated by reduction in productivity losses, but this may not be the case if animal-health-care services are of poor quality and the treatment is not applied correctly. This is a serious problem in many remote regions in developing countries, where veterinary services are scarce.

Livestock in developing countries are exposed to a range of diseases that affect productivity. For example, in Africa, CBPP and peste des petits ruminants (PPR) affect cattle and sheep, respectively; both diseases now appear to be spreading, killing local livestock. In Viet Nam, classical swine fever (CSF) causes serious losses to small-scale pig producers but has little impact on export trade as Viet Nam exports only small amounts of pig meat. Foot-and-mouth disease in India and elsewhere in Asia causes considerable loss of production; it is a particular problem when it infects draught animals during the ploughing season, limiting their ability to work. This reduces farmers' incomes from renting out draught animals and causes a reduction in the area of land that can be planted to staple food crops.

Markets, trade and rural economies
Animal diseases that cause high mortality in animals and spread rapidly nationally and internationally into disease-free areas can exact particularly high economic costs.

BOX 16
Animal health and welfare

The way people treat animals is influenced by beliefs and values regarding the nature of animals and their moral significance, which vary from culture to culture. The view of animals as "sentient beings" is spreading through scientific and veterinary education and provides an additional impetus to safeguard animal welfare.

Good animal welfare management includes implementation of practices that prevent and mitigate pain and distress, prevent and treat diseases and injuries and provide living conditions that allow animals to express natural behaviours. Often, such practices have multiple benefits for people as well as animals: they can contribute to productivity, livelihoods, food security and safety, human health and psychological well-being. However, they can also carry costs in the form of investment for welfare-friendly animal housing and training of staff, longer time periods to produce outputs or less output per unit space allocated to animals. An approach to animal welfare that focuses on benefits to people, rather than to the animals, is more likely to succeed, especially in parts of the world where many people suffer from poverty and starvation.

A wide range of standards and programmes have been created to ensure the implementation of good animal welfare practices, including: voluntary welfare codes, often created by industry organizations; corporate programmes; product differentiation programmes that allow consumers to purchase selectively; legislated standards; and international agreements created by treaties or intergovernmental organizations. The different types of programme serve different political and commercial purposes and have different strengths and weaknesses; a legislative approach, for example, will be effective only if sufficient resources are devoted to its administration and enforcement.

Animal welfare is increasingly being linked to trade and market access. There is a concern in some developing countries that animal welfare may become another non-tariff barrier limiting their access to markets. Developed-country producers, on the other hand, are concerned that the extra costs they incur to comply with legislation and standards in their domestic markets makes their products uncompetitive compared with imports. However, meat, eggs and dairy products produced in compliance with high animal-

These so-called transboundary and emerging diseases can be vectored by birds, rodents and insects and carried by live animals and animal products or on the clothes, shoes and vehicle tyres of people moving through an affected area. The emergence of new diseases that are not understood or for which control technology is not available are of particular concern. Because of their dramatic effects on animal mortality and their high economic costs, they tend to attract the greatest attention from public animal-health programmes and national and international regulations.

The main strategy used to reduce the impact of transboundary and emerging diseases involves eliminating them from a population and then preventing their reintroduction, for example, through vaccination and sanitary measures aimed at protecting susceptible species from exposure from infected populations. The international institutions most directly involved are the Agreement on the Application of Sanitary and Phytosanitary Measures (SPS) of the World Trade Organization (WTO) and the OIE. The framework for international trade in livestock and livestock products allows countries that are free of a given notifiable disease to require their trading partners to have equivalent disease-free status. This system, based on strict definitions and evidence, works well for protecting trade, but it creates a major market barrier for

welfare standards can provide access to new, valuable market opportunities. Capacity needs to be built in lower-income countries to ensure that producers in these countries are better positioned to participate in such trade. Capacity building is also needed to prevent small- and medium-scale producers from being put at a competitive disadvantage relative to large, industrialized producers.

Currently, standards are being applied primarily in large-scale intensive systems, with poultry and pig systems being strongly targeted for improvements at the farm level. However, welfare concerns also apply to the animals kept by small-scale producers. With the increasing shift toward larger-scale livestock production in developing and emerging economies, there is an urgent need to work with producers and governments in such countries to improve animal health and welfare. The World Organisation for Animal Health (OIE) identified animal welfare as a strategic priority in 2001 and produced a set of standards for animal transport and slaughter in 2008 (OIE, 2008b). These are currently being expanded to cover on-farm animal welfare as well. The endorsement by the 2nd Global Conference on Animal Welfare, entitled "Putting the OIE Standards to Work", held in Cairo in October 2008, represented a significant step in the direction of global awareness in animal welfare. However, efforts need to be made to ensure implementation, compliance and enforcement of these standards.

FAO is committed to raising awareness, strengthening synergies and fostering partnerships, building capacities and creating and disseminating information related to animal welfare. As a starting point, FAO, in collaboration with key international partners in animal welfare, including the European Commission, OIE, animal welfare non-governmental organizations, producers and professional associations, launched in May 2009 a participatory portal to facilitate information sharing and improve access to knowledge and capacity building tools (www.fao.org/ag/animalwelfare.html).

Sources: FAO, 2008a; OIE, 2008b.

countries with weak animal-health systems. Such countries are rarely if ever free of all notifiable diseases.

The discovery of a notifiable disease in a country that exports livestock or livestock products can create severe market shocks. Control measures typically include market and trade bans, restrictions on the movement of livestock and culling of affected herds or flocks. Consumers may also shun products of the livestock species involved if the disease is perceived to have possible human-health implications. Sharp falls in consumption can affect producers and traders far outside the area where the outbreak occurs (Yalcin, 2006; Hartono, 2004). Control measures can also devastate tourism and associated industries.

It may take weeks or months until markets and production cycles are re-established, and producers may lose market share to others in the meantime.

Foot-and-mouth disease, a well-known disease of ruminant livestock and pigs, has caused serious trade disruptions in several meat-exporting countries of Europe and South America over the past 20 years, but most of these countries have managed to regain disease-free status. However, the costs of FMD outbreaks and control measures are significant, reaching perhaps €90 billion for countries in the EU since 2001 (Table 15). In much of Africa and Asia, FMD is endemic and remains a perpetual obstacle to the export of meat and other livestock products. Other transboundary diseases can be equally devastating. Thailand lost its export market for unprocessed poultry meat in 2004 during the first wave of highly pathogenic avian influenza (HPAI) outbreaks. It has since recaptured some markets by exporting processed poultry meat. Some countries in the Horn of Africa depend on livestock exports to the Near East, but periodic outbreaks of Rift Valley fever and the resulting trade bans can seriously harm livestock producers. Bovine spongiform encephalitis (BSE) has infected relatively few animals, but its association with the human variant Creutzfeldt-Jakob disease has had a huge impact on international beef trade, estimated at US$11 billion for exports from the United States of America alone (see Table 15). Control measures aimed at tracing and eliminating animals infected with BSE have imposed regulations that poorer countries find difficult to meet.

The OIE recently defined the concept of "compartments" to help countries overcome trade barriers associated with notifiable diseases (OIE, 2008a). While some countries may be unable to attain full disease-free status, they may be able to eliminate notifiable diseases from some subpopulations of animals. A compartment is a subpopulation held under a common biosecurity management system for which disease-free status can be certified. In theory at least, animals could be traded from a disease-free compartment even if the rest of the country were not free of disease. An even more recent idea is that of "commodity-based trade", which would allow a livestock commodity to be certified as safe because of the particular conditions under which it was produced and processed, no matter the overall disease status of the country.

Livelihoods
Animal disease affects all livestock-owning households by threatening their assets and making their income less secure. For many families in the poorest quintile, livestock disease is particularly damaging because it threatens the very asset that they use for dealing with other crises. It also affects people who are employed by livestock owners, small-scale traders of livestock and poor consumers. The measures used by veterinary authorities to combat disease can

have severe consequences for people living in poverty, including depriving poor producers of their livelihoods, in the case of culls, and driving up costs of livestock products to poor consumers.

Some diseases that can be prevented or controlled by wealthier farmers are a continuing problem in the flocks and herds of poor households. For example, brucellosis is often present in sheep and goat flocks under extensive management in many parts of the world, but vaccination is not widely practised by extensive herders because of the high cost.

Likewise, Newcastle disease in poultry is kept under control by segregation and vaccination in commercial flocks but no economically viable control system has yet been found for scavenging flocks. Peste des petits ruminants (PPR) causes high mortality in sheep and goats, and, while it is preventable by vaccination or by keeping infected flocks away from healthy ones, it is still capable of taking communities by surprise as the outbreaks in North and Eastern Africa in 2007–08 demonstrated.

Other diseases affect rich and poor alike but have very particular effects on the poor. For example, FMD, a disease that disrupts international trade, is not usually a major cause for concern among extensive herders and mixed farmers, but it does have a large impact when it occurs in traction animals during land preparation (Thuy, 2001). Classical swine fever is a problem for pig producers who want to trade on the international markets, but at a very low level of incidence it is an accepted risk for small-scale pig producers.

Diseases affect the amount, timing and certainty of income from livestock enterprises, depriving small producers in particular of access to credit to buy feed, animals or their replacements. Poor people are more likely to be chronically affected by health problems that can be caused by contact with sick animals, such as brucellosis or internal parasites. Many poor people earn wages from working in intensive livestock production or marketing enterprises. Animal disease can jeopardize this source of income.

For these reasons, reducing the incidence of livestock diseases can help alleviate poverty. However, as noted above, livestock keepers have different objectives and face different risks and incentives. Policy-makers need to consider these differences in formulating responses, even as health objectives remain foremost. It must be recognized that poorly planned and executed measures may seriously harm poor livestock owners and fail to achieve animal health objectives. For example, a hastily introduced ban on poultry keeping in a Southeast Asian capital resulted in a loss of income for many families, but failed to eradicate poultry from the city because of incomplete compliance (ICASEPS, 2008).

In recent years, the scientific community has developed a variety of animal-health technologies and interventions that can reduce the threat of disease. However, these have tended to overlook the specific animal-health requirements of poor livestock keepers in developing countries. In addition, there are financial and institutional constraints that impede the delivery of new technology to small-scale producers.

Developing countries, and particularly their poorer farmers, are suffering from a contraction of government services and intervention in the last two or three decades. Government veterinary services are very poorly funded, legislation governing the livestock sector is often out of date, and private animal health services are very limited. Many farmers never call a veterinarian, particularly in remote rural areas, and they may need to travel far to obtain access to drugs or vaccines. In addition, when there is a crisis that the government veterinary service needs to respond to, the service is hard-pressed to mobilize the people, transport and equipment to deal with it. Similarly, nations with limited resources that focus their efforts on supporting food exports may neglect the infrastructure needed to ensure domestic food-safety systems. In order to be able to sustain the infrastructure required for overall food safety, nations must have food-safety systems that work for both their domestic and export markets.

Despite the global shift towards intensive livestock production, the many poor people who will continue to rely on small numbers of poultry or other livestock for income diversity and security still require better animal-health services than those available at present. One of the greatest challenges will be to find ways to provide and sustain these services in countries where investment in such services has been falling for many years. Recently, for example, funding that was made available to tackle HPAI helped to strengthen support for community-level animal-health services in a number of countries by providing training and support programmes for community animal-health workers; however, unless financial support is sustained, these gains could be short-lived.

In Africa, where the shortage of public funds for agricultural services is particularly acute, the advent of structural adjustment programmes led to the withdrawal of highly subsidized animal-health services, including communal dipping of cattle and provision of clinical services and drugs. The reach of clinical veterinary services became restricted, in particular failing to cover remote and marginal areas of arid and semi-arid lands where the majority of pastoralists live. Prices of veterinary drugs increased and support services formerly provided by government during droughts were withdrawn. Community-based organizations and non-governmental organizations often step into the existing institutional voids left by retreating public services. Incorporating these organizations more fully into national animal-health systems represents a further challenge that needs to be addressed.

A priority in the development agenda must be to understand the relationship between animal health/disease and the livelihoods of poor livestock keepers. Moreover, animal-health concerns need to be integrated in overall rural development policy, because failure to consider disease can seriously reduce rural growth.

Human-health threats
Threats to human health from animals arise mainly from existing and emerging zoonotic diseases (those that pass between animals and humans), from food-borne illnesses and from residues left by the improper use of veterinary medicines (e.g. antibiotics), hormones and toxic substances.

During the early stages of intensification of livestock production, large-scale livestock production units tend to be established near to growing urban centres, which places large livestock populations in close proximity to large human populations. This brings both public-health and environmental hazards. In some cities in poorer countries, a significant proportion of city-dwellers keep livestock, often in cramped and unsanitary conditions and in close proximity to people. This can foster the emergence and spread of diseases affecting both animals and humans (Waters-Bayer, 1995).

Zoonotic diseases and pandemic threats
Emerging zoonotic diseases (from wild or domestic animals) can spread out of their natural ecosystem due to many reasons, such as human and animal demographic changes, ecosystem encroachment, climate fluctuations and trade flows. These diseases cause sickness and death in humans and are an issue of growing importance to medical and veterinary authorities. A very large number of new diseases in animals are able to infect and affect humans. At least half of the 1 700 known causes of infectious disease in humans have a reservoir in animals, and many new infections are zoonotic diseases. More than 200 zoonotic diseases have been described, caused by bacteria, parasites, viruses, fungi and unconventional agents (e.g. prions). About 75 percent of the new diseases that have affected humans over the past ten years are caused by pathogens originating from animals or from products of animal origin. Many of these diseases have the potential to spread by various means over long distances and to become global problems. Treatment can be costly or long-term; some, such as new-variant Creutzfeldt-Jakob disease and rabies, are incurable. Highly infectious zoonotic diseases have received a considerable amount of attention because of their sudden appearance and potential high impact, while vaccines and effective treatments may not be available.

In recent years, the world has experienced the emergence of severe acute respiratory syndrome (SARS), HPAI (caused by the A[H5N1] virus) and an influenza caused by the A(H1N1) virus, all causing considerable concern about the risk of a major global pandemic. Major national and international efforts have succeeded in containing SARS effectively. However, although H5N1 HPAI has disappeared from most countries, it is stubbornly persisting in several countries.

The influenza caused by the A(H1N1) virus has recently been declared a worldwide pandemic by the WHO; infections and deaths continue to rise. The worldwide dispersal of BSE was avoided, but occasional cases continue to be detected beyond the British Isles. The end of 2008 marked the detection of the Ebola Reston virus circulating in pigs and pig workers in the Philippines. In addition, outbreaks of the Ebola virus flare up occasionally in the Democratic Republic of the Congo, Uganda and other countries in Africa, killing humans and large numbers of great apes.

Some zoonotic diseases are being brought under control in some countries and yet are expanding in others. Rabies has been largely controlled in Europe since the introduction of oral vaccines to control the disease in foxes, the main reservoir of the virus. For example, in France, the number of rabies cases in domestic animals fell from 463 in 1990 to a single case in 2007. In contrast, rabies is growing in importance in many developing countries. A recent outbreak in Bali, Indonesia, appears to be difficult to control because of a lack of general awareness about the outbreak and the challenge to agree on a strategy that works: the choice of the right vaccine and whether to vaccinate, sterilize or cull stray dogs.

Another group of zoonotic diseases, often referred to as "neglected" because of their endemicity, includes cysticerocosis, echinococcosis and brucellosis. Little attention is paid to them, and they often persist in the poorest and most vulnerable populations. The lack of awareness and government commitment tends to aggravate the situation.

Food-borne illnesses
Although several of the diseases previously mentioned can be transmitted through food, food-borne diseases are considered as a specific group. Organisms such as salmonella (particularly *S. enteritidis* and *S. typhimurium*), *Campylobacter* and *E. coli* O157:H7 are major food-borne threats, causing illness in millions of people worldwide every year.

The global incidence of food-borne diseases in foods of animal origin is difficult to estimate. However, Maxwell and Slater (2003) found that up to 30 percent of people in industrialized countries suffer from food-borne illnesses every year. Consumer attitudes to risk, as well as the food-safety risk levels, priorities and approaches to food safety and quality vary significantly between developed and developing countries. Countries have responded in different ways to growing public concerns over food safety. Some have approached the problem from the perspective of domestic consumer welfare, while others with a strong export orientation have addressed the issue as a threat to their export markets.

The major food-safety hazards in livestock products are biological and chemical contaminants. These contaminants can originate from air, soil, water, feedstuffs, fertilizers (including natural fertilizers), pesticides, veterinary drugs or any other agent used in primary production, or from diseased animals.

Biological contaminants in livestock products include: abnormal proteins, such as those associated with BSE; bacteria, such as *Salmonella* and *Brucella* species and some types of *E. coli*; and parasites, such as *Echinococcus* species. Chemical and biological contaminants include: veterinary drug residues, such as antimicrobials, and pesticides; chemicals; heavy metals; and naturally occurring mycotoxins and bacterial toxins.

In developing countries, the quality and safety of food supplies are put at risk by demands for more, cheaper food, driven by growing population and increasing urbanization, combined with a lack of resources to deal with issues related to food safety and lower or less rigorously enforced regulatory standards. Human and financial resources that are dedicated by national authorities to the support of regulatory and non-regulatory food-safety programmes generally fall well short of needs. Commonly, many of the resources available are used for quality control of food for export, rather than products for domestic consumption, leaving the domestic market more vulnerable to unacceptable levels of food-safety hazards. In many developing countries, there is a substantial informal market that generally escapes any food-safety controls.

Informal food production systems, such as unregulated slaughter in developing countries, make available food that has not met food-safety standards. Many rural and urban poor people buy food in informal and uncontrolled markets and, therefore, face a higher chance of contracting zoonotic and food-borne diseases, resulting in illness and wage loss as well as medical expenses to treat the illnesses (FAO, 2005). Moreover, food-borne illnesses often affect aged, young and malnourished people most severely. The failure by national governments in developing countries to invest adequately in food-safety systems has greater impact on the poor than the better-off.

The ultimate goal of food-safety management systems is to prevent unsafe food from entering the food supply. This is achieved by applying good hygiene practices at all stages of the food chain. The role of national authorities is to define the food-safety standards that the industry must meet and to provide the necessary oversight to ensure that the standards are met. Development of appropriate food-safety management and information strategies also depends on a thorough knowledge of the market and of the forces affecting stakeholders' behaviour and choices. The ability of both public and private sectors to carry out their roles effectively depends on the availability of adequate facilities for food processing and handling and of enough appropriately trained people.

The FAO/WHO Codex Alimentarius Commission develops internationally agreed standards and guidelines for safe food that provide the benchmark for food-safety regulation in international trade. However, governments vary in their investment in developing an internationally acceptable food-safety system. Many developing countries focus their efforts on meeting the requirements of importing countries for selected key exports, motivated by the desire to maximize export earnings and trade-led growth. However, neglect of food safety on domestic markets has its own cost. Food-safety concerns about domestic products can lead importers to question a country's ability to impose and enforce acceptable food-safety standards on any food product.

Increasingly, private food-safety standards are being imposed by buyers. These prescribe food-safety management procedures to be followed that are consistent with the principles laid out in Codex standards and guidelines but generally go further. While these private standards are "voluntary", the concentration within the retail sector is such that many producers in developing countries are forced to comply with them in order to be able to export.

As economies develop, food processing and preparation tends to shift outside the home, and supermarkets increasingly dominate urban food retailing. In many developing countries, this has led to demands from the growing affluent middle-class driving improvements in food safety.

For example, the Government of China has established "green food" certification for a wide range of products, including beef, in response to food-safety concerns raised by affluent urban consumers. A survey revealed that affluent consumers are prepared to pay premiums of 20–30 percent for "green foods". At the production level, the certificate prohibits use of growth promoters, imposes withholding periods for some veterinary products and sets national standards to be met on the use of feed additives and antibiotics (Brown and Waldron, 2003).

Developing countries commonly lack the technical and institutional capacity – food laboratories, human and financial resources, national legislative and regulatory frameworks, enforcement capacity, management and coordination – to ensure compliance with international standards, which compromises food safety. Such systemic weaknesses not only threaten public health but may also reduce access to global food markets. Umali-Deininger and Sur (2007) also noted that cultural issues, such as religious beliefs, may constrain the adoption of appropriate food-safety measures.

The complexity of food safety makes it difficult to identify the right policies to alleviate problems in the sector, especially where little is known of the magnitude of the problems. While food-safety risks can be minimized, we cannot expect risk to be eliminated when it comes to food safety – implying that policy-makers, together with scientists and the food industry, will have to define acceptable levels of risk.

Disease control and risk management

Managing livestock disease and improving social welfare requires action on several fronts. Dealing with transboundary diseases requires regional cooperation or "cluster" approaches that take into consideration the rapid spread and evolution of these diseases. Mechanisms for reducing risks from livestock diseases include: relocating intensive livestock production facilities away from urban population centres; strengthening animal-health and food-safety systems, including information and early warning; engaging all stakeholders, including poor people, in decision-making on animal-health programmes; developing animal-health strategies tailored to specific local circumstances; improving collaboration between national and international animal-health and food-safety authorities; and investing in technologies to mitigate risk.

Location of production

The geographic concentration of production units near urban centres increases the risks of epidemic disease outbreaks in the livestock population, especially when people and animals move between traditional and intensive production systems, and increases the exposure of the urban population to livestock diseases. Animal-health protection in large, clustered livestock production units is straightforward in some respects. There are few units to monitor and it is cost-effective for veterinarians to visit them or to be employed by them. If there is a disease outbreak, there are relatively few critical points for timely intervention and proper monitoring. There is also a strong incentive for farmers to invest in disease prevention, reducing the range of animal-health hazards. It may be necessary, however, to encourage the relocation of these units away from urban centres in the interests of human health. It is important to recall that pathogens that are circulating in smallholder livestock, including in scavenging poultry, are not normally seen to jump to a higher level of virulence, A mutation into a more aggressive disease agent is far more probable where pathogens gain access to an abundance of susceptible host animals, as may occur in medium- to large-scale commercial plants if biosecurity measures are breached. Most extensive livestock production is characterized by relatively small herds and flocks of genetically diverse, robust and more disease-resistant animals.

Meanwhile, backyard livestock production continues in many urban and peri-urban areas. There have been instances where governments have tried to ban such enterprises in light of human-health concerns. This has been the case, for example, in recent efforts to control HPAI (ICASEPS, 2008). Where implemented without careful consultation with producers, this approach has damaged livelihoods and resulted in non-compliance. Some governments have modified or removed these restrictions and are trying instead to provide incentives to encourage safer production practices.

Animal health, food safety and early-warning systems

Many developing countries lack mechanisms for gathering information about the incidence of animal-health and food-safety problems or any form of early-warning system for disease outbreaks. This limits their ability to diagnose and prioritize animal-health problems and deliver appropriate interventions.

Many of the basic elements for a global information system already exist. Regional organizations in Southeast Asia and South America for instance, have played an important role in promoting cross-border and regional animal-health surveillance programmes. The Global Early Warning System (GLEWS), operated by FAO, OIE and WHO, provides warnings based on the most up-to-date scientific information available; these permit national decision-makers and the international scientific community to make more accurate assessments of risks of disease outbreaks. Global and regional networks of laboratories and epidemiologists – for example, the OIE/FAO Network of Expertise on Animal Influenza (OFFLU) and regional laboratory and epidemiology networks in Africa and Asia – have also been set up to facilitate the sharing of information and samples.

However, these systems function where reliable local information is available. Gathering such information requires an effective surveillance system based on a sensitized, alert and engaged community, suitably trained and equipped staff and well-equipped laboratories. Regrettably, few developing countries have such systems in place. Some developing countries have had successful experiences with participatory disease surveillance involving villagers or community animal-health workers, for example in Africa during the 1990s to detect residual pockets of rinderpest (Mariner and Roeder, 2003) and in Indonesia in 2004–05 to discover the extent of H5N1 HPAI infection (Alders et al., in press). However, sustained investment and government commitment are needed to create such systems, and given the contribution that good disease intelligence makes to global public goods, at least part of the investment should come from the international community.

Strengthening animal-health and food-safety systems requires consistent, sustained funding. This will have to be provided at the local and national levels as well as by the international community. Stronger planning, advocacy and monitoring of impacts of the systems will be important, together with closer engagement between public and private sectors in countries where the private sector is sufficiently robust. There are a few examples of combined public and private animal-health funds, but none are in developing countries. The best known example is in Australia, where a not-for-profit public company has been established by the federal government, state and territory governments and major national livestock industry organizations to manage national animal-health programmes on behalf of its members (AHA, 2009). Responsible behaviour by individuals is needed to reduce externalities, and a shared public–private fund ensures that both risks and responsibilities are shared. Many disease-control issues represent a mixture of private and public goods. Private actions taken by livestock owners to preserve their own herds and flocks, such as voluntary vaccination, or the application of biosecurity measures can also create a public benefit

BOX 17
Global Rinderpest Eradication Programme (GREP) – elements of a success

The virus that causes rinderpest is arguably the most dreaded cattle disease on account of its epidemic history that caused massive depopulations of livestock and wildlife in three continents and was responsible for several famines in agricultural communities of the eighteenth, nineteenth and twentieth centuries. With the launching in 1994 of the Global Rinderpest Eradication Programme (GREP), FAO spearheaded an initiative to consolidate gains in rinderpest control and to move towards disease eradication. In close association with the World Organisation for Animal Health (OIE), the International Atomic Energy Agency (IAEA), the African Union's Inter-African Bureau for Animal Resources (AU-IBAR) and other partners, the GREP, a key unit within the Emergency Prevention System for Transboundary Animal and Plant Pests and Diseases (EMPRES), was conceived as an international coordination mechanism to promote the global eradication of rinderpest and verification of rinderpest freedom, while providing technical guidance to achieve these goals. From the outset, the GREP was a time-bound programme, with a focus on global declaration of freedom in 2010.

Target achieved. The last reported outbreak of rinderpest was in Kenya in 2001 and the last known use of vaccines against this disease was in 2007. Not only has eradication proved feasible, it is probable that it has been achieved. However, the process for international

recognition must be upheld and processes respected to ensure that country dossiers are submitted for evaluation by the international community as determined by the OIE. An international declaration of Global Rinderpest Freedom is expected to be made in 2010. This would be only the second time that a disease has been eradicated worldwide (the first being smallpox in humans).

Partnership and donor support. The GREP has been able to count on the partnership with the OIE, economic blocs and regional specialized organizations (e.g. the African Union and the South Asian Association for Regional Cooperation) and numerous donor agencies, such as the European Commission, United States Agency for International Development, Department for International Development (United Kingdom) and the Governments of Ireland and Italy. However, the most important partners of the GREP have been the countries themselves. In several situations, FAO's Technical Cooperation Programme project funding has been used to control rinderpest outbreaks rapidly or undertake activities to promote diagnostic laboratory strengthening, emergency preparedness planning, surveillance and capacity building. The GREP has also been instrumental in drafting and revising the OIE Pathway (a standard-setting activity to determine international disease status as it relates to rinderpest viral activity), surveillance strategies and other guidelines that lead to confirming eradication.

by limiting disease spread to animals or people.

Engaging the poor in animal-health programmes
Consultative processes are required to ensure that government, non-governmental organizations, academia and the private-sector groups involved in community-based programme development collectively

provide inputs into the animal-health and food-safety management process. High priority should be given to research that emphasizes both basic and applied aspects of food quality and safety. Countries need to pursue the development of simple, inexpensive analytical methods/techniques for all hazardous substances and micro-organisms. These should be applicable in wider community contexts in order to

Promoting vaccination. The strategy adopted early in the global rinderpest eradication was the implementation of widespread vaccination campaigns of cattle and buffaloes; this has entailed the use of heat-stable vaccines and, most importantly, the determination of post-vaccinal immunity, which has been carefully monitored to make sure that the campaigns covered the appropriate proportion of cattle population.

Virus characterization. Following molecular analyses, rinderpest virus strains were grouped into three distinct lineages: lineages I and II in Africa, and lineage III consisting of virus strains isolated from Asia and the Near East.

Rinderpest eradication campaign coordination. It was agreed during the FAO Expert Consultation meeting held in Rome in 1992 that regional coordination of campaigns would be the only realistic approach to rinderpest control, as isolated national actions would only lead to sporadic and unsustainable or temporary improvements. The GREP incorporated the concept of a coordinated Pan-African Rinderpest Campaign (PARC), which covered 34 countries in Africa until 1999, and a West Asian Rinderpest Eradication Campaign (WAREC), which covered 11 countries in the Near East region. The WAREC coordinated activities between 1989 and 1994. The PARC has been followed by the programme for Pan-African Control of Epizootics (30 countries),

while the Somali Ecosystem Rinderpest Eradication Coordination Unit (SERECU) regrouped Ethiopia, Kenya and Somalia as an area that showed the possible maintenance of viral activity. These efforts include epidemiological support and technical assistance in collaboration with the Pan-African Vaccine Centre based in Debre Zeit, Ethiopia, and those of the joint FAO/IAEA Division in Vienna, Austria.

Network in epidemiology and laboratories. Only through international coordination can transboundary animal diseases such as rinderpest be eliminated. It is concerted efforts by national authorities that have placed the world on the threshold of worldwide eradication of rinderpest. Their efforts have benefited from the assistance of reference laboratories (for confirmatory diagnosis, vaccine development and quality control) and from investment by the international community (for the establishment of regional approaches and networks of laboratories and epidemiological units).

Disease surveillance and participatory disease search. Aspects of epidemiology, risk-based surveillance and participatory disease search techniques have been developed and proved essential for detecting the last foci of rinderpest, for providing the epidemiological understanding of disease maintenance, and for gaining assurance of the disappearance or eradication of the disease.

offer both cultural and economic advantages.

Efforts to reduce the impacts of livestock disease on people living in poverty must take into account the wide range of diseases that affect the lives of poor people, including currently neglected diseases. They must also aim to minimize damage done by control measure used to deal with outbreaks of emerging zoonotics and transboundary

diseases. Achieving these goals will require the close engagement of poor people and their representatives in planning and delivery of disease-prevention and control measures; this will help ensure that more of the solutions proposed will be appropriate to, and wanted by, local communities.

This approach is essential both to protect the livelihoods of poor people and to increase the likelihood of disease-control efforts succeeding. Several examples have been cited above of the problems that may arise when the poor are not engaged in the planning and delivery of disease-control measures, ranging from non-compliance to creating household food-security problems.

It must be recognized, however, that the approach is particularly difficult to apply when faced with a rapidly developing disease threat, because of the urgency of the need to halt a growing problem before it becomes too great. For example, poor livestock keepers were hardly engaged in planning and delivering the emergency measures used to combat HPAI, but a great deal of effort is now going into finding ways to prepare for emergencies that will allow local conditions to be considered, and to plan for a smoother transition from immediate crisis response back to development efforts.

Measures that will help poor livestock keepers include: reducing the shock of control measures, e.g. avoiding extensive culls where possible; compensating those affected; and investing more heavily in local institutions that will help to provide better coping mechanisms. Public–private partnerships need to create space for the poor to become more engaged in order to capture local knowledge about prevailing diseases and impacts, and, where possible, to encourage them to develop their own measures to prevent and control livestock disease outbreaks.

Developing animal-health protection tailored to local circumstances
Animal-health protection should be tailored to specific local circumstances. Blanket solutions work well for some but not for others, setting up the conditions for tensions and non-compliance. Vaccination, for example, is relatively simple to apply in large, intensively managed flocks and herds, but tends to be much less cost-effective in small-scale systems because of the costs of delivering it to many small production units. Smallholders may be reluctant to participate in vaccination programmes when they perceive little immediate benefit. Much of the information that is currently available on financially viable protection measures is relevant only to large-scale, intensive farms – a gap that the international community is

attempting to fill, for instance for poultry in the wake of H5N1 HPAI (FAO, World Bank and OIE, 2008).

A more nuanced set of responses is needed that takes account of the needs and strengths of small-, medium- and large-scale producers in different types of production and marketing chains. Animal-health solutions need to be developed in and for local situations, and they must be seen in the context of wider developments in the livestock sector and beyond. Experience also underlines the need for those involved in animal-health systems to be constantly evaluating and learning from experience.

In all of these efforts, two-way communication is essential. Communication strategies to promote behaviours at the community and household levels aimed at preventing and controlling outbreaks of livestock disease include: informing communities of new or emerging health threats and how to recognize them; engaging local people in responding to such threats and in developing preventive practices for new diseases; and national public education campaigns to promote awareness of the impact of livestock diseases and what the public can do to help prevent and control outbreaks.

Improving collaboration between national and international animal-health and food-safety authorities
Efforts to control zoonotic diseases and food-safety problems related to the livestock sector must involve both human- and animal-health sectors. There is also a need to collaborate with wildlife or environmental experts in order to understand the origins and reservoirs of diseases. For this reason, many current efforts are focused on improving collaborative arrangements at the national, regional and international levels.

"One World, One Health" is an interdisciplinary and cross-sectoral approach to dealing with emerging infectious diseases, developed by the Wildlife Conservation Society (see Box 18). It has been adopted by a number of recent initiatives against zoonotic disease that bring together a wide range of stakeholders from human- and animal-health sectors, medical and veterinary communities, wildlife and environmental organizations, the private sector and advanced research

BOX 18
One World, One Health

"One World, One Health" is an interdisciplinary and cross-sectoral approach aimed at promoting and developing a better understanding of the drivers and causes surrounding the emergence and spread of infectious diseases (www.oneworldhealth.org). The concept was developed by, and is a trademark of, the Wildlife Conservation Society. It was adopted in October 2008 as the basis for a strategic framework for reducing risks of infectious diseases at the animal–human–ecosystems interface by a group of international agencies – including FAO, the World Organisation for Animal Health (OIE), the World Health Organization (WHO), the United Nations Children's Fund (UNICEF) – and by the World Bank and the UN System Influenza Coordinator (UNSIC) (FAO *et al.*, 2008).

The main goal of the One World, One Health approach is to reduce the risk and global impact of disease outbreaks by improving livestock and wildlife intelligence, surveillance, and emergency response through stronger public and animal health systems. The approach calls on broad cooperation among disciplines and sectors and puts a high priority on "hot spots" for emerging infectious diseases.

The strategic framework focuses on emerging infectious diseases at the animal–human–ecosystems interface, where there is the potential for epidemics and pandemics that could result in wide ranging impacts at the country, regional and international levels. The objective of the framework is to establish ways to reduce the risk and global impact of epidemics and pandemics of emerging infectious diseases. This requires better disease intelligence, surveillance and emergency response systems at all levels, which, in its turn, calls for strong public and animal health services together with effective communication strategies.

National authorities play a key role in devising, financing and implementing these strategies.

There are five elements to the strategic framework:
- to build robust and well-governed public- and animal-health systems compliant with the WHO International Health Regulations (WHO, 2005) and OIE international standards, through the pursuit of long-term interventions;
- to prevent regional and international crises by controlling disease outbreaks through improved national and international emergency response capabilities;
- a shift in focus from developed to developing economies and from potential to actual disease problems, as well as an enhanced focus on the drivers of a broader range of locally important diseases;
- to promote wide-ranging collaboration across sectors and disciplines; and
- to develop rational and targeted disease-control programmes through the conduct of strategic research.

The overall objective of the strategic framework represents an international public good. While it does not prioritize diseases to target, it does have a clear aim to benefit the poor by helping to reduce the risks of infectious diseases that are important locally – e.g. Rift Valley fever, tuberculosis, brucellosis, rabies, foot-and-mouth disease, African swine fever and peste des petits ruminants. The One World, One Health paradigm is aimed at improving global, national and local public health, food safety and security and the livelihoods of poor farming communities everywhere while protecting fragile ecosystems.

Source: FAO *et al.*, 2008.

institutions at the country, regional and international levels (Box 18).

In most countries, sector-specific institutions have clear roles and responsibilities, but mechanisms for cross-sectoral collaboration are not clearly identified or developed. However, significant progress in cross-sectoral collaboration has been achieved regionally and at the international level. Regionally, collaboration occurs through organizations such as ASEAN, ECO, OIRSA, IICA, APEC, SAARC and AU-IBAR,[5] among others. Internationally, collaboration exists among many organizations or institutions, such as WHO, FAO, UNICEF, OIE, WWF, WCS and IUCN[6] and advanced research organizations and laboratories, including those of the Consultative Group on International Agriculture Research (CGIAR) system. FAO, the International Atomic Energy Agency (IAEA) and OIE reference laboratories and collaborating centres support diagnostic services, research in epidemiology and development of vaccines. OIE and FAO promoted joint Regional Animal Health Centres to support harmonized strategies and approaches for transboundary animal diseases and emerging infectious diseases across countries in regions with similar problems and challenges.

The more localized or endemic human-health problems of animal origin have so far received less attention of this nature, although there is growing awareness that the control of endemic human diseases of animal origin may contribute cost-effectively to poverty alleviation. Control of neglected zoonotic diseases requires coordination between veterinary and human-health services. Where cost recovery is not possible and the diseases particularly affect poor people, government funds are needed to support their prevention, detection and control.

---

[5] ASEAN: Association of South East Asian Nations; ECO: Economic Cooperation Organization; OIRSA: Organismo Internacional Regional de Sanidad Agropecuaria; IICA: Instituto Interamericano de Cooperación para la Agricultura; APEC: Asia-Pacific Economic Cooperation; SAARC: South Asian Association for Regional Cooperation; AU-IBAR: African Union Inter-African Bureau for Animal Resources.
[6] UNICEF: United Nations Children's Fund; WWF: World Wide Fund for Nature; WCS: Wildlife Conservation Society; IUCN: International Union for Conservation of Nature.

A risk management approach to food-safety risks from animal products is essential to allocate efficiently the limited funds available for food-safety systems. Involvement of all members of the food supply chain in understanding risks and identifying priority areas for controls and mitigations will go a long way to ensuring social acceptance of, and responsibility for, food safety along the food supply chain. This cross-sector involvement helps to deal with business practices that may threaten food safety.

Technological innovation

New technologies can support better management of animal-health risks. Advances in proteomics, transcriptomics and genomics will probably result in many new products in the next few years. The recent rush to develop a vaccine following the outbreak and spread of bluetongue serotype 8 (not previously seen in Europe) in Belgium, France, Germany, the Netherlands and the United Kingdom in 2006 has shown that the pharmaceutical industry can respond rapidly when appropriate incentives are in place. The Government of the United Kingdom issued a tender in November 2007 to develop and supply 22.5 million doses of bluetongue vaccine. The company that won the tender developed the vaccine in just two years.

The market for animal-health inputs such as vaccines and pharmaceuticals is not large in the developing world. This is not surprising given the low incomes of the majority of livestock producers. As a result, there is little incentive for international pharmaceutical companies to develop new technologies to address livestock health in the developing world.

This raises two questions. First, how can pharmaceutical companies be persuaded to invest in the development of new products suited to poor livestock keepers who have limited resources? Second, what can governments do to assist the spread of technology to control the diseases that are a priority for the poor? Workable solutions to these questions are key to progress towards improved animal-health services for all.

For example, in large tracts of the developing world, there is scope to contain transboundary animal diseases at the regional level, involving groups of countries that share livestock production challenges and disease risks. In these situations, there is often a need for customized vaccines protecting against several transboundary animal diseases. These may be manufactured by the industry on a sustainable basis provided that prior public agreement has been reached by the countries involved to progressively control and eliminate the concerned disease.

Key messages of the chapter

- Animal diseases, the lack of adequate food hygiene and resulting food-borne illnesses are a problem for everyone because they can threaten human health, disrupt markets and trade, reduce productivity and deepen poverty. Improving the management of livestock with a view to preventing and controlling diseases can provide significant economic, social and human-health benefits for the poor and for society at large.
- Pathogens evolve unpredictably, and it is impossible to prevent this. New pathogenic agents will continue to emerge, and the risk of spread has to be addressed specifically. An adequate global framework is necessary to address emerging zoonotic and transboundary animal diseases.
- Public animal-health and food-safety systems need to recognize that the impacts of livestock disease and food-borne illnesses vary across countries and production systems depending on their economic status. The capacities of different groups to respond to these challenges, and the incentives needed to encourage them to do so, must be considered in the design of disease-control and risk-management strategies.
- Large, strategic and sustained investment is needed in national animal-health and food-safety infrastructure in developing countries to reduce the risks to human health and to allow growth in trade and markets, in ways that can contribute to lifting small livestock keepers out of poverty.
- The capacity of poorer countries to participate in the design of animal-

health and food-safety standards should be enhanced so that they are better able to improve their animal-health and food-safety systems and gain greater access to markets for their livestock products.
- Producers of all levels and capacities must be engaged in the design and implementation of programmes to prevent and control animal disease and improve food safety. Poor livestock keepers need to be more engaged in disease-control efforts, to the benefit of themselves and others.
- Location matters. The concentration of intensive production systems in close proximity to urban population centres increases the risk of emergence of diseases and their transmission, both among animals and to humans. This is particularly the case when people and animals move between traditional and intensive systems. Incentives and regulations may be required to encourage the location of livestock production units in less densely populated areas.

6. Conclusions: balancing society's objectives for livestock

The livestock sector supports almost one billion of the world's poorest people and is likely to do so for decades to come. Many people who rely on livestock for their sustenance and livelihoods are under extreme pressure from the global economic forces of growth, competition and global integration that are driving rapid structural change. The environmental and human-health hazards associated with livestock production are creating risks of systemic failure.

A growing awareness of the challenges faced by the livestock sector offers an opportunity for change. Governments and donors are increasingly recognizing the importance of agriculture in rural development and poverty reduction, and the central role of livestock in the livelihoods of poor men and women. At the same time, recent human-health scares related to potentially pandemic outbreaks of zoonotic diseases have captured headlines and frightened travellers around the world. Meanwhile, contingency programmes have been prepared in a large number of countries. Within governments, civil society and the scientific community, a strengthening consensus that climate change is a reality is leading the search for effective ways of mitigating the effects of climate change and adapting to it. Recognizing the urgency of a situation is the first step towards dealing with it (Kotter, 2005).

The livestock sector requires a delicate balance of policy interventions and institutional and technological innovations if it is to continue to meet the multiple, often competing, demands of society.

Balancing opportunities against risks

Rapid growth in the livestock sector offers clear opportunities for poverty reduction; agriculture is the key to pro-poor economic development and the livestock sector is one of the fastest-growing agricultural activities. However, livestock pose environmental and health risks that must be mitigated. The sector is consuming a large share of the world's resources and is contributing a significant portion of global GHG emissions.

Steps are needed to improve the environmental performance of the livestock sector. It must use resources more efficiently, and capture the wastes it generates and turn them into resources. In economic terms, the positive and negative externalities long generated by the livestock sector should be internalized so that producers and consumers pay the real price of the impacts of livestock production on natural resources and the environment.

Animal-health systems should help reduce the growing risk of human pandemics of diseases that originate in animals and should deal better with the endemic diseases that constantly undermine the livelihoods of the poor. Rich and poor producers face different risks and incentives in the area of livestock health. Measures taken to control transboundary diseases may serve the public good by controlling potential pandemics, but, unless properly designed, they may also destroy the livelihoods, assets and safety nets of millions of smallholders. This aspect must be considered in the planning and implementation of such measures.

Balancing the needs of different smallholders

Growth in the livestock sector can promote broader economic growth, alleviate poverty and reduce food insecurity, but the traditional livestock "ladder" that smallholders once climbed to escape from poverty is now missing several rungs. Increasing competition, economies of scale and rising health and food-safety standards mean that smallholders face enormous challenges in remaining competitive with larger, more-intensive production systems, and a widening gulf is emerging between those who can take advantage of growing demand for livestock products and those who cannot. Policy-makers need to recognize that not all smallholders will be able to benefit from the opportunities offered by growth, and that men and women may face different risks and opportunities. They should use scarce public resources, not in fighting insuperable forces of change, but rather in helping smallholders adapt to change in ways that produce better social outcomes. Specific gender-sensitive policy interventions can efficiently and effectively support the needs of different types of smallholders.

Some smallholders are competitive in the changing economic environment and can remain so if they receive the right kind of policy, financial and institutional support. They need institutional innovations to overcome the higher transaction costs associated with being small operators. These institutions should help them gain access to inputs on more favourable terms and provide a go-between with large-scale consolidators and retailers to overcome technical barriers that block smallholders' access to growing urban and international markets. Policy support should promote productivity growth and market access for smallholders. The development and dissemination of new technologies tailored for small-scale producers, and the establishment of market and communications infrastructure and animal-health and food-safety systems would help smallholders navigate the changing landscape in which they operate.

Most smallholder livestock producers will eventually leave the sector, as has been seen in OECD countries and many rapidly growing developing and transition economies. This is a natural part of the evolution of the agriculture sector and can be considered a sign of progress. When and where small-scale livestock producers face rising opportunity costs for their labour, they naturally move out of the sector and into more remunerative employment elsewhere. Broader rural development policies can promote a dynamic economy that offers attractive alternatives for livestock keepers who cannot compete in the sector.

Concerns arise when competitive forces push people out of the sector before the broader economy can create alternative employment opportunities. The very rapid pace of change in the livestock sector in many countries is driving an exodus that is faster in some areas than the overall economy can absorb.

The smallest livestock keepers, who rely on livestock primarily as a safety net, need particular attention that recognizes the multiple roles that livestock play in their livelihoods. At a minimum, the safety-net function played by livestock must not be destroyed without compensation or without the creation of alternative social safety nets.

Balancing food security and nutrition

Livestock products make an important contribution to household food security and they are especially important in meeting the micronutrient requirements of women and young children. Adding a small amount of animal-based foods to a plant-based diet can yield large improvements in maternal health and child development. Undernutrition, including inadequate levels of consumption of food of animal origin, remains a huge and persistent problem in the developing world. Inadequate diets hamper the mental and physical development of children and result in increased morbidity and mortality from infectious diseases. There are also significant economic costs in terms of reduced work performance and productivity in adults. Income growth can help to improve nutrition: as the incomes of the poor increase, they generally purchase more and better-quality food, including that of animal origin. However, waiting for economic growth to improve nutrition is not an acceptable solution. Action is needed that ensures immediate access to adequate diets; this can make an indispensable contribution to assisting the poor to escape the undernourishment/undernutrition–poverty trap.

On the other hand, many countries in the world, including developing countries, are experiencing an epidemic of obesity and diet-related non-communicable diseases that impose costly economic and health burdens on society. Excessive consumption of high-fat and processed-meat products contributes to this problem, although, of course, other dietary and lifestyle choices are also implicated. Agricultural and trade policies can influence dietary choices by making certain products more or less readily available and affordable. Typically, agricultural policy is aimed at increasing the availability and accessibility of food, but there may be a need to promote a better balance in the choices people make.

Balancing the trade-offs among systems, species, goals and impacts

The trade-offs among the use of various livestock production systems and species, the goals set for the sector and livestock's social and environmental impacts must be recognized. Intensive production systems are extremely efficient converters of resources – feed, water, etc. – into high-quality, low-cost meat, milk and eggs. This is particularly the case for poultry and pigs. Intensive production systems also produce less GHG per unit of output than extensive systems. The demand for foods of animal origin in rapidly growing developing countries can be met most efficiently and with least contribution to climate change through intensive systems. But intensive production also comes at a cost.

Intensive systems are associated with the production of large amounts of waste products that often exceed the nutrient absorption capacity of local land. Stronger measures are required to ensure that these wastes are captured and returned to the land as fertilizers or used productively in other ways.

The amounts of resources used by intensive and extensive systems vary according to the livestock species and location, but, in all areas, improved management practices can reduce the environmental impact of livestock production.

The geographic concentration of intensive livestock production systems near urban centres creates a potent breeding ground for novel diseases, especially when small-scale, traditional producers remain nearby. It also increases exposure of urban populations to diseases carried by livestock, increasing the risk of transfer of zoonotic diseases

to the human population. Much stronger animal-health systems are required in order to mitigate and manage these health risks. A first step would be to encourage the relocation of intensive livestock production units away from urban areas and to reduce the risk of pathogens moving between systems.

Balancing objectives in different societies

This report has considered the role of livestock in meeting society's objectives in terms of delivery of private and public goods. Often, the multiple objectives of society are interrelated. Managing animal diseases, for example, may be crucial for securing the livelihoods of people living in poverty. Improving human nutrition through, *inter alia*, an appropriate contribution of livestock products to diets may also contribute to promoting social development. However, frequently there are trade-offs, especially in the short run, that require prioritization of objectives. Promoting livestock production and incomes may imply increased stress on natural resources. Tighter environmental restrictions may increase production costs for livestock products, reducing their accessibility to poorer population groups.

Different countries and societies may prioritize objectives differently, depending on factors such as income levels, relative role of smallholders in the sector, importance of and prospects for exports, and degree of pressure on and degradation of natural resources. In general, the objectives will tend to be prioritized differently according to the country's stage of economic development (Figure 16). Countries at low levels of economic development typically emphasize the role of livestock in economic and social development and poverty alleviation and design policies accordingly. Enhancing the contribution of livestock as a source of income, employment and insurance against risks for poor population groups with few other immediate livelihood options is likely to be a key objective for such countries. Other dimensions, such as managing livestock diseases, may also need consideration by low-income countries in order to support sustainable livelihoods.

FIGURE 16
Balancing policy objectives

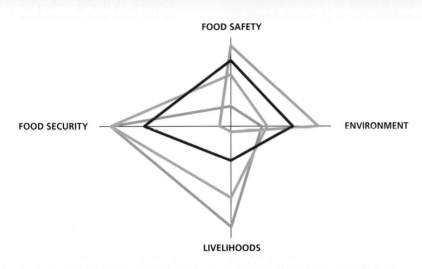

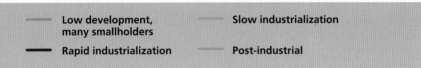

Low development, many smallholders	Slow industrialization
Rapid industrialization	Post-industrial

Source: FAO.

At subsequent stages of development, the policy emphasis is likely to shift towards other objectives, such as: provision of food to growing, especially urban, populations; addressing human-health risks from animal diseases; and protecting the environment and natural resources. In advanced economies, in which livestock production represents a small share of the overall economy, society's concerns are likely to focus heavily on human health, food safety and the environment.

It is important at the international level to recognize the legitimacy of such differences in prioritization and to ensure that international policies and agreements do not focus exclusively on the priorities of a narrow group of affluent countries.

The way forward: towards an agenda for action for the livestock sector

The livestock sector is expected to provide safe, cheap and plentiful food and fibre for growing urban populations, to provide a livelihood for poor producers, to preserve natural resources and use them efficiently, and to minimize health risks to human populations.

This edition of *The State of Food and Agriculture* has argued that the livestock sector is not contributing as well as it might to the provision of the private and public goods that are expected of it, largely because the necessary policy changes and investments have not been made. The rapid growth of the sector, in a setting of weak institutions and governance, has given rise to systemic risks that may have catastrophic implications for livelihoods, human and animal health and the environment. To meet the challenges and constraints it faces, the livestock sector requires renewed attention and investments from the agricultural research and development community and robust institutional and governance mechanisms that reflect the diversity within the sector and the multiple demands placed upon it.

Action is required at all levels, from the local level, through the regional and national levels to the international level. Multilateral institutions need to be involved, as well as civil society. However, no single entity is in a position to carry out its task in isolation.

Bringing together the multiple stakeholders, including the private sector, in a coordinated effort is indispensable.

There is a clear need to focus attention at the international level on the livestock sector and the challenges it faces. Developing an agenda for action for the livestock sector, supported by governments, international institutions, multilateral and bilateral donors and civil-society stakeholders is a crucial first step towards a livestock sector characterized by: better governance; a clearer focus on the problems and issues; a more inclusive development process; levels of investment commensurate with the importance of the sector and the challenges it faces; and improved international cooperation.

Indeed, considering the very substantial positive and negative impacts of the livestock sector on social, environmental and public health targets, and the importance of global governance for agriculture as a whole, such a framework may be an appropriate avenue for concerted international action to guide the development of the livestock sector.

Key messages of the report

- **The livestock sector is changing.** The livestock sector is one of the most dynamic parts of the agricultural economy. It has expanded rapidly in recent decades and demand for animal products is expected to continue growing strongly through the middle of this century, driven by population growth, rising affluence and urbanization. Urgent action is required if the sector is to meet this demand in ways that contribute to poverty reduction, food security, environmental sustainability and human health. The opportunities and challenges offered by the sector should be carefully balanced.
  - The potential for increasing demand for livestock products is substantial and implies challenges in terms of efficient use of natural resources, managing animal- and human-health risks, alleviating poverty and ensuring food security.
  - Growing demand for livestock products and the implementation of

technological changes along the food chain have spurred major changes in livestock production systems. Small-scale mixed production systems are facing increased competition from large-scale specialized production units based on purchased inputs. These trends present major competitive challenges for smallholders and have implications for the ability of the sector to promote poverty reduction.
  - The shift from small-scale mixed production systems, based on locally available resources, to large-scale industrial systems has also changed the location of livestock production units. As the constraint of locally available natural resources is removed, the spatial distribution of livestock production facilities is becoming more clustered to exploit linkages along the supply chain. This has increased the efficiency of production but has implications for natural-resource use.
  - The increasing concentration of production and growth in trade are leading to new challenges in the management of animal diseases.
- **The livestock sector contributes to food security and poverty reduction.** However, it could do more with judicious policy and institutional reforms and significant public and private investments that consider three objectives: (i) to enhance the ability of smallholders to take advantage of the opportunities offered by growth in the sector; (ii) to protect the poorest households for whom livestock serve as a crucial safety net; and (iii) to enact broader rural development policies to ease the transition of many rural households out of the sector.
  - Livestock are important to the livelihoods of a large percentage of rural women, men and children living in poverty. They play a number of different roles, from income generation and the provision of inputs into mixed cropping systems to providing a buffer against environmental and economic shocks. Policy-makers need to consider the multiple roles of livestock in the livelihoods and food security of the poor.

– Smallholders need support in order to take advantage of the opportunities provided by an expanding livestock sector and to manage the risks associated with increasing competition and closer linkages with modern value chains. This requires significant and sustained innovation in national, regional and global food and agricultural systems, and a mix of policy and institutional change, capacity building, technological innovation and investment that is gender-sensitive and responsive.

– Policy-makers need to consider the different capacities of smallholders to respond to change. Some smallholders may be unable to compete in a rapidly modernizing sector and will give up their livestock, as opportunity costs for family labour rise. Broader rural development strategies aimed at creating off-farm employment for women, men and youths can ease their transition out of the livestock sector.

– Policy-makers need to recognize and protect the safety-net function performed by livestock for the very poor. Within the livestock sector, poor people are particularly vulnerable to risks related to zoonotic diseases and environmental hazards.

- **The livestock sector must improve its environmental performance.** Governance of the livestock sector should be strengthened to ensure that its development is environmentally sustainable. Livestock production is placing increasing pressures on land, air, water and biodiversity. Corrective action is needed to encourage the provision of public goods, such as valuable ecosystem services and environmental protection. This will involve addressing policy and market failures and developing and applying appropriate incentives and penalties. Livestock contribute to and are a victim of climate change. The sector can play a key role in mitigating climate change. For example, adoption of improved technologies, encouraged by appropriate economic incentives, can lead to reduced emissions of GHGs by livestock.

– There is an urgent need for governments and institutions to develop and enact appropriate policies, at the national and international levels, that focus more on and account for livestock–environment interactions. Continued growth in livestock production will otherwise exert enormous pressures on ecosystems, biodiversity, land and forest resources and water quality, and will contribute to global warming.

– A key policy focus should be on correcting market distortions and policy failures that encourage environmental degradation. For example, subsidies that directly or indirectly promote overgrazing, land degradation, deforestation, overuse of water or GHG emissions should be reduced or eliminated. Market-based policies, such as taxes and fees for natural-resource use, should cause producers to internalize the costs of environmental damages caused by livestock production.

– Some negative environmental consequences from livestock production stem from problems associated with open-access common-property resources. Clarifying property rights and promoting mechanisms for cooperation are vital to sustainable management of common property.

– The application of technologies that improve the efficiency of land use and feed use can mitigate the negative effects of livestock production on biodiversity, ecosystems and global warming. Technologies that increase livestock efficiency include improved breeds, improved grazing-land management, improved herd-health management and silvipastoralism.

– Payments from public or private sources for environmental services can be an effective means to promote better environmental outcomes, including soil conservation, conservation of wildlife and landscapes and carbon sequestration.

– The livestock sector has enormous potential to contribute to climate change mitigation. Realizing this potential will require new and extensive initiatives at the national and international levels, including: the promotion of research on and development of new mitigation technologies; effective and enhanced means for financing livestock activities; deploying, diffusing and transferring technologies to mitigate GHG emissions; and enhanced capacities to monitor, report and verify emissions from livestock production.

- **Livestock diseases pose systemic risks that must be addressed.** Some animal-health services are public goods in that they protect human and animal public health and thus benefit society as a whole. Animal diseases reduce production and productivity, disrupt local and national economies, threaten human health and exacerbate poverty, but producers face a range of risks and differ in the incentives they are offered and their capacities to respond. Animal-health systems have been neglected in many parts of the world, leading to institutional weaknesses and information gaps as well as inadequate investments in animal-health-related public goods. Producers at every level, including poor livestock keepers, must be engaged in the development of animal-disease and food-safety programmes.
  - Animal diseases, the lack of adequate food hygiene and resulting food-borne illnesses are a problem for everyone because they can threaten human health, disrupt markets and trade, reduce productivity and deepen poverty. Improving the management of livestock with a view to preventing and controlling diseases can provide significant economic, social and human-health benefits for the poor and for society at large.
  - Pathogens evolve unpredictably, and it is impossible to prevent this. New pathogenic agents will continue to emerge, and the risk of spread has to be addressed specifically. An adequate global framework is necessary to address emerging zoonotic and transboundary animal diseases.
  - Public animal-health and food-safety systems need to recognize that the

impacts of livestock disease and food-borne illnesses vary across countries and production systems depending on their economic status. The capacities of different groups to respond to these challenges, and the incentives needed to encourage them to do so, must be considered in the design of disease-control and risk-management strategies.
  - Large, strategic and sustained investment is needed in national animal-health and food-safety infrastructure in developing countries to reduce the risks to human health and to allow growth in trade and markets, in ways that can contribute to lifting small livestock keepers out of poverty.
  - The capacity of poorer countries to participate in the design of animal-health and food-safety standards should be enhanced so that they are better able to improve their animal-health and food-safety systems and gain greater access to markets for their livestock products.
  - Producers of all levels and capacities must be engaged in the design and implementation of programmes to prevent and control animal disease and improve food safety. Poor livestock keepers need to be more engaged in disease-control efforts, to the benefit of themselves and others.
  - Location matters. The concentration of intensive production systems in close proximity to urban population centres increases the risk of emergence of diseases and their transmission, both among animals and to humans. This is particularly the case when people and animals move between traditional and intensive systems. Incentives and regulations may be required to encourage the location of livestock production units in less densely populated areas.

Part II

WORLD FOOD AND AGRICULTURE IN REVIEW

Part II

World food and agriculture in review

This is a period of grave concern for the fate of the world's hundreds of millions of poor and hungry people. When the 2008 edition of *The State of Food and Agriculture* (FAO, 2008b) was being prepared, the world's attention was focused on the global food crisis as rapidly rising prices of staple foods posed major threats to global food security. At the G8 Summit in Japan in July 2008, the leaders of the world's most industrialized nations voiced their deep concern "that the steep rise in global food prices, coupled with availability problems in a number of developing countries, is threatening global food security". The devastating effects of high food prices compounded an already worrisome trend of rising numbers of undernourished people throughout the world.

The episode of "soaring food prices" was followed in rapid succession by the most severe global financial crisis and deepest economic recession witnessed in the last 70 years. The crisis has hit large parts of the world simultaneously, pushing millions of more people into hunger and undernourishment. The impact has been particularly severe owing to the overlap with the food crisis of 2006–08, which had pushed basic food prices beyond the reach of millions of poor people. While food commodity prices in world markets have declined substantially in the wake of the financial crisis, food prices in domestic markets have often come down more slowly. Months of unusually high food and fuel prices have stretched the coping mechanisms of many poor households to the limit, as they have been forced to draw down their assets (financial, physical and human) in not-always successful attempts to avoid large declines in consumption.

By mid-2009, the severity, depth and breadth of the crisis make a swift recovery unlikely. In April 2009, the International Monetary Fund (IMF, 2009) projected a global decline in gross domestic product (GDP) in 2009 and a re-emergence of growth only in 2010, but expected it to remain sluggish compared with past economic recoveries. The IMF also emphasized the extreme uncertainty of the outlook and the concern that economic policies might not be sufficient to arrest the vicious spiral of deteriorating financial conditions and weakening economies.

Both the prospects for recovery from the economic crisis and developments in agricultural markets are critical for the world's poor and hungry and for the possibility of moving towards rapid and sustained progress in hunger reduction. While the outlook for the global economy remains uncertain, agricultural market uncertainties have grown over the past year, making the agricultural outlook particularly unclear. The sources of, and risks associated with, the high food price episode of 2006–08 remain latent in 2009. Real energy prices still remain above trend levels while resumed income growth in developing countries could put renewed upward pressure on food prices. Biofuel feedstock demand is being sustained, if not by economic fundamentals, then by a plethora of consumption mandates, fuel blending requirements, subsidies and tax incentives in many countries (biofuels and their relationships with agriculture were reviewed in depth in the 2008 edition of *The State of Food and Agriculture* [FAO, 2008b]). Commodity prices have dropped considerably from their peak in mid-2008, but most of them still remain at or above trend levels. More seriously, while international indicator prices have fallen, commodity prices – and particularly retail food prices – inside many countries have been slow in coming down. Although consumer food price increases have calmed, retail food prices have not dropped in line with lower commodity prices. In addition, many of the various policies implemented by numerous countries to protect domestic consumers from high prices, several of which constituted a disincentive to a possible supply response, have been slow to be removed. Policy concerns about how to prevent a future food price crisis also remain. In short, considerable uncertainty persists in agricultural markets across the globe.

Beyond the overriding question of the timing and speed of recovery from the severe economic recession, some issues particular to agriculture and agricultural markets appear as critical for the future of global agriculture and food security in 2009–2010 and beyond. How efficient are global and domestic food markets in transmitting price signals to producers and consumers? Will resumed growth of the global economy lead to a renewed phase of soaring food prices? What is the capacity of global agriculture to expand in the face of higher agricultural commodity prices? How much have policies initiated to protect domestic consumers from the effect of higher food prices distorted international markets, thereby exacerbating the problem and hampering an efficient supply response?

TRENDS IN GLOBAL FOOD SECURITY[7]

The incidence of hunger and undernourishment in the world has been dramatically affected by the two successive crises. FAO's current estimate of the number of undernourished people in the world in 2008 is 915 million (FAO, 2009c), the highest number estimated over the past 3–4 decades (although in terms of the percentage of

the world's population, the share of hungry people is still far below that of 1970). Projections by FAO based on work by the United States Department of Agriculture Economic Research Service point to an increase in the number of undernourished people in the world to 1.02 billion during 2009. Figure 17 shows the regional breakdown of this number.

This sharp increase comes on top of an already worrisome upward trend observed over the past decade in the estimated number of undernourished people. The number of undernourished people had declined significantly in the 1970s, 1980s and early 1990s, in spite of rapid population growth, as the proportion of undernourished people in the developing countries fell from one-third in 1970 to less than 20 percent in the 1990s. However, since the mid-1990s, the number of undernourished people has been increasing despite a continued decline in the proportion of undernourished people to 16 percent of the developing country population and 13 percent of the world's population in 2004–06. Moreover, the recent crisis has led to an increase for the first time in decades in both the absolute number and in the proportion of undernourished people.

---

[7] FAO (2009c) provides a more thorough analysis of trends in global undernourishment and the impact of the crisis on global food security.

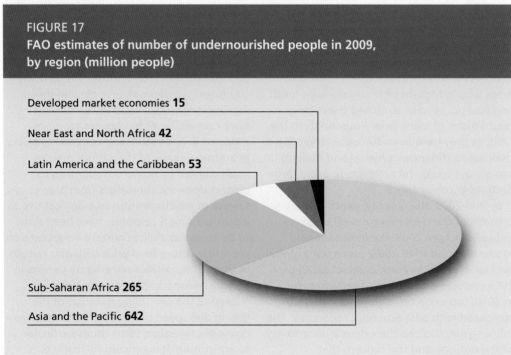

FIGURE 17
FAO estimates of number of undernourished people in 2009, by region (million people)

Developed market economies **15**

Near East and North Africa **42**

Latin America and the Caribbean **53**

Sub-Saharan Africa **265**

Asia and the Pacific **642**

Source: FAO, 2009c.

BOX 19
Food emergencies

One indicator of vulnerability is the number of countries in crisis requiring external assistance. As of April 2009, 31 countries were in this situation, of which 20 in Africa, 9 in Asia and the Near East and 2 in Latin America and the Caribbean. These are countries that are expected to lack the resources to deal with reported critical problems of food insecurity. Food crises are nearly always caused by a combination of factors. However, for the purposes of response planning, it is important to establish whether the nature of the food crises is predominantly related to lack of food availability, limited access to food, or severe but localized problems (see map).

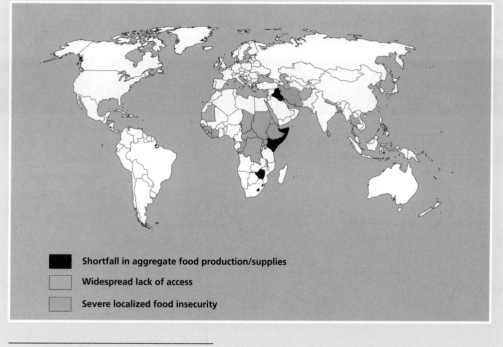

■ **Shortfall in aggregate food production/supplies**

□ **Widespread lack of access**

▨ **Severe localized food insecurity**

Source: FAO, 2009d.

The crisis is affecting large population segments. Those who were most affected by the high food prices crisis – rural landless, female-headed households and the urban poor (FAO, 2008c) – are in a particularly precarious situation. In many cases, they have already reached or come very close to the limit of their ability to cope. Both rural and urban areas are being affected by a reduction in numerous sources of income, including remittances. The urban poor are likely to be particularly affected as urban areas are linked more directly to world markets and may suffer more directly from declining export demand and reduced foreign direct investment. However, rural areas may also be affected by possible declines in agro-industrial activity and return migration.

AGRICULTURAL PRICE DEVELOPMENTS – HIGH VARIABILITY OF BASIC FOOD PRICES

After a phase with soaring prices, international food commodity prices have come down (Figure 18). However, international food prices remain high by historical standards and, in many cases, domestic consumer prices have been slow in receding. Prices began rising slowly in the early years of this decade but accelerated precipitously in late 2006. The FAO food price index of internationally traded basic food commodities (base = 100 in 2002–04) attained a historical peak in June 2008 of 214, more than twice the level of the base period and 139 percent above the average of the year 2000. From June 2008 to the end of the first quarter of 2009, the index fell a full 35 percent, returning to its level of the first quarter of 2007. In May 2009, after a renewed surge in international prices of several major basic food commodities (excluding rice and meat), the index stood at 152, almost 30 percent below the peak level of June 2008. However, this was still 152 percent above the base value and almost 70 percent higher than in 2000.

Most agricultural prices moved higher during the episode of high prices, but the fact that basic foods, especially cereals and vegetable oils, rose the most and displayed the highest variability received particular attention as these food commodities represent the core components of both rural incomes and the diets of poor populations in developing countries. Other agricultural prices also displayed variability but, with the exception of dairy products, to a much lesser extent. Raw materials, which are important to the economies of some developing countries, barely rose during the critical 2006–08 period. In addition, in relative terms, these prices have been the most affected during the recession, given their strong dependence on income-sensitive

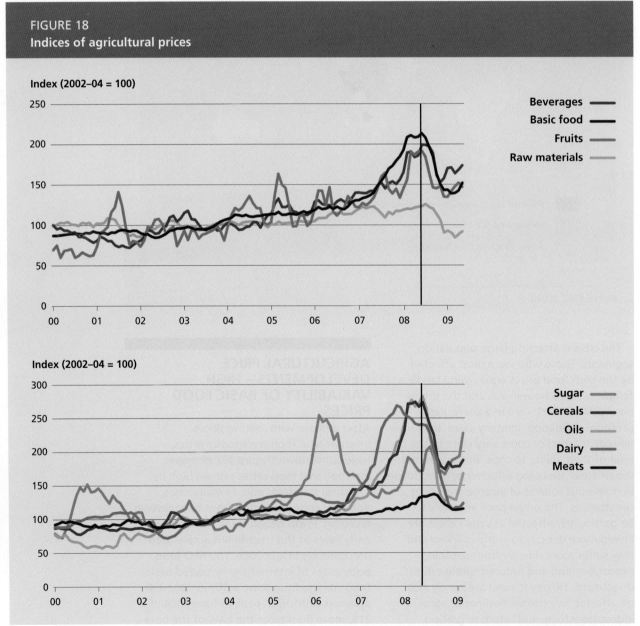

FIGURE 18
Indices of agricultural prices

Index (2002–04 = 100)

Beverages
Basic food
Fruits
Raw materials

Index (2002–04 = 100)

Sugar
Cereals
Oils
Dairy
Meats

Source: FAO food price indices; IMF raw material and beverage indices (rebased); fruit index constructed, FAO.

sectors. An example is hides and skins for leather used in durable consumables such as cars, the demand for which has fallen drastically since the onset of the global recession.

The essential causes of the price declines of food commodities have been widely attributed to faltering consumer/import demand under global recession and conditions of limited credit, as well as to lower biofuel feedstock demand resulting from lower energy prices. However, supply-side indicators have also made an important contribution to price declines, especially given a significant crop supply response in 2008, and to lower input prices, particularly for transport. Major uncertainty remains as to how these factors will evolve in the near term and affect the future of agriultural markets.

DOMESTIC FOOD PRICES IN DEVELOPING COUNTRIES
In spite of lower international prices for agricultural commodities, the transmission of these lower prices to domestic markets appears to have been low or delayed in many developing and low-income food-deficit countries, particularly in sub-Saharan Africa. In many cases, domestic prices were still higher in early 2009 than a year earlier and, where they had declined, price reductions had been relatively smaller than those on international markets (see Box 20, page 110). Such low price transmission is a symptom of inefficient markets, and it also tends to heighten variability in international markets.

Retail-level food price increases became a major factor of concern in both developing and developed economies in 2008. Evidence suggests that food price inflation has been tapering off significantly, following the drop in basic commodity prices in mid-2008. However, retail food prices have continued to increase in some countries and have fallen only marginally in others (Figure 19). "Stickiness" of retail prices is a common attribute of food markets, as changes in these prices also reflect the greater importance of other factors of production involved in the processing and distribution of food products.

Thus, at the same time as the economic crisis is dramatically reducing incomes, persistent high food prices continue to constrain access to food for large numbers of low-income population groups, exactly those who tend to spend a large portion of their income on food. Most affected are the urban poor and net food buyers in rural areas.

MEDIUM-TERM PROSPECTS FOR INTERNATIONAL AGRICULTURAL COMMODITY PRICES
Although significantly below the peak levels of June 2008, commodity prices for food products remain high in 2009 by the standards of the past ten years. The Organisation for Economic Co-operation and Development (OECD) and FAO project food commodity prices to remain at these levels or to increase in the medium term, thus continuing to exceed in real terms the price levels preceding the price hikes of 2007–08 (OECD–FAO, 2009). The OECD–FAO projections also indicate that these expectations are relatively resilient to the global recession, although more income-sensitive commodities such as vegetable oils, meats and dairy products may be more affected by economic conditions should these deteriorate further.

Prospects that real agricultural commodity prices may remain at these higher levels over the medium term are largely contingent on three important factors. First, biofuel consumption mandates in several countries – which specify market shares for ethanol and biodiesel in proportion to total fuel consumption, irrespective of market conditions – as well as various subsidies and tax incentives appear likely to perpetuate the influence of biofuel production on agricultural prices. This is despite the fact that the price prospects for crude oil appear lower than they did in early 2008. As energy markets are large compared with agricultural markets, energy prices will tend to drive the prices of biofuels and their agricultural feedstocks (FAO, 2008b). Second, while crude oil prices are at levels that would not induce further increases in biofuel production in the short term, they still remain high in real terms by historical standards. This will

FIGURE 19
Consumer food price inflation 2007–2009, selected countries

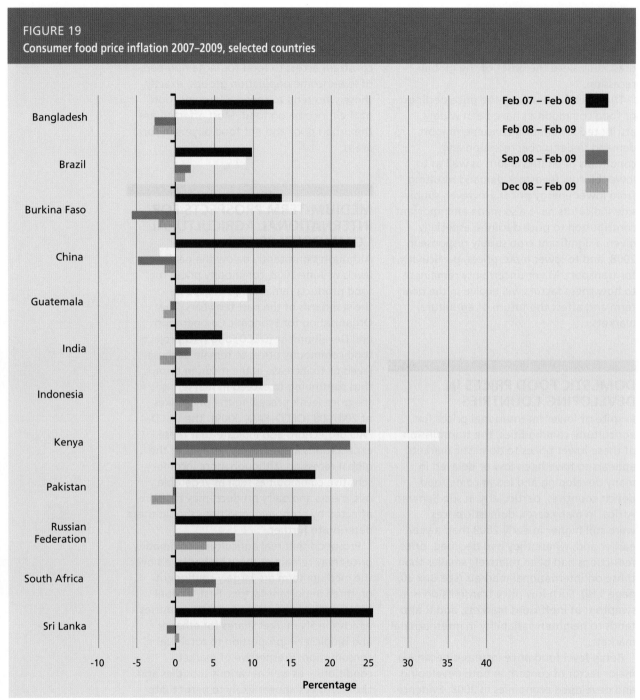

Source: OECD–FAO, 2009.

continue to translate into high input prices for chemicals and fertilizers as well as high transportation costs. Finally, agricultural productivity growth appears to be slowing, implying that, at the margin, increased production will require higher real costs per unit. Analysis of developments in real crop prices shows that the declining long-term trend, which had been evident for many

decades, may have stopped by 2000, and projections do not suggest a resumption of the downward trend in the medium term (see Figure 20).

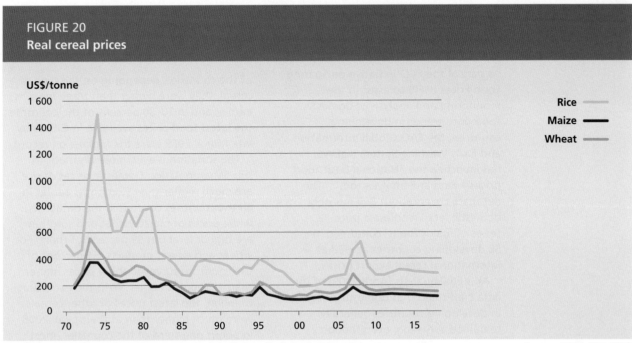

FIGURE 20
Real cereal prices

US$/tonne

Rice
Maize
Wheat

Note: Wheat, HRW No. 2 US Gulf; maize, No. 2 US Gulf; rice milled, Grade B, Bangkok. Deflated by the USA GDP deflator.

Source: OECD–FAO, 2009, for projections from 2009 to 2018.

AGRICULTURAL PRODUCTION

How has agriculture responded to the price crisis of 2007–08, and how may it respond in the context of the global recession and beyond? According to estimates based on FAO production index numbers[8] and OECD–FAO (2009), global agricultural production grew by 3.9 percent in 2008 relative to 2007 as a number of countries expanded production in response to the higher prices of 2007 and even better price prospects for 2008 (Figure 21). This response followed two successive years (2006 and 2007) of performance below the global trend growth for the decade of about 2.2 percent.

The agricultural supply response in 2008 differed by region. Most of the supply response originated in the European countries of the Commonwealth of Independent States (CIS) and in the industrialized countries. Growth in the former group is estimated at 13 percent, although this high rate is largely the result of excellent crop conditions after several years of low growth. The most significant quantitative response came from industrialized countries, which also dominate

export markets. Output from this group grew by almost 6 percent in 2008.

Among the developing countries, growth in Africa was significant, at 4 percent, mainly representing a rebound after negative growth in 2007. Estimates for the developing countries as a group indicate almost no above-trend production, with below-trend growth in Latin America and a small decline in output in Asia. Indeed, low price transmission in many developing countries along with supply-side constraints, particularly limited availability and use of modern inputs, lack of access to markets and weak infrastructures in many countries reduces the supply response to improved incentives.

While global agriculture did expand in 2008, the expansion was fairly modest and mostly confined to a limited number of countries that have been traditional cereal exporters supplying global markets. The prospects for growth in agricultural production in 2009 also appear limited, particularly under the severe economic recession, with weak demand and the difficulty in replicating the performance of 2008 in the developed countries. Moreover, the waiving of set-aside requirements for cropland set aside in the European Union (EU) was a significant factor behind the

---

[8] FAOSTAT production index numbers of net agricultural production (FAO, 2009b).

BOX 20
Domestic food prices in developing countries remain high

As part of the FAO Initiative on Soaring Food Prices (ISFP) to assist in the monitoring and analysis of domestic food price trends in developing countries, the FAO Global Information and Early Warning System (GIEWS) has launched the "National basic food prices – data and analysis tool".[1] The database covers about 800 monthly domestic retail/wholesale price series of major foods[2] consumed in 58 developing countries as well as international cereal export prices.

An initial analysis (April 2009) of the data confirmed that domestic prices in developing countries generally remained very high, even though international prices were considerably lower than in 2008. International export prices of maize, sorghum, wheat and rice were, respectively, 31, 38, 39 and 30 percent lower than 12 months earlier and between 37 and 53 percent below their 2008 peaks. The situation for domestic cereal prices in developing countries contrasted sharply with this trend. In about 80 percent of the countries covered by the database, the latest nominal domestic price quotations[3] were higher than 12 months earlier. In 35–65 percent of the countries, depending on the type of cereal, they were higher than three months earlier, and in 10–30 percent of the countries the latest food prices available in GIEWS by late March 2009 were the highest on record.

The situation is even more dramatic in sub-Saharan Africa. Domestic prices of rice are much higher than 12 months earlier in all the countries covered in the database, while prices of maize, millet and sorghum are higher in about 89 percent of them. For wheat and wheat products, 71 percent of the countries surveyed show prices higher than 12 months earlier. With the exception of millet, the latest prices of other cereals were much higher than at their peak 2008 in about one-third of the countries, most of them in Eastern and Southern Africa. However, food prices remain at high levels also in other regions, particularly in Asia for rice and in Central and South America for maize and wheat.

---

[1] Available at www.fao.org/giews/pricetool
[2] Mainly cereals and cereal products but also beans, cassava, potatoes and some animal products.
[3] The most recent price quotation refers, with few exceptions, to the period between January and April 2009.
Source: FAO, 2009d.

expansion in production. Production in the CIS and the industrialized countries will not reach the level attained in 2008. By contrast, production response in many developing countries may be stronger if higher prices persist in these regions.

Looking to the medium term, according to OECD–FAO (2009), agricultural output growth in the coming decade will not match that of the previous decade, with average annual growth falling from 2.0 percent in 1999–2008 to 1.7 percent in 2009–2018. This implies identical rates of growth on a per capita basis (of 0.6 percent).

The industrialized countries have seen the slowest growth in agricultural output in the past decade, particularly because of stagnant production growth in Europe. In fact,

agricultural output in the EU-27 is estimated to be lower in 2009 than it was in 2000. Despite a depreciated exchange rate, which tends to increase export demand, agricultural output in the United States of America is estimated to have increased by only about 12 percent over the same period. Moreover, in the coming decade, growth in agricultural production is projected to be slowest in the industrialized countries, while Latin America, Asia and the CIS countries will see much more rapid growth. By 2018, agricultural output in these regions is projected to be, respectively, 75, 53 and 58 percent higher than in 2000, compared with an increase of only 12 percent in industrialized economies. Brazil, whose agricultural output is estimated to have grown by a remarkable 50 percent

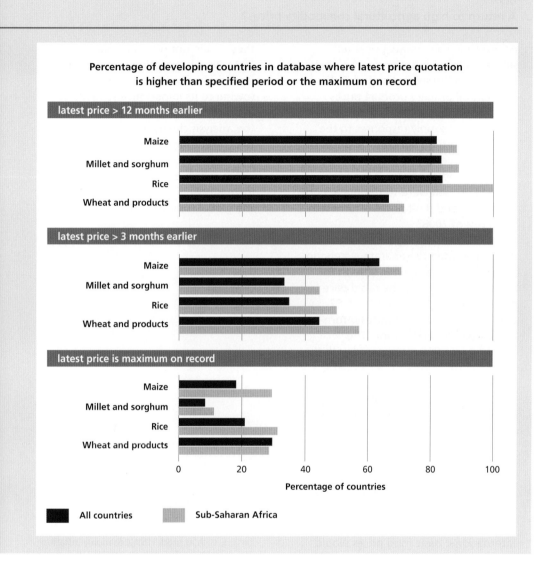

Percentage of developing countries in database where latest price quotation
is higher than specified period or the maximum on record

latest price > 12 months earlier

Maize
Millet and sorghum
Rice
Wheat and products

latest price > 3 months earlier

Maize
Millet and sorghum
Rice
Wheat and products

latest price is maximum on record

Maize
Millet and sorghum
Rice
Wheat and products

0   20   40   60   80   100

Percentage of countries

■ All countries   ▨ Sub-Saharan Africa

since 2000, may expand by another
50 percent in the next ten years.

Longer-term growth opportunities in
agriculture appear to lie in regions outside
of the industrial countries (Figure 22). In this
regard, investments are now being made
in these potential supply regions by higher-
income developing countries concerned
about their own long-term food security.
Such investments may offer the potential
for development of the agriculture sector
and may further change the long-term
location of agriculture. However, in the
context of underdeveloped land markets,
for these investments to be sustainable
and lead to equitable outcomes, they will
require significantly improved frameworks
to protect domestic resources and local

populations from exploitation (FAO, IIED
and IFAD, 2009).

AGRICULTURAL TRADE

In the short term, trade volumes are very
sensitive to economic conditions and to
production changes by region, particularly
in the net exporting regions. At the time of
writing (June 2009), very little information
was available on a global basis on changes
in agricultural trade during the price crisis
of 2008. It is also unclear how trade may
be affected by recession in 2009 and 2010,
considering also that availability of credit
for importers, particularly in developing
countries, is an important limiting factor.

BOX 21
A return to high agricultural commodity prices?

Agricultural commodity prices fell substantially with the onset of global recession in the second half of 2008. Virtually all primary product prices fell precipitously in the face of weak demand and supply responses to the often record-high agricultural prices of the two previous years. What would be the likelihood of a resurgence of prices if world growth were to resume a more rapid pace and if oil prices returned to the levels of 2008?

The OECD–FAO's Aglink-Cosimo model was used to generate a scenario in which world economic growth for all countries resumes the rapid pace experienced in the period 2004–07 and in which world oil prices return to the level of US$100/bbl.[1] The resulting scenario is compared with the baseline projection of the *OECD–FAO Agricultural Outlook 2009–2018* (OECD–FAO, 2009), in which economic growth of developed and developing countries is some 1 and 2 percent lower, respectively, and in which world oil prices range from US$60/bbl in 2012 to US$70/bbl in 2018.

The model simulations indicate that under this simple scenario of resumed growth and higher crude oil prices, international basic food prices would increase by some 20–25 percent relative to the baseline projection. However,

they would not return to the levels of 2007–08. An exception is maize, which is more closely linked to crude oil prices (owing to its importance as feedstock in ethanol production). However, the analysis clearly demonstrates the current high sensitivity of the agriculture sector to increases in energy prices, which affect the supply side and increasingly also the demand side of the global food economy.

---

[1] More precisely, in the scenario, growth resumes in 2011 and world oil prices move up to US$100/bbl by 2012. All other conditioning factors, such as productivity, economy inflation and exchange rates, remain constant as documented in OECD–FAO, 2009.
Source: FAO.

For the medium term, projections based on OECD–FAO (2009) indicate that real food commodity trade values will continue to expand slowly (Figure 23).[9]

Medium-term trends in trade in food commodities imply a changing landscape of international trading patterns (Figure 24). With relatively slow growth in agricultural

output and stagnating food demand, real net food commodity exports from industrialized countries have been stagnant in recent years, a pattern that is not expected to change in the medium term. As a group, industrial countries will remain excess suppliers, exporting to other countries, while developing countries will remain, as a group, net food commodity buyers.

However, within the developing countries, a continued significant expansion in net trade is projected from Latin American countries, notably Argentina and Brazil, while the Asia Pacific and Africa regions will see a widening of their net import

---

[9] Real food trade value (like the net agricultural production indices) is estimated at constant reference prices averaged for 1999–2001 from basic food commodities. Annual trade from these estimates is approximate as they combine both marketing-year-basis data for crops with calendar data for other commodities. Estimates are used to examine recent trends, not annual trade performance.

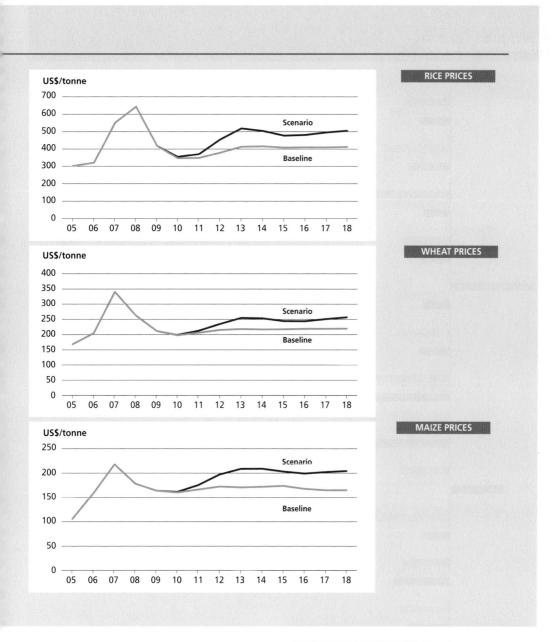

position. The net food surplus of Brazil has grown almost four times since 2000, and is expected to grow another 50 percent in the next ten years. The CIS countries are expected to emerge as net suppliers of food, reversing their position from that of net importers to that of net exporters in the medium term. An area of particular concern is the continued significant food deficit of the least-developed countries (LDCs), particularly those in Africa, which is anticipated to increase in real terms by over 50 percent in the next ten years, thus further increasing their dependence on foreign supplies.

POLICY RESPONSES TO HIGHER FOOD PRICES AND THEIR IMPACT ON AGRICULTURAL MARKETS

Faced with high and rising world food prices in 2007 and 2008, many countries adopted policy measures designed to reduce the impact on their domestic populations (FAO, 2009e). These measures, involving different key commodity sectors, can be classified into four broad categories: trade, production, consumption and stock policies. Most of these policy measures were implemented for limited periods. However, some introduced in 2007 still remain in effect in 2009 despite

FIGURE 21
Growth in agricultural production, by region

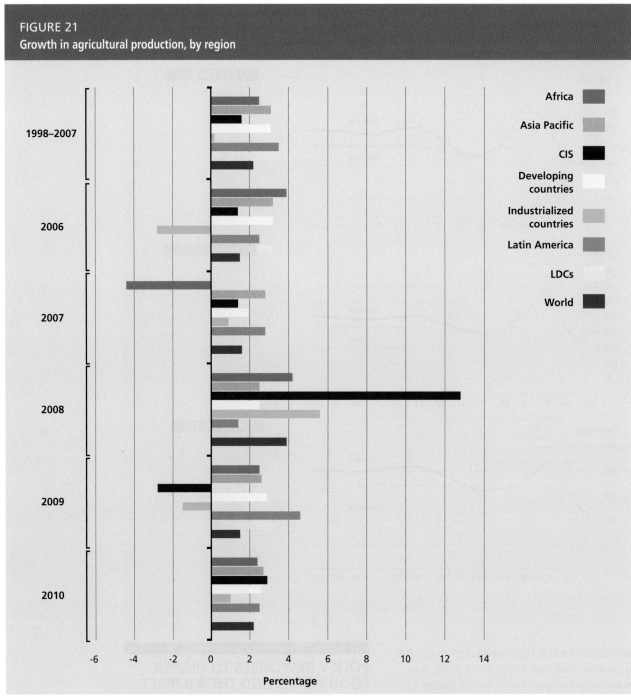

Source: FAOSTAT net agricultural production index to 2007 (FAO, 2009b). Extrapolation based on OECD–FAO, 2009.

the substantial retreat of international prices.

An important question concerns the combined impact of these policy responses on both international and domestic markets and whether uncoordinated policy actions may have had the effect of destabilizing international markets by introducing greater price volatility. The question is important for at least two reasons. First, actions by

one country or group of countries may impede or reduce the effectiveness of actions taken by others. Second, some policy measures may simply be ineffective, if not counterproductive, in addressing the key problem – the impact of high food prices on poor consumers.

This section reviews the various policy measures put in place by various countries and discusses their different anticipated

FIGURE 22
Long-term trends in agricultural production, by region

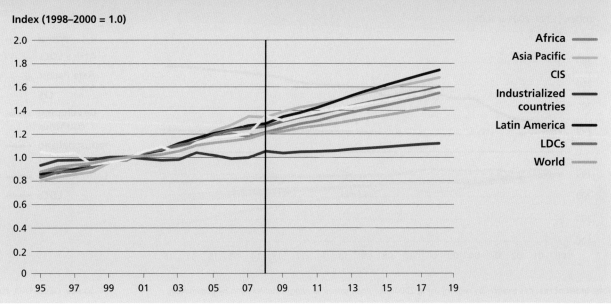

Index (1998–2000 = 1.0)

Africa
Asia Pacific
CIS
Industrialized countries
Latin America
LDCs
World

Source: FAOSTAT net agricultural production index to 2007 (FAO, 2009b). Extrapolation based on OECD–FAO, 2009.

FIGURE 23
Changes in global real food commodity exports

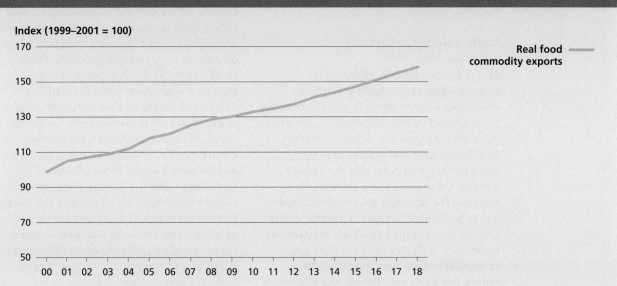

Index (1999–2001 = 100)

Real food commodity exports

Note: Index of real exports using 1999–2001 reference prices to weight exports by commodity, measures changes in exports in constant US dollars.

Source: OECD–FAO, 2009.

FIGURE 24
Changes in real food commodity net trade, by region

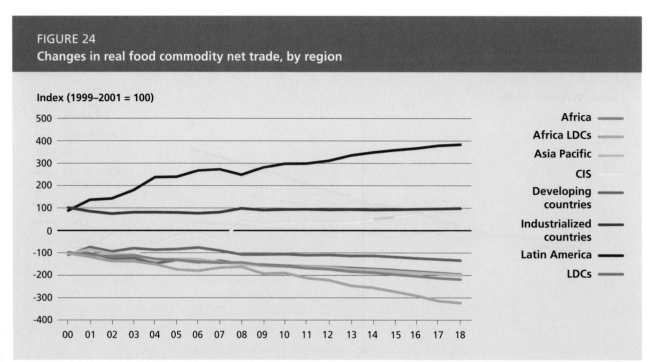

Index (1999–2001 = 100)

Africa
Africa LDCs
Asia Pacific
CIS
Developing countries
Industrialized countries
Latin America
LDCs

Note: Index of real net exports by region, using 2000 reference prices to weight net exports by commodity.   *Source:* OECD–FAO, 2009.

impacts. It concludes by presenting some simple scenario analysis, based on the OECD–FAO Aglink-Cosimo model, in order to gauge the nature and magnitude of the impact of these measures on agricultural markets.

Trade-related measures
Export measures
Export policies include export taxes and subsidies, export bans and other quantitative restrictions. They have typically been applied by net exporting countries to enhance supply on the domestic market. Such taxes, bans and quotas are highly distortionary, particularly in the case of bans (as these completely sever the link between the domestic and international markets). Depending on the specific policy and the exact degree to which they restrict trade, such policies tend to reduce prices to domestic consumers. However, they reduce the gains and, hence, the incentives to producers from higher prices, thus limiting their longer-term supply response. Moreover, by curtailing exports, they tend to increase prices on international markets. On the other hand, export taxes may increase the government's fiscal capacity to implement targeted social programmes or safety nets.

India, the world's third-largest rice exporter, banned exports of non-basmati rice and restricted those of basmati rice, thus significantly reducing global exportable supplies. In addition, India banned maize exports. China eliminated rebates on value added taxes on exports of wheat, rice, maize and soybeans and imposed an export tax on a series of grains and products. Prior to 20 December 2007, exports of these agricultural products were entitled to a 13 percent rebate of their declared value at exporting ports. Bangladesh, Cambodia, Egypt, Indonesia and Viet Nam banned exports of rice, while India, Pakistan, Serbia and Ukraine banned those of wheat. Kazakhstan and the Russian Federation raised export taxes on wheat and the Russian Federation imposed an export tax on barley of 30 percent. Similarly, Malaysia imposed export taxes on palm oil, while Argentina raised taxes on exports of wheat, maize, soybeans and soybean products.

Import measures
One of the most commonly applied policy measures, typically adopted by net importing countries, was the removal or reduction of import duties and taxes on food commodities. Like export policies, these policies have the effect of reducing both

consumer and producer prices. However, the magnitude of the price reduction tends to be less pronounced than for export bans and taxes as the extent of the reduction is limited by the size of the existing tariff or tax. Governments see a decline in revenues from such measures. In the case of food commodities, the reduction in taxes is progressive relative to income as poorer people tend to spend a larger share of their income on food. However, targeting is not as efficient as it may be in the case of targeted safety net programmes.

A number of countries (and the EU) reduced or eliminated food tariffs or taxes. They included Bangladesh, Egypt, India, Indonesia, the Islamic Republic of Iran, Mali, Mexico, Morocco, Pakistan, Peru, the Philippines, Senegal and Turkey. In some cases, the tariff cuts were very substantial. Nigeria slashed duties on rice imports from 100 to 2.7 percent and Turkey cut import taxes on wheat from 130 to 8 percent and those on barley from 100 to zero percent, while India removed a 36 percent import tariff on wheat flour.

Several countries suspended or reduced domestic taxes on food commodities. Brazil reduced its taxation of wheat, wheat flour and bread. Similarly, valued-added tax was reduced on a range of basic imported foodstuffs and other goods in the Congo, on rice in Madagascar, on rice and bread in Kenya and on foodgrains and flour in Ethiopia.

Production policies

With a view to encouraging an expansion in production, various forms of producer support measures were introduced, including input subsidies, output price support and an easing of cropland set-aside requirements. Some of these policies are expensive, and the impact on domestic consumer prices is limited in the context of open markets but more substantial if linkages to international markets are weak. If not well administered, input subsidies may also lead to an increase in input prices as demand for inputs increases, thus benefiting input suppliers more than agricultural producers. The easing of set-aside requirements, which may otherwise constrain the production response to higher prices, is most effective at increasing

production and may effectively reduce domestic prices in a closed-market situation. In the case of major exporters, such as the EU, it may also have a significant dampening effect on international prices.

Countries that increased input subsidies include Bangladesh, China, Dominican Republic, Indonesia and Madagascar. In some cases, this was accompanied by measures to improve access to funds and credit, as well as by border measures such as reduced import taxes and higher export duties on inputs. China increased its floor price for rice and wheat. It also expanded non-price government support, including direct payments, seed subsidies, subsidies for farm machinery, and subsidies for fuels used on farms as well as fertilizers to farmers in 2008 (Fang, 2009). Total subsidies in 2008 reached RMB102.9 billion (US$14.8 billion), double the level of the previous year. The Government imposed chemical fertilizer export taxes several times in 2008 in order to control exports and satisfy domestic demand from farmers. India increased the minimum support for common paddy rice by as much as 37 percent between 2006/07 and 2008/09 (from Rs6 200/tonne to Rs8 500/tonne) (Gulati and Dutta, 2009). In order to increase production, Indonesia launched a rice intensification programme involving the State Board of Logistics (Bulog), private companies, banks and groups of farmers. The fertilizer subsidy was also increased by 240 percent. The EU waived its 5 percent mandatory set-aside requirement for cropland for the 2008/09 crop, a measure that was an important factor in the sizeable expansion in EU cereal production in 2008.

Concerns over the reliability of international markets as a source of food supplies has resulted in a renewed focus in many countries on food self-sufficiency as a means of achieving national food security. Many net food-importing countries around the world are adjusting their agricultural development strategies and giving priority to expanding production in order to reduce import dependence. The Philippines has decided to promote food production with the aim of achieving self-sufficiency in staple foods by 2010. Armenia announced an attempt to reach self-sufficiency in wheat by 2009/10 through subsidies for expansion of cropland and irrigation. The Government of Kazakhstan planned to inject US$3 million into the agriculture sector to help farmers withstand the impact of the global credit crisis. Malaysia allocated US$1.29 billion to promote rice-growing while also increasing government minimum prices for rice.

Consumption policies

Policies to support consumers and vulnerable groups have included:
- direct consumer subsidies;
- tax reductions;
- distribution from public stocks;
- price subsidies;
- public-sector salary increases;
- social safety net programmes.

Targeted transfer programmes can potentially reach the poor much more efficiently and effectively than tax reductions and price subsidies. Examples of such food assistance are direct food transfers, food stamps or vouchers and school feeding.

Self-targeting food-for-work programmes have been put in place by countries such as Bangladesh, Cambodia, Ethiopia, Haiti, India, Liberia, Madagascar and Peru, while Afghanistan, Angola, Bangladesh and Cambodia have distributed emergency food aid. School feeding programmes have been implemented in Brazil, Burkina Faso, Cape Verde, China, Honduras, Kenya, Mexico and Mozambique. Countries such as Dominican Republic, Egypt, Ethiopia, Indonesia, Jordan, Lebanon, Mongolia, Morocco, the Philippines and Saudi Arabia have sold food at subsidized prices to targeted groups.

Stock policies

Building and releasing public stocks in order to stabilize domestic food prices have been common measures implemented to contain the problem of rising food prices. Increasing and holding stocks could lead to higher food prices, while releasing stocks to the market has the opposite effect. In a context of closed domestic markets, depending on buying and selling behaviour, stock policies may stabilize or destabilize domestic prices. At the global level, higher stock demand, either by national intervention programmes, companies or individual producers speculating on higher prices, may cause

higher prices. However, in the longer term, higher stock levels have been associated with lower international prices.

Bangladesh, Cameroon, China, Ethiopia, India, Indonesia, Pakistan and Senegal all released food from public stocks to lessen price increases and offered targeted and untargeted subsidies for staple food. However, several countries contributed to higher international prices by building up stocks through purchases from the international market with a view to stabilizing their domestic market. The national grain reserve systems in China increased temporary grain stocks. The Food Corporation of India made record purchases of rice and wheat in 2008, allowing it to release sufficient stocks into the domestic market to stabilize prices. India's stocks of wheat and rice are expected to be 40–45 million tonnes by July 2009 (against a norm of 26 million tonnes). The Government of the Philippines, the world's largest rice importer, increased its imports for 2008 to 2.4 million tonnes (from 2.1 million tonnes in the previous year) in a bid to ensure at least a 30-day stockpile until the end of the year. The Government of Saudi Arabia, one of the major importers of rice in the Near East, proposed that rice importers consider raising their stocks of grain by 50 percent in 2008 to meet national consumption requirements for a 6–8-month period.

IMPACT OF POLICY RESPONSES ON GLOBAL MARKETS

Measuring the impacts of the complex assortment of policy responses to confront the high food prices is difficult. Even more difficult is disentangling these impacts from the other factors underlying the volatile market situation in 2007–08, in which these policies were implemented. However, there are important lessons to be learned from such an examination. The OECD–FAO Aglink-Cosimo model of international commodity markets was used to study some of the more important policy initiatives implemented in response to the high commodity prices. Policies were examined against a baseline scenario into which key policies were then introduced. Thus, the analysis compared two scenarios – one with and one without these key policies in place.[10]

The policy measures that are the subject of the analysis were introduced into the model according to the time in which they were put in place, starting in the 2007/08 marketing year, and maintained until the time they were discontinued. In the case of policies still in place, they were maintained within the modelling framework throughout the baseline period to 2012.[11] The analysis focused on global rice and wheat markets, as these were the main markets most affected by policies. Estimated impacts for individual countries may vary substantially from these aggregate projection scenarios.[12]

The scenario impacts on global rice and wheat markets, presented in Figure 25, illustrate some important issues. Rice markets, which are relatively "thin" compared with global production and consumption levels, saw a clear destabilizing effect of policies implemented to address high food prices, with significantly higher international prices in 2007 and 2008 than in the baseline scenario. The most distortionary policies in the case of rice were border policies implemented in 2007 and 2008. These alone drove international rice prices higher by an estimated 12 percent on an annualized basis in both 2007 and 2008. Had the policies been maintained throughout both marketing years, the measured effects would have been much greater. Stock policies are estimated to have driven global rice stocks up by some 30–35 percent in both years, adding some 5 and 3 percent to international rice prices in the 2007 and 2008 marketing years, respectively. Production policy measures, relatively minor in the case of rice markets, are estimated not to have

affected international prices at all in the first few years of the scenario period. Moreover, consumption-enhancing measures had little impact on market prices. Overall, the policies examined are estimated to have increased global rice production in 2007–09 but to have led to decreased global consumption in 2007.

For wheat markets, effects on world prices are estimated to have been smaller than for rice. With the exception of the initial period, where border measures drive prices up by 4–5 percent, the most significant impact on markets is attributable to production policies, which indeed reduced prices by as much as 6 percent (in 2009) and induced both higher consumption and production of wheat. In the case of wheat, border measures are estimated to be much less important than for rice. This is because the prevalence of such measures was less than that for rice but also because international wheat markets are much less "thin" than those for rice.

In conclusion, the analysis suggests that implemented policy measures increased wheat production and consumption, with lower global reference prices. However, it also suggests that they destabilized rice markets, without any significant longer-term effect on consumption levels. It is important to add that the reduction to zero of mandatory cropland set aside in the EU was not included in this analysis. Had it been included, the estimated positive impact on crop production and consumption would have been significantly higher, especially for wheat and other major crops in Europe.

CONCLUSIONS

The rapid succession of two major crises – the global food crisis and the subsequent financial crisis and economic recession – has delivered the hardest blow to world food security in decades. The two crises have led to a sharp increase in the number of people suffering from chronic hunger and undernourishment in the world and a reversal of the previously declining trend in the proportion of the world's population without access to adequate food for a healthy and active life.

The financial crisis – and the consequent economic downturn – originated far

[10] Model simulations are based on information contained in FAO (2009f), but coverage of policies focuses on those that were adaptable to the modelling environment and that were expected to have a measurable market impact.
[11] The OECD–FAO Aglink-Cosimo model is annual. The impacts of policies that were in place in part of two or more years were introduced proportionately in the different marketing years. However, in the case of policies that were in place only for short periods, this procedure may have had the effect of underestimating the magnitude of the short-term effects by distributing them over two years.
[12] A forthcoming report will assess impacts for other commodity sectors and refine the analysis.

FIGURE 25
Estimated impact of production, consumption, stock and border measures on rice and wheat markets

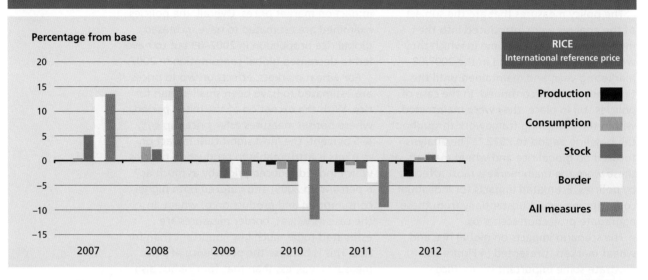

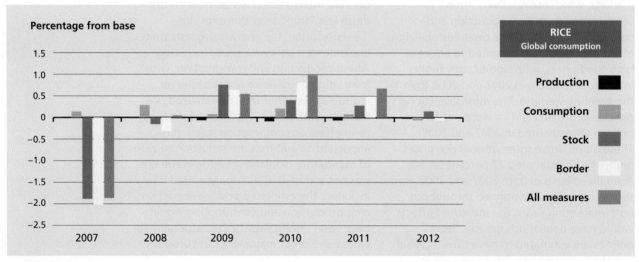

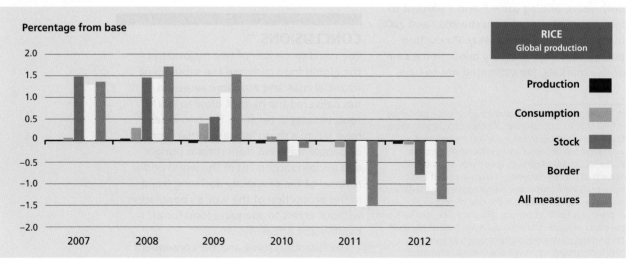

(Cont.)

FIGURE 25 *(cont.)*
Estimated impact of production, consumption, stock and border measures on rice and wheat markets

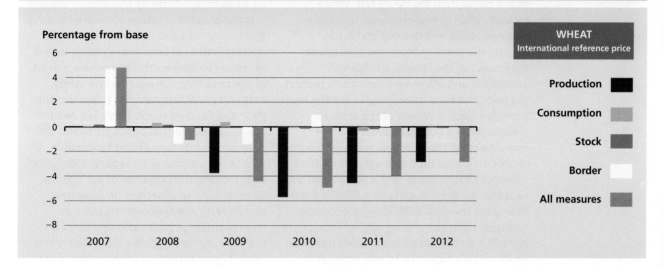

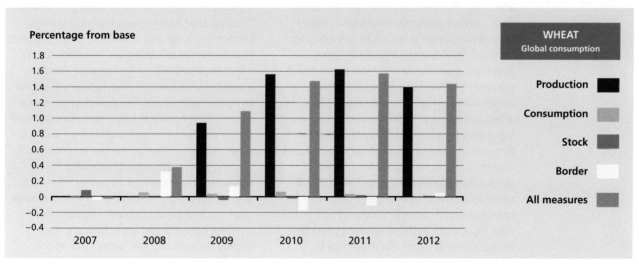

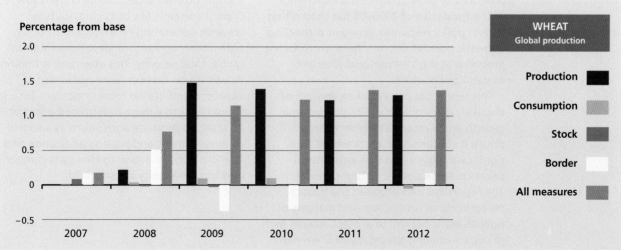

Source: FAO.

from the agriculture sector and far from the developing countries, where its most devastating effects on the poorest segments of the population are being felt. While recovery from global economic recession, however rapid, will depend on factors beyond the areas of food and agriculture, the impact of the recession requires immediate and effective measures to protect the poor and food-insecure who are the most severely affected victims of the crisis.

Beyond the – hopefully swift – recovery from the crisis, there remain many problems related to global food and agriculture that have been highlighted in this report and are cause for concern. In spite of a decline from their peak levels of 2008 and the economic recession notwithstanding, global food prices are still high compared with recent historical levels and are expected to stay high, at least over the medium term. At the same time, various currently latent underlying factors may cause a return to even higher food prices. Resumed income growth in developing countries will lead to renewed expansion of demand for agricultural commodities. Higher real energy prices may affect agricultural food production through input and transportation costs as well as through increased demand for agricultural commodities as feedstock for biofuel production. Consumption mandates and other incentives for biofuel production and consumption in several countries will in their own right contribute to upward pressure on agricultural prices. To these can be added concerns over declining agricultural productivity growth, while the experience of the food crisis of 2006–08 has shown that several policy responses aimed at protecting domestic populations may have exacerbated problems at the international level and destabilized markets.

This report has presented an analysis of the likely consequences of higher income growth and a return to higher energy prices. It confirms that there would be a significant impact and that agricultural prices could be pushed to higher levels. The report has also analysed the impact on agricultural production and markets of policies implemented to protect against high prices, concluding that many of them had a destabilizing effect. Similarly, *The State of Food and Agriculture 2008* (FAO, 2008b)

also analysed the impact on agricultural markets of growing biofuel demand as well as the implications of different scenarios for agricultural productivity growth.

In the present situation of severe hardship and future risks and uncertainties, efforts are required in at least four directions. It is necessary to address the immediate impact of the crisis through appropriate safety nets and social programmes to protect the poor and food-insecure. There is a need to step up investment in agriculture with the dual purpose of stimulating sustainable productivity increases to expand supply and of exploiting the potential of agriculture to contribute to economic development and poverty alleviation in the LDCs. In this regard, high prices also represent an opportunity for agricultural producers and imply higher returns to investments in the agriculture sector, whether public or private. The fact that hunger was increasing even before the food and economic crises suggests that technical solutions are insufficient. To lift themselves out of hunger, the food-insecure need control over resources, access to opportunities and improved governance at the local, national and international levels based on right-to-food principles. Finally, it is necessary to strengthen the international trading system in order to prevent measures implemented to protect domestic populations from destabilizing international markets and penalizing other countries.

These broad areas for action are now widely recognized and supported at the international level. If it is possible to point to a single positive aspect of the current severe crisis, it certainly lies in its contribution towards generating renewed attention on agriculture, agricultural development and global food security. This attention is finding its expression on ever more numerous occasions and in ever more important fora. It should lead to a more determined effort at all levels to promote agriculture as a source of development and poverty alleviation and to more decisive action to eliminate hunger and food insecurity in the world.

STATISTICAL ANNEX

1986   1990

1999   1989

Part III

TABLE A1
Production of livestock products, 1995–2007

	Meat			Milk			Eggs		
	(Thousand tonnes)		(Annual % growth)	(Thousand tonnes)		(Annual % growth)	(Thousand tonnes)		(Annual % growth)
	1995	2007	1995–2007	1995	2007	1995–2007	1995	2007	1995–2007
WORLD	206 853	285 700	2.7	540 207	671 274	1.8	46 853	67 751	3.1
DEVELOPED COUNTRIES	99 572	110 250	0.9	345 533	357 774	0.3	17 317	18 860	0.7
FORMER CENTRALLY PLANNED ECONOMIES	19 541	18 993	–0.2	107 554	101 505	–0.5	4 375	5 078	1.2
Albania	67	81	1.6	968	1 064	0.8	14	27	5.7
Armenia	49	71	3.1	428	636	3.4	11	30	8.7
Azerbaijan	81	171	6.5	827	1 328	4.0	25	52	6.1
Belarus	657	818	1.8	5 070	5 909	1.3	189	181	–0.4
Bosnia and Herzegovina	39	62	3.9	372	607	4.2	10	16	4.3
Bulgaria	477	226	–6.0	1 448	1 327	–0.7	110	100	–0.8
Croatia	125	139	0.9	598	883	3.3	49	48	–0.1
Czech Republic	862	719	–1.5	3 143	2 707	–1.2	152	87	–4.6
Estonia	68	62	–0.7	709	606	–1.3	20	11	–5.2
Georgia	115	108	–0.5	475	758	4.0	15	16	0.3
Hungary	1 046	914	–1.1	1 992	1 807	–0.8	189	168	–1.0
Kazakhstan	985	838	–1.3	4 619	5 073	0.8	103	149	3.1
Kyrgyzstan	180	184	0.2	864	1 241	3.1	8	21	8.0
Latvia	123	84	–3.1	948	842	–1.0	24	39	4.3
Lithuania	209	247	1.4	1 828	2 004	0.8	44	55	1.9
Montenegro		2			190			2	
Poland	2 758	3 353	1.6	11 644	11 823	0.1	351	538	3.6
Republic of Moldova	135	109	–1.8	837	604	–2.7	20	39	5.8
Romania	1 252	1 104	–1.0	5 021	5 926	1.4	284	334	1.4
Russian Federation	5 796	5 602	–0.3	39 305	32 206	–1.6	1 898	2 110	0.9
Serbia		758			1 716			73	
Serbia and Montenegro	1 007			1 997			90		
Slovakia	340	247	–2.6	1 205	1 018	–1.4	91	75	–1.6
Slovenia	180	149	–1.5	610	656	0.6	19	17	–0.7
Tajikistan	44	60	2.5	382	584	3.6	3	6	6.9
The former Yugoslav Republic of Macedonia	31	26	–1.6	204	452	6.9	24	18	–2.4
Turkmenistan	111	211	5.6	727	1 333	5.2	15	34	7.0
Ukraine	2 294	1 924	–1.5	17 274	12 552	–2.6	547	790	3.1
Uzbekistan	509	722	3.0	4 057	5 658	2.8	69	41	–4.3
OTHER DEVELOPED COUNTRIES	80 031	91 257	1.1	237 979	256 268	0.6	12 942	13 782	0.5
Australia	3 297	4 164	2.0	8 460	10 350	1.7	138	166	1.5
Austria	874	854	–0.2	3 168	3 167	0.0	103	90	–1.1

TABLE A1 *(cont.)*

	Meat			Milk			Eggs		
	(Thousand tonnes)		*(Annual % growth)*	*(Thousand tonnes)*		*(Annual % growth)*	*(Thousand tonnes)*		*(Annual % growth)*
	1995	2007	1995–2007	1995	2007	1995–2007	1995	2007	1995–2007
Belgium		1 722			3 000			224	
Belgium–Luxembourg	1 751			3 644			220		
Canada	3 102	4 416	3.0	7 920	8 000	0.1	326	392	1.6
Denmark	1 854	2 061	0.9	4 676	4 600	–0.1	95	78	–1.6
Finland	311	401	2.1	2 468	2 300	–0.6	75	57	–2.2
France	6 347	5 064	–1.9	26 093	24 549	–0.5	1 025	765	–2.4
Germany	5 822	7 053	1.6	28 629	27 935	–0.2	836	800	–0.4
Greece	530	494	–0.6	1 971	2 030	0.2	116	100	–1.3
Iceland	20	24	1.5	106	115	0.7	2	3	2.0
Ireland	879	982	0.9	5 347	5 200	–0.2	31	33	0.6
Israel	311	659	6.5	1 200	1 220	0.1	96	95	–0.1
Italy	3 989	3 977	0.0	12 260	11 865	–0.3	721	670	–0.6
Japan	3 164	2 952	–0.6	8 382	8 140	–0.2	2 549	2 525	–0.1
Luxembourg		27			313			1	
Malta	16	16	0.1	26	44	4.4	7	7	–0.3
Netherlands	2 860	2 360	–1.6	11 294	10 750	–0.4	602	610	0.1
New Zealand	1 324	1 448	0.8	9 285	15 842	4.6	44	54	1.8
Norway	242	300	1.8	1 934	1 572	–1.7	49	51	0.2
Portugal	659	718	0.7	1 837	2 049	0.9	103	119	1.2
Spain	3 975	5 362	2.5	6 762	7 565	0.9	615	886	3.1
Sweden	558	533	–0.4	3 304	3 000	–0.8	105	102	–0.2
Switzerland	448	449	0.0	3 929	4 024	0.2	34	39	1.1
United Kingdom	3 830	3 411	–1.0	14 844	14 450	–0.2	634	608	–0.4
United States of America	33 868	41 809	1.8	70 439	84 189	1.5	4 417	5 308	1.5
DEVELOPING COUNTRIES	107 281	175 450	4.2	194 675	313 500	4.1	29 536	48 891	4.3
EAST AND SOUTHEAST ASIA	58 411	106 248	5.1	13 627	42 909	10.0	20 130	34 626	4.6
Brunei Darussalam	6	21	11.8	0.0	0.1	5.4	4	7	5.1
Cambodia	152	239	3.8	19	24	1.8	13	17	2.1
China, mainland	46 130	88 681	5.6	9 112	36 770	12.3	16 767	30 080	5.0
China, Hong Kong Special Administrative Region	250	248	–0.1	0.4	0.1	–11.4	1	0	–9.2
China, Macao Special Administrative Region	16	8	–5.5				1	1	3.9
China, Taiwan Province of	1 854	1 641	–1.0	345	343	–0.1	316	373	1.4
Democratic People's Republic of Korea	174	338	5.7	85	90	0.5	62	142	7.1
Indonesia	1 903	2 568	2.5	731	993	2.6	736	1 298	4.8
Lao People's Democratic Republic	68	111	4.2	6	7	1.7	5	13	8.8
Malaysia	1 011	1 296	2.1	45	47	0.4	365	476	2.2
Mongolia	212	214	0.1	337	400	1.4	0	1	8.5
Myanmar	354	1 279	11.3	556	1 120	6.0	54	230	12.8

TABLE A1 *(cont.)*

	Meat			Milk			Eggs		
	(Thousand tonnes)		*(Annual % growth)*	*(Thousand tonnes)*		*(Annual % growth)*	*(Thousand tonnes)*		*(Annual % growth)*
	1995	2007	1995–2007	1995	2007	1995–2007	1995	2007	1995–2007
Philippines	1 414	2 431	4.6	12	13	0.3	430	603	2.9
Republic of Korea	1 430	1 754	1.7	2 005	2 145	0.6	460	574	1.9
Singapore	172	100	–4.4				19	23	1.3
Thailand	1 856	2 097	1.0	307	684	6.9	759	563	–2.5
Timor–Leste	28	14	–5.6	1	0	–8.4	1	2	2.4
Viet Nam	1 384	3 211	7.3	66	274	12.6	136	225	4.3
LATIN AMERICA AND THE CARIBBEAN	27 449	40 262	3.2	49 768	68 733	2.7	4 281	6 317	3.3
Antigua and Barbuda	1	1	1.9	6	5	–0.9	0	0	2.3
Argentina	3 908	4 439	1.1	8 771	10 500	1.5	286	480	4.4
Bahamas	8	9	0.8	2	2	0.7	1	1	2.1
Barbados	15	17	1.1	8	7	–1.1	1	2	5.6
Belize	9	19	6.1	1	4	8.8	1	3	5.6
Bolivia, Plurinational State of	326	436	2.5	233	361	3.7	68	59	–1.1
Brazil	12 808	20 082	3.8	17 126	25 464	3.4	1 447	1 765	1.7
Chile	777	1 351	4.7	1 900	2 460	2.2	93	125	2.5
Colombia	1 411	1 704	1.6	5 078	6 800	2.5	347	500	3.1
Costa Rica	178	218	1.7	583	790	2.6	51	49	–0.4
Cuba	237	198	–1.5	639	422	–3.4	68	105	3.7
Dominica	1	1	1.0	6	6	0.0	0	0	0.0
Dominican Republic	280	451	4.0	385	872	7.0	45	80	4.9
Ecuador	358	600	4.4	1 935	2 609	2.5	60	78	2.2
El Salvador	80	160	5.9	291	495	4.5	45	70	3.8
Grenada	1	1	0.4	1	1	0.0	1	1	0.0
Guatemala	173	256	3.3	308	294	–0.4	93	85	–0.8
Guyana	12	27	6.8	13	30	7.2	2	0	–9.4
Haiti	66	96	3.2	57	70	1.6	4	5	1.4
Honduras	123	230	5.4	444	1 800	12.4	34	41	1.7
Jamaica	69	124	5.0	168	187	0.9	6	7	1.6
Mexico	3 799	5 572	3.2	7 538	9 764	2.2	1 242	2 300	5.3
Netherlands Antilles	1	1	–3.3	0	0	1.9	1	1	0.3
Nicaragua	85	187	6.8	188	646	10.9	27	21	–1.9
Panama	136	164	1.5	155	187	1.6	13	21	4.0
Paraguay	393	362	–0.7	358	375	0.4	41	101	7.7
Peru	604	1 125	5.3	877	1 521	4.7	115	205	4.9
Saint Kitts and Nevis	1	1	–1.1				0	0	–3.8
Saint Lucia	2	3	2.6	1	1	–0.8	1	1	5.8
Saint Vincent and the Grenadines	1	1	–1.4	1	1	–0.4	1	1	0.1
Suriname	7	10	3.0	18	9	–6.1	4	3	–3.8
Trinidad and Tobago	33	64	5.7	9	11	1.5	3	4	2.1
Uruguay	459	677	3.3	1 254	1 650	2.3	32	43	2.6

TABLE A1 *(cont.)*

	Meat			Milk			Eggs		
	(Thousand tonnes)		*(Annual % growth)*	*(Thousand tonnes)*		*(Annual % growth)*	*(Thousand tonnes)*		*(Annual % growth)*
	1995	2007	1995–2007	1995	2007	1995–2007	1995	2007	1995–2007
Venezuela, Bolivarian Republic of	1 087	1 678	3.7	1 413	1 390	−0.1	149	160	0.6
NEAR EAST AND NORTH AFRICA	**6 610**	**9 693**	**3.2**	**25 442**	**36 413**	**3.0**	**2 011**	**2 999**	**3.4**
Afghanistan	286	318	0.9	1 365	2 288	4.4	15	18	1.8
Algeria	497	588	1.4	1 168	1 647	2.9	132	170	2.1
Bahrain	16	14	−1.2	16	11	−3.4	3	2	−1.5
Cyprus	87	86	0.0	181	202	0.9	10	10	0.0
Egypt	991	1 428	3.1	2 732	4 608	4.5	162	240	3.3
Iran, Islamic Republic of	1 330	2 323	4.8	4 540	7 596	4.4	466	880	5.4
Iraq	111	179	4.1	341	630	5.2	21	50	7.6
Jordan	124	144	1.3	148	313	6.4	44	45	0.1
Kuwait	66	75	1.0	35	45	2.1	11	22	5.7
Lebanon	91	201	6.9	208	241	1.3	26	47	5.1
Libyan Arab Jamahiriya	168	144	−1.3	159	203	2.1	44	60	2.6
Morocco	494	745	3.5	920	1 565	4.5	195	168	−1.2
Occupied Palestinian Territory		92			204			38	
Oman	29	51	5.0	94	136	3.2	6	9	3.2
Saudi Arabia	472	723	3.6	662	1 242	5.4	132	174	2.4
Syrian Arab Republic	264	396	3.4	1 414	1 977	2.8	103	170	4.3
Tunisia	183	249	2.6	591	1 012	4.6	62	82	2.4
Turkey	1 181	1 586	2.5	10 602	12 075	1.1	550	744	2.5
United Arab Emirates	93	91	−0.2	59	100	4.4	12	17	3.0
Yemen	128	259	6.0	207	318	3.7	18	52	8.9
SOUTH ASIA	**7 159**	**9 353**	**2.3**	**87 655**	**140 614**	**4.0**	**1 965**	**3 369**	**4.6**
Bangladesh	370	502	2.6	1 985	2 888	3.2	116	161	2.7
India	4 631	6 322	2.6	65 368	102 923	3.9	1 496	2 670	4.9
Nepal	205	270	2.3	1 008	1 397	2.8	20	28	2.9
Pakistan	1 857	2 161	1.3	19 006	33 230	4.8	285	459	4.1
Sri Lanka	95	99	0.3	288	176	−4.0	49	52	0.5
SUB–SAHARAN AFRICA	**7 129**	**9 291**	**2.2**	**17 635**	**24 319**	**2.7**	**1 106**	**1 539**	**2.8**
Angola	112	140	1.9	147	195	2.4	4	4	0.4
Benin	45	58	2.2	24	37	3.8	6	11	4.4
Botswana	74	56	−2.3	109	106	−0.2	3	3	0.5
Burkina Faso	142	240	4.5	140	234	4.4	34	48	2.7
Burundi	27	20	−2.3	37	26	−2.9	4	3	−1.3
Cameroon	180	221	1.7	183	189	0.3	13	13	0.3

TABLE A1 *(cont.)*

| | Meat | | | Milk | | | Eggs | | |
| | *(Thousand tonnes)* | | *(Annual % growth)* | *(Thousand tonnes)* | | *(Annual % growth)* | *(Thousand tonnes)* | | *(Annual % growth)* |
	1995	2007	1995–2007	1995	2007	1995–2007	1995	2007	1995–2007
Cape Verde	10	9	–0.4	7	12	4.5	2	2	–0.2
Central African Republic	89	118	2.4	50	65	2.2	1	1	0.6
Chad	95	134	2.9	172	256	3.4	4	5	2.3
Comoros	1.9	2.1	0.8	4	5	0.3	1	1	0.9
Congo	22	31	2.6	1	1	0.8	1	1	0.4
Côte d'Ivoire	200	156	–2.1	22	25	1.0	16	35	6.7
Democratic Republic of the Congo	212	157	–2.4	7	5	–2.5	9	6	–2.9
Eritrea	25	31	1.8	47	57	1.6	5	2	–6.6
Ethiopia	468	615	2.3	1 022	1 816	4.9	28	38	2.4
Gabon	28	32	1.1	1	2	1.0	2	2	1.2
Gambia	7	7	0.7	7	8	0.6	1	1	2.3
Ghana	145	138	–0.4	25	37	3.2	14	26	5.7
Guinea	39	65	4.4	62	105	4.5	10	21	6.6
Guinea-Bissau	16	21	2.2	17	20	1.4	1	1	7.0
Kenya	358	529	3.3	2 157	3 672	4.5	50	53	0.5
Lesotho	25	25	0.1	27	25	–0.6	1	2	2.1
Liberia	17	25	3.2	1	1	0.3	4	5	1.7
Madagascar	273	302	0.9	510	520	0.2	16	20	1.8
Malawi	47	59	1.9	32	36	1.0	18	20	0.9
Mali	184	291	3.9	426	636	3.4	12	11	–1.0
Mauritania	54	90	4.4	284	355	1.9	5	5	1.2
Mauritius	24	40	4.5	8	4	–6.2	5	5	0.9
Mozambique	82	94	1.2	66	69	0.4	12	14	1.3
Namibia	64	68	0.5	74	110	3.4	2	3	2.6
Niger	105	138	2.3	286	339	1.4	9	11	1.0
Nigeria	847	1 108	2.3	380	468	1.8	390	553	2.9
Rwanda	24	47	5.7	94	144	3.7	2	2	1.6
Sao Tome and Principe	1	1	3.0	0	0	1.0	0	0	3.3
Senegal	100	127	2.0	106	121	1.1	12	32	8.8
Seychelles	2	2	–0.7	0	0	–1.9	2	2	0.7
Sierra Leone	20	23	1.2	19	17	–0.7	7	8	1.5
Somalia	145	204	2.9	2 220	2 166	–0.2	2	3	0.8
South Africa	1 397	2 111	3.5	2 794	3 000	0.6	251	385	3.6
Sudan	555	756	2.6	4 452	7 324	4.2	38	47	1.8
Swaziland	19	21	0.5	36	39	0.6	0	1	9.9
Togo	25	36	3.2	8	10	1.7	6	8	2.0
Uganda	232	239	0.2	458	795	4.7	17	21	1.6
United Republic of Tanzania	341	365	0.6	684	955	2.8	37	37	0.0
Zambia	112	129	1.2	81	65	–1.8	32	47	3.2
Zimbabwe	139	210	3.5	350	250	–2.8	20	22	1.0

Notes: Data values rounded to nearest whole number. Totals for developing countries and the world include a few countries not included in the regional aggregates.

TABLE A2
Production of main categories of meat, 1995–2007

	Pig (Thousand tonnes)		Poultry (Thousand tonnes)		Cattle (Thousand tonnes)		Sheep (Thousand tonnes)	
	1995	2007	1995	2007	1995	2007	1995	2007
WORLD	80 123	115 454	54 602	86 772	54 191	61 881	10 436	14 038
DEVELOPED COUNTRIES	35 990	39 457	27 746	36 956	30 774	29 398	3 498	3 233
FORMER CENTRALLY PLANNED ECONOMIES	8 407	7 742	2 917	5 135	6 968	5 078	948	774
Albania	14	10	4	8	31	42	18	20
Armenia	5	12	7	6	30	43	7	10
Azerbaijan	2	1	14	49	41	76	23	46
Belarus	263	368	69	155	316	290	4	1
Bosnia and Herzegovina	11	11	11	24	16	25	1	2
Bulgaria	256	75	106	105	63	23	45	24
Croatia	56	56	39	46	26	32	2	2
Czech Republic	502	360	152	236	170	80	4	2
Estonia	35	35	6	12	26	14	1	1
Georgia	44	35	10	15	53	49	8	9
Hungary	578	490	387	379	58	34	2	1
Kazakhstan	113	218	53	52	548	384	206	125
Kyrgyzstan	28	19	3	6	85	92	54	47
Latvia	63	40	11	21	48	23	1	1
Lithuania	93	114	26	73	87	60	2	1
Montenegro		2						
Poland	1 962	2 100	384	878	386	355	6	1
Republic of Moldova	60	54	25	35	47	17	3	3
Romania	673	526	286	318	202	186	75	61
Russian Federation	1 865	1 788	859	1 769	2 733	1 828	261	160
Serbia		560		96		80		21
Serbia and Montenegro	644		107		227		29	
Slovakia	243	130	31	87	59	25	2	1
Slovenia	61	57	67	54	51	36	1	2
Tajikistan	1	3	1	1	32	27	11	29
The former Yugoslav Republic of Macedonia	9	9	5	4	7	7	10	7
Turkmenistan	3	0	4	13	51	102	50	97
Ukraine	807	650	235	670	1 186	563	40	15
Uzbekistan	16	19	16	25	392	586	83	89
OTHER DEVELOPED COUNTRIES	27 583	31 716	24 830	31 820	23 806	24 320	2 550	2 459
Australia	351	378	489	850	1 803	2 261	631	652
Austria	566	515	99	114	196	210	7	8
Belgium		1 000		454		262		2

TABLE A2 *(cont.)*

	Pig (Thousand tonnes)		Poultry (Thousand tonnes)		Cattle (Thousand tonnes)		Sheep (Thousand tonnes)	
	1995	2007	1995	2007	1995	2007	1995	2007
Belgium–Luxembourg	1 043		315		357		5	
Canada	1 276	1 894	870	1 207	928	1 279	10	18
Denmark	1 494	1 750	173	175	182	130	2	2
Finland	168	210	43	100	96	90	2	1
France	2 144	1 982	2 071	1 473	1 683	1 450	148	102
Germany	3 602	4 670	642	1 026	1 408	1 190	42	47
Greece	137	110	163	148	72	73	143	153
Iceland	3	5	2	6	3	3	9	9
Ireland	212	210	100	139	477	560	89	72
Israel	11	16	253	513	41	120	7	10
Italy	1 346	1 600	1 097	947	1 180	1 100	76	62
Japan	1 300	1 165	1 252	1 290	601	491	0	0
Luxembourg		9		0		18		0
Malta	9	9	5	4	2	1	0	0
Netherlands	1 622	1 296	641	666	580	382	16	16
New Zealand	51	51	91	151	623	632	535	575
Norway	96	120	29	62	84	88	27	26
Portugal	305	332	217	252	104	106	27	24
Spain	2 175	3 222	924	1 087	508	705	242	236
Sweden	309	270	82	99	143	140	3	4
Switzerland	251	250	40	54	147	135	6	7
United Kingdom	1 017	700	1 405	1 523	1 002	850	394	330
United States of America	8 097	9 953	13 827	19 481	11 585	12 044	130	105
DEVELOPING COUNTRIES	**44 133**	**75 996**	**26 855**	**49 817**	**23 417**	**32 483**	**6 938**	**10 805**
EAST AND SOUTHEAST ASIA	**37 793**	**68 355**	**12 522**	**22 158**	**4 530**	**8 768**	**2 007**	**5 202**
Brunei Darussalam	0	0	4	18	1	2	0	0
Cambodia	82	140	20	25	40	63		
China, mainland	32 000	60 000	8 000	15 320	3 265	7 250	1 745	4 850
China, Hong Kong Special Administrative Region	159	185	59	41	25	15	0	0
China, Macao Special Administrative Region	9		5	7	1	1	0	0
China, Taiwan Province of	1 233	965	610	666	5	6	4	4
Democratic People's Republic of Korea	115	169	24	45	31	21	4	12
Indonesia	572	597	876	1 356	312	418	94	148
Lao People's Democratic Republic	29	47	10	21	13	23	0	1
Malaysia	283	226	707	1 042	16	22	1	1
Mongolia	1	0	0	0	69	52	112	111

TABLE A2 *(cont.)*

	Pig (Thousand tonnes)		Poultry (Thousand tonnes)		Cattle (Thousand tonnes)		Sheep (Thousand tonnes)	
	1995	2007	1995	2007	1995	2007	1995	2007
Myanmar	116	380	117	726	95	122	8	24
Philippines	805	1 501	419	649	97	170	31	35
Republic of Korea	799	915	402	596	221	237	3	3
Singapore	86	19	86	81	0	0	0	0
Thailand	489	700	1 007	1 136	254	198	1	1
Timor-Leste	9	10	1	2	1	1	1	0
Viet Nam	1 007	2 500	176	428	83	166	4	11
LATIN AMERICA AND THE CARIBBEAN	**5 044**	**6 149**	**8 894**	**17 249**	**12 595**	**15 773**	**439**	**456**
Antigua and Barbuda	0	0	0	0	1	1	0	0
Argentina	211	230	817	1 204	2 688	2 830	88	62
Bahamas	0	0	7	8	0	0	0	0
Barbados	3	2	11	15	1	0	0	0
Belize	1	1	7	15	1	3	0	0
Bolivia, Plurinational State of	62	108	97	134	140	170	20	24
Brazil	2 800	3 130	4 154	8 907	5 710	7 900	125	120
Chile	172	470	321	614	258	240	15	17
Colombia	133	130	553	760	702	790	14	14
Costa Rica	24	39	60	97	94	82	0	0
Cuba	107	100	57	31	67	56	4	10
Dominica	0	0	0	0	0	1	0	0
Dominican Republic	62	79	137	297	80	74	1	2
Ecuador	89	165	105	210	149	210	7	13
El Salvador	11	17	40	109	29	34	0	0
Grenada	0	0	0	1	0	0	0	0
Guatemala	9	27	105	160	54	65	3	2
Guyana	1	1	7	24	4	2	1	1
Haiti	23	33	7	8	24	42	4	7
Honduras	8	10	50	145	64	75	0	0
Jamaica	7	9	45	102	17	14	0	1
Mexico	922	1 200	1 315	2 543	1 412	1 650	68	95
Netherlands Antilles	0	0	1	0	0	0	0	0
Nicaragua	5	7	29	88	49	90	0	0
Panama	17	22	59	85	61	57		
Paraguay	130	99	34	39	226	220	3	4
Peru	80	108	355	800	107	165	26	42
Saint Kitts and Nevis	0	0	0	0	0	0	0	0
Saint Lucia	1	1	1	1	1	1	0	0
Saint Vincent and the Grenadines	1	1	0	0	0	0	0	0
Suriname	1	2	4	6	2	2	0	0
Trinidad and Tobago	2	3	30	60	1	1	0	0
Uruguay	22	19	41	46	338	570	52	32

TABLE A2 *(cont.)*

	Pig (Thousand tonnes)		Poultry (Thousand tonnes)		Cattle (Thousand tonnes)		Sheep (Thousand tonnes)	
	1995	2007	1995	2007	1995	2007	1995	2007
Venezuela, Bolivarian Republic of	139	138	445	740	316	430	7	10
NEAR EAST AND NORTH AFRICA	**51**	**54**	**2 901**	**5 291**	**1 370**	**1 832**	**1 811**	**1 963**
Afghanistan			12	16	130	175	132	115
Algeria	0	0	208	260	101	121	178	196
Bahrain			5	5	1	1	10	7
Cyprus	43	50	30	24	5	4	8	7
Egypt	3	2	407	666	215	320	91	61
Iran, Islamic Republic of	0		660	1 444	255	354	377	496
Iraq			37	97	40	50	31	28
Jordan			108	133	4	4	12	7
Kuwait			26	42	2	2	38	31
Lebanon	4	1	58	130	18	53	11	17
Libyan Arab Jamahiriya			103	100	22	6	36	34
Morocco	1	1	197	410	122	160	132	137
Occupied Palestinian Territory				69		5		18
Oman			4	6	3	4	17	35
Saudi Arabia			310	560	26	24	88	99
Syrian Arab Republic			93	133	34	57	137	205
Tunisia	0	0	68	124	50	58	54	66
Turkey	0		506	915	292	351	372	317
United Arab Emirates			22	36	11	10	51	30
Yemen			47	123	41	73	38	60
SOUTH ASIA	**509**	**515**	**1 103**	**2 988**	**1 929**	**2 105**	**1 490**	**1 545**
Bangladesh			103	116	148	184	107	198
India	495	497	624	2 273	1 365	1 282	663	770
Nepal	11	16	10	15	46	50	34	46
Pakistan			313	519	342	562	683	529
Sri Lanka	2	2	54	65	27	27	3	2
SUB-SAHARAN AFRICA	**634**	**805**	**1 336**	**2 031**	**2 941**	**3 962**	**1 176**	**1 630**
Angola	26	28	7	9	65	85	6	11
Benin	7	4	11	17	15	23	6	8
Botswana	0	0	8	5	46	31	9	7
Burkina Faso	12	40	22	33	67	116	33	46
Burundi	5	4	6	6	10	6	5	4
Cameroon	12	16	21	30	73	92	28	32
Cape Verde	8	8	1	0	0	0	0	1
Central African Republic	10	13	3	4	48	74	8	13

TABLE A2 *(cont.)*

	Pig (Thousand tonnes)		Poultry (Thousand tonnes)		Cattle (Thousand tonnes)		Sheep (Thousand tonnes)	
	1995	2007	1995	2007	1995	2007	1995	2007
Chad	0	1	4	5	63	86	24	38
Comoros			0	1	1	1	0	0
Congo	2	2	6	5	1	2	1	1
Côte d'Ivoire	13	12	24	69	37	52	11	9
Democratic Republic of the Congo	28	24	13	11	16	13	23	21
Djibouti					3	6	4	5
Eritrea			4	2	10	17	10	11
Ethiopia	1	2	36	48	235	350	61	124
Gabon	2	3	3	4	1	1	1	1
Gambia	0	1	1	1	3	3	1	1
Ghana	11	4	12	30	21	24	11	22
Guinea	1	2	3	6	25	41	6	12
Guinea-Bissau	10	12	1	2	4	5	1	2
Kenya	8	12	20	17	239	390	59	75
Lesotho	3	3	2	2	11	11	6	6
Liberia	4	6	5	10	1	1	1	2
Madagascar	65	70	48	72	146	147	10	9
Malawi	16	21	14	15	15	16	3	7
Mali	2	2	26	38	85	134	48	89
Mauritania	0	0	4	4	10	23	21	39
Mauritius	1	1	19	37	3	2	0	0
Mozambique	12	13	30	40	37	38	3	3
Namibia	2	2	3	8	48	42	7	12
Niger	1	1	24	29	25	45	35	44
Nigeria	130	212	169	233	267	287	180	254
Rwanda	2	5	1	2	10	22	2	5
Sao Tome and Principe	0	0	0	1	0	0	0	0
Senegal	4	11	17	31	44	49	23	29
Seychelles	1	1	1	1	0	0	0	0
Sierra Leone	2	2	9	11	6	5	1	3
Somalia	0	0	3	4	50	66	57	90
South Africa	127	150	604	982	508	805	146	155
Sudan			25	28	225	340	237	334
Swaziland	1	1	1	5	14	13	3	2
Togo	5	5	7	13	6	6	3	8
Uganda	66	60	36	38	86	106	26	35
United Republic of Tanzania	10	13	35	47	246	247	37	41
Zambia	10	11	25	37	44	42	3	5
Zimbabwe	13	28	19	40	73	97	11	14

Note: Totals for developing countries and the world include a few countries not included in the regional aggregates.

TABLE A3
Per capita consumption of livestock products, 1995–2005

	Meat (kg/person/year)		(Annual % growth)	Milk (kg/person/year)		(Annual % growth)	Eggs (kg/person/year)		(Annual % growth)
	1995	2005	1995–2005	1995	2005	1995–2005	1995	2005	1995–2005
WORLD	35.7	41.2	1.5	75.6	82.1	0.8	7.3	9.0	2.1
DEVELOPED COUNTRIES	77.3	82.1	0.6	198.3	207.7	0.5	12.3	13.0	0.6
FORMER CENTRALLY PLANNED ECONOMIES	50.6	51.5	0.2	156.6	176.0	1.2	9.6	11.4	1.7
Albania	27.6	40.9	4.0	289.8	296.4	0.2	5.4	5.7	0.6
Armenia	23.0	29.2	2.4	70.8	107.5	4.3	3.6	6.9	6.7
Azerbaijan	13.5	19.4	3.7	98.5	132.3	3.0	4.3	5.5	2.6
Belarus	59.4	60.9	0.3	252.0	191.9	−2.7	16.5	14.5	−1.3
Bosnia and Herzegovina	23.8	21.7	−0.9	97.3	172.6	5.9	4.2	4.9	1.6
Bulgaria	59.0	51.2	−1.4	157.8	158.0	0.0	11.5	12.1	0.6
Croatia	35.2	38.9	1.0	163.0	197.2	1.9	9.5	10.2	0.7
Czech Republic	84.2	86.6	0.3	200.9	195.7	−0.3	13.1	9.5	−3.2
Estonia	49.2	59.7	2.0	273.3	254.6	−0.7	13.4	10.4	−2.5
Georgia	27.6	31.2	1.2	90.0	149.1	5.2	5.7	7.3	2.6
Hungary	77.9			155.3			16.8		
Kazakhstan	54.3	56.0	0.3	171.0	245.7	3.7	5.7	8.7	4.3
Kyrgyzstan	37.7	34.9	−0.8	172.4	202.9	1.6	1.7	3.4	6.8
Latvia	57.3	57.5	0.0	243.4	280.1	1.4	9.3	13.3	3.6
Lithuania	52.5	70.6	3.0	140.8	230.6	5.1	10.0	10.6	0.6
Poland	69.0	76.8	1.1	194.3	178.7	−0.8	8.6	12.0	3.4
Republic of Moldova	22.5	38.2	5.4	140.0	158.0	1.2	4.1	9.7	9.0
Romania	54.7	63.9	1.6	194.6	246.5	2.4	9.9	14.3	3.7
Russian Federation	52.9	52.1	−0.1	129.0	168.8	2.7	11.9	13.9	1.5
Serbia and Montenegro	94.1	82.0	−1.4	151.3	161.9	0.7	7.9	7.1	−1.1
Slovakia	65.0	64.7	0.0	136.0	125.8	−0.8	16.5	12.5	−2.7
Slovenia	91.6	93.9	0.2	208.5	253.1	2.0	7.0	6.0	−1.5
Tajikistan	11.0	11.9	0.8	67.0	81.8	2.0	0.5	0.8	6.2
The former Yugoslav Republic of Macedonia	37.2	37.9	0.2	103.9	127.4	2.1	10.5	8.9	−1.7
Turkmenistan	30.1	42.8	3.6	127.5	146.9	1.4	3.5	6.7	6.7
Ukraine	39.3	38.6	−0.2	180.8	162.7	−1.0	10.0	13.4	2.9
Uzbekistan	29.3	24.5	−1.8	162.6	157.8	−0.3	2.9	3.9	2.9
OTHER DEVELOPED COUNTRIES	90.2	95.8	0.6	218.7	221.8	0.1	13.6	13.8	0.1
Australia	105.7	117.6	1.1	246.6	233.9	−0.5	6.2	5.2	−1.7
Austria	106.3	109.1	0.3	271.0	226.6	−1.8	13.5	13.3	−0.2
Belgium		82.4			244.5			11.4	
Belgium–Luxembourg	88.7			200.9			13.9		
Canada	93.7	96.3	0.3	204.7	201.2	−0.2	10.3	11.6	1.3
Denmark	101.7	100.7	−0.1	253.8	296.8	1.6	16.1	19.0	1.6

TABLE A3 *(cont.)*

	Meat			Milk			Eggs		
	(kg/person/year)		(Annual % growth)	(kg/person/year)		(Annual % growth)	(kg/person/year)		(Annual % growth)
	1995	2005	1995–2005	1995	2005	1995–2005	1995	2005	1995–2005
Finland	61.5	70.8	1.4	361.5	339.3	−0.6	11.2	8.3	−2.9
France	97.4	88.6	−0.9	269.5	263.3	−0.2	15.8	13.0	−1.9
Germany	83.2	83.3	0.0	238.2	248.7	0.4	12.3	11.8	−0.4
Greece	80.1	79.2	−0.1	257.3	271.3	0.5	9.8	9.2	−0.6
Iceland	70.0	83.7	1.8	256.6	233.7	−0.9	7.3	8.7	1.8
Ireland	84.6	100.7	1.8	246.7	254.5	0.3	7.6	7.0	−0.9
Israel	66.3	99.7	4.2	218.0	183.9	−1.7	13.2	9.2	−3.6
Italy	83.6	88.0	0.5	232.2	252.1	0.8	11.9	11.6	−0.3
Japan	43.6	45.4	0.4	68.3	64.5	−0.6	19.6	19.0	−0.3
Luxembourg		142.5			316.5			7.5	
Malta	77.2	82.4	0.6	172.5	186.5	0.8	20.5	12.0	−5.2
Netherlands	91.2	77.8	−1.6	365.8	313.2	−1.5	16.5	16.9	0.2
New Zealand	122.6	104.0	−1.6	103.9	92.0	−1.2	9.7	10.8	1.1
Norway	57.7	65.7	1.3	263.9	260.4	−0.1	10.5	10.1	−0.4
Portugal	74.8	86.0	1.4	168.8	216.5	2.5	8.5	9.7	1.4
Spain	101.9	107.9	0.6	162.0	160.4	−0.1	13.9	15.5	1.0
Sweden	64.8	77.1	1.8	346.8	367.7	0.6	11.3	11.1	−0.2
Switzerland	73.6	72.3	−0.2	319.4	302.6	−0.5	9.8	10.1	0.3
United Kingdom	73.5	83.9	1.3	216.1	248.9	1.4	9.9	10.2	0.3
United States of America	117.1	126.6	0.8	258.2	256.5	−0.1	13.3	14.6	1.0
DEVELOPING COUNTRIES	**24.0**	**30.9**	**2.6**	**41.1**	**50.5**	**2.1**	**6.0**	**8.0**	**3.1**
EAST AND SOUTHEAST ASIA	**32.3**	**48.2**	**4.1**	**9.1**	**21.0**	**8.7**	**10.2**	**15.4**	**4.2**
Brunei Darussalam	70.2	60.6	−1.5	78.9	138.8	5.8	17.4	14.6	−1.7
Cambodia	13.3	16.4	2.1	4.7	5.5	1.5	1.1	1.1	0.6
China, mainland	38.2	59.5	4.5	6.6	23.2	13.4	12.8	20.2	4.7
China, Hong Kong Special Administrative Region	121.2	134.2	1.0	60.5	58.2	−0.4	12.9	11.6	−1.1
China, Macao Special Administrative Region	84.4	97.2	1.4	53.6	55.9	0.4	9.3	15.2	5.0
China, Taiwan Province of	75.0	78.7	0.5	51.5	35.6	−3.6	12.1	12.4	0.2
Democratic People's Republic of Korea	8.1	14.6	6.0	3.7	4.8	2.5	2.6	5.5	7.6
Indonesia	9.7	10.0	0.3	7.4	9.5	2.5	3.0	3.8	2.4
Lao People's Democratic Republic	14.4	17.6	2.0	4.6	5.1	0.9	0.8	1.9	9.3
Malaysia	52.2	51.3	−0.2	60.2	44.8	−2.9	12.4	9.6	−2.5
Mongolia	87.8	72.3	−1.9	106.5	126.6	1.7	0.1	0.5	20.8
Myanmar	8.2	23.0	10.8	13.9	22.3	4.9	1.0	3.5	13.0
Republic of Korea	38.1	48.9	2.5	20.5	26.8	2.7	9.2	9.9	0.8
Singapore	23.9	29.6	2.2	22.0	16.0	−3.1	5.8	6.4	1.1

TABLE A3 *(cont.)*

	Meat			Milk			Eggs		
	(kg/person/year)		(Annual % growth)	(kg/person/year)		(Annual % growth)	(kg/person/year)		(Annual % growth)
	1995	2005	1995–2005	1995	2005	1995–2005	1995	2005	1995–2005
Thailand	28.5	26.7	–0.6	26.4	26.0	–0.2	10.4	9.4	–1.0
Timor-Leste	38.0	34.0	–1.1	11.7	24.7	7.8	1.2	2.3	6.4
Viet Nam	18.8	34.9	6.4	4.0	11.2	11.0	1.6	2.1	2.5
LATIN AMERICA AND THE CARIBBEAN	**54.8**	**61.9**	**1.2**	**106.1**	**109.7**	**0.3**	**7.5**	**8.6**	**1.3**
Antigua and Barbuda	68.3	78.8	1.4	142.7	136.9	–0.4	2.5	4.3	5.6
Argentina	90.9	88.6	–0.3	211.5	186.1	–1.3	7.1	6.5	–0.8
Bahamas	90.0	98.8	0.9	102.0	70.5	–3.6	3.2	3.8	1.7
Barbados	72.6	73.4	0.1	99.8	116.2	1.5	3.0	5.4	6.0
Belize	41.3	49.2	1.8	84.4	92.9	1.0	5.6	3.3	–5.2
Bolivia, Plurinational State of	43.2	51.3	1.7	35.7	41.0	1.4	7.5	4.8	–4.4
Brazil	75.3	80.8	0.7	114.7	120.8	0.5	7.4	6.8	–0.9
Chile	57.0	70.6	2.2	120.4	104.3	–1.4	4.6	5.8	2.4
Colombia	37.1	38.2	0.3	110.2	120.3	0.9	7.8	9.3	1.7
Costa Rica	42.8	39.5	–0.8	158.5	164.7	0.4	13.3	9.2	–3.7
Cuba	24.1	31.6	2.8	95.0	73.0	–2.6	5.5	7.6	3.3
Dominica	65.6	71.2	0.8	141.1	147.2	0.4	2.6	2.6	0.1
Dominican Republic	34.9	47.7	3.2	75.9	80.7	0.6	4.4	5.9	3.1
Ecuador	31.6	46.5	3.9	97.5	94.0	–0.4	4.5	5.0	1.3
El Salvador	15.9	24.9	4.6	74.8	102.6	3.2	6.5	8.8	3.1
Grenada	51.9	65.4	2.3	95.3	140.6	4.0	7.3	6.9	–0.6
Guatemala	17.6	24.6	3.4	41.1	42.2	0.3	8.6	6.2	–3.2
Guyana	25.5	36.9	3.8	61.6	161.3	10.1	1.8	1.5	–1.9
Haiti	9.3	14.1	4.2	15.8	13.3	–1.7	0.5	0.5	–1.1
Honduras	21.4	36.5	5.5	90.0	105.9	1.6	6.2	4.8	–2.6
Jamaica	38.8	61.2	4.7	107.7	109.0	0.1	2.3	2.9	2.6
Mexico	44.9	62.2	3.3	94.5	117.1	2.2	11.6	16.6	3.6
Netherlands Antilles	83.4	95.2	1.3	164.4	130.9	–2.3	3.1	3.9	2.2
Nicaragua	12.2	20.3	5.2	43.0	87.4	7.4	5.5	3.5	–4.3
Panama	51.5	57.7	1.1	59.5	67.5	1.3	3.4	6.5	6.7
Paraguay	77.3	32.3	–8.4	82.5	63.9	–2.5	7.8	16.1	7.5
Peru	18.8	25.9	3.3	51.0	49.9	–0.2	3.5	4.7	3.2
Saint Kitts and Nevis	73.5	85.4	1.5	80.5	85.5	0.6	5.5	3.5	–4.5
Saint Lucia	88.0	88.1	0.0	99.8	111.0	1.1	3.4	8.2	9.1
Saint Vincent and the Grenadines	63.9	76.7	1.8	54.9	73.5	3.0	5.2	5.0	–0.4
Suriname	32.2	45.4	3.5	57.8	44.5	–2.6	9.1	5.0	–5.8
Trinidad and Tobago	33.6	41.8	2.2	103.5	99.5	–0.4	1.9	3.3	6.0
Uruguay	99.2	68.4	–3.6	196.2	150.0	–2.6	8.3	10.9	2.8
Venezuela, Bolivarian Republic of	48.2	60.8	2.3	89.4	68.2	–2.7	4.9	5.5	1.0

TABLE A3 *(cont.)*

	Meat (kg/person/year)		(Annual % growth)	Milk (kg/person/year)		(Annual % growth)	Eggs (kg/person/year)		(Annual % growth)
	1995	2005	1995–2005	1995	2005	1995–2005	1995	2005	1995–2005
NEAR EAST AND NORTH AFRICA	**22.6**	**27.3**	**1.9**	**74.8**	**81.6**	**0.9**	**5.4**	**6.3**	**1.5**
Afghanistan	15.7	13.6	−1.4	68.2	63.0	−0.8	0.7	0.7	0.3
Algeria	18.8	21.6	1.4	102.8	119.2	1.5	4.0	4.7	1.5
Cyprus	99.4	104.4	0.5	176.4	162.8	−0.8	10.7	9.6	−1.1
Egypt	19.5	22.3	1.4	40.9	50.6	2.2	2.2	2.7	1.8
Iran, Islamic Republic of	22.2	30.4	3.2	53.7	70.5	2.8	6.4	8.9	3.4
Iraq	5.3	7.1	2.9	17.2	42.9	9.6	0.9	2.6	11.1
Jordan	34.2	36.5	0.7	64.7	65.4	0.1	7.4	4.4	−5.2
Kuwait	66.3	92.9	3.4	175.4	82.4	−7.3	12.2	12.8	0.5
Lebanon	32.1	54.5	5.5	94.8	110.0	1.5	5.3	7.9	4.2
Libyan Arab Jamahiriya	34.7	27.6	−2.3	86.5	110.5	2.5	7.5	9.2	2.0
Morocco	18.6	23.8	2.5	32.9	38.1	1.5	6.2	5.2	−1.8
Occupied Palestinian Territory		27.0			56.2			8.9	
Saudi Arabia	46.3	54.5	1.6	70.8	85.5	1.9	5.2	5.0	−0.5
Syrian Arab Republic	18.5	19.5	0.5	85.2	104.9	2.1	6.1	7.3	1.7
Tunisia	20.9	25.7	2.1	78.1	98.4	2.3	5.8	7.2	2.3
Turkey	19.4	21.2	0.9	137.4	125.3	−0.9	7.8	9.1	1.6
United Arab Emirates	94.4	72.4	−2.6	141.7	97.0	−3.7	12.3	10.0	−2.1
Yemen	9.7	17.1	5.8	23.7	36.5	4.4	1.1	1.8	5.2
SOUTH ASIA	**5.6**	**5.8**	**0.3**	**59.8**	**69.5**	**1.5**	**1.3**	**1.7**	**2.6**
Bangladesh	2.9	3.1	0.7	13.1	15.1	1.4	0.7	0.9	1.6
India	4.7	5.1	0.8	57.7	65.2	1.2	1.3	1.8	3.0
Maldives	11.1	19.4	5.7	45.0	90.8	7.3	5.6	9.9	5.9
Nepal	9.4	9.7	0.3	36.4	40.7	1.1	0.8	1.0	2.0
Pakistan	14.5	12.2	−1.7	126.1	158.3	2.3	1.8	2.2	1.7
Sri Lanka	5.3	7.1	3.0	31.5	30.8	−0.2	2.4	2.0	−1.6
SUB-SAHARAN AFRICA	**12.4**	**13.3**	**0.7**	**27.9**	**30.1**	**0.7**	**1.6**	**1.6**	**0.3**
Angola	11.3	18.8	5.3	18.6	12.8	−3.7	0.3	1.1	13.3
Benin	10.3	12.3	1.8	6.2	8.8	3.6	0.8	0.9	1.2
Botswana	32.3	26.0	−2.1	113.7	82.3	−3.2	1.7	2.8	5.3
Burkina Faso	13.9	15.9	1.4	18.1	16.3	−1.0	2.4	2.4	−0.3
Burundi	4.3	3.7	−1.5	7.1	3.5	−6.9	0.4	0.3	−4.1
Cameroon	12.9	13.5	0.4	14.4	13.7	−0.5	0.7	0.5	−2.4
Cape Verde	29.3	33.7	1.4	88.7	94.6	0.6	4.9	3.4	−3.7
Central African Republic	25.8	31.0	1.8	14.2	16.2	1.4	0.4	0.3	−1.2
Chad	13.3	12.6	−0.6	23.0	22.5	−0.2	0.4	0.3	−3.3
Comoros	7.9	11.2	3.6	11.8	9.0	−2.7	1.0	0.9	−1.8

TABLE A3 *(cont.)*

	Meat			Milk			Eggs		
	(kg/person/year)		(Annual % growth)	(kg/person/year)		(Annual % growth)	(kg/person/year)		(Annual % growth)
	1995	2005	1995–2005	1995	2005	1995–2005	1995	2005	1995–2005
Congo	18.3	21.0	1.4	10.1	20.9	7.5	0.3	0.8	9.8
Côte d'Ivoire	13.7	13.0	−0.5	8.5	10.0	1.6	0.9	1.2	3.2
Democratic Republic of the Congo	5.4	4.6	−1.6	0.9	1.3	3.2	0.1	0.1	−0.2
Djibouti	15.2	20.9	3.2	58.2	53.1	−0.9	0.8	0.3	−9.1
Eritrea	7.8	7.1	−0.9	16.9	13.1	−2.5	1.2	0.4	−11.0
Ethiopia	7.8	8.3	0.7	16.3	22.4	3.2	0.4	0.4	−0.2
Gabon	57.0	64.4	1.2	26.1	37.5	3.7	1.3	1.2	−0.8
Gambia	5.9	8.7	4.0	14.6	19.9	3.1	1.0	1.6	4.2
Ghana	9.5	10.6	1.1	2.8	7.2	10.0	0.6	0.8	4.0
Guinea	5.8	7.5	2.6	14.2	13.1	−0.8	1.1	1.8	4.8
Guinea-Bissau	13.8	12.9	−0.7	16.5	13.2	−2.2	0.4	0.6	3.9
Kenya	13.0	15.4	1.7	73.5	75.8	0.3	1.5	1.4	−1.1
Lesotho	17.8	17.1	−0.4	18.2	19.5	0.7	0.7	0.7	0.5
Liberia	9.4	9.5	0.2	3.4	3.8	1.1	1.8	2.3	2.6
Madagascar	19.2	14.2	−2.9	35.6	27.6	−2.5	0.9	0.8	−1.1
Malawi	4.7	4.6	−0.2	3.7	5.1	3.1	1.5	1.3	−1.4
Mali	21.1	22.4	0.6	52.7	56.7	0.7	0.8	0.4	−6.1
Mauritania	24.3	32.2	2.8	145.4	151.4	0.4	1.7	1.5	−1.3
Mauritius	31.4	42.4	3.1	110.8	118.1	0.6	3.0	3.8	2.6
Mozambique	5.3	5.7	0.8	6.9	4.5	−4.2	0.6	0.5	−1.7
Namibia	14.7	30.1	7.4	38.1	82.6	8.1	0.8	1.5	5.7
Niger	11.3	11.4	0.1	33.1	29.6	−1.1	0.7	0.5	−2.3
Nigeria	7.8	7.5	−0.4	12.4	6.2	−6.6	3.3	3.3	−0.1
Rwanda	4.3	5.6	2.7	18.1	15.4	−1.6	0.3	0.2	−3.2
Sao Tome and Principe	7.9	13.7	5.7	11.3	34.7	11.8	1.7	3.0	6.0
Senegal	11.2	12.4	1.1	26.5	26.6	0.1	1.0	1.9	6.7
Seychelles	22.9	29.0	2.4	95.3	78.8	−1.9	6.1	6.1	0.0
Sierra Leone	5.2	4.9	−0.7	6.4	4.2	−4.0	1.4	1.3	−0.8
Somalia	22.3	23.5	0.5	247.5	191.4	−2.5	0.3	0.2	−1.6
South Africa	37.3	46.2	2.2	56.1	54.1	−0.4	4.6	5.8	2.3
Sudan	18.6	22.0	1.7	141.8	202.7	3.6	1.1	1.1	0.1
Swaziland	25.1	32.6	2.7	43.0	82.3	6.7	2.0	4.9	9.3
Togo	6.2	6.5	0.5	5.2	4.3	−1.8	1.1	0.7	−3.5
Uganda	10.9	10.2	−0.7	21.2	24.3	1.4	0.6	0.5	−2.2
United Republic of Tanzania	11.4	9.5	−1.8	22.7	24.3	0.7	1.1	0.8	−2.8
Zambia	12.1	13.4	1.0	8.9	7.4	−1.8	3.1	3.6	1.6
Zimbabwe	9.6	16.9	5.9	17.4	17.1	−0.2	1.3	1.4	1.0

TABLE A4
Per capita calorie intake from livestock products, 1995–2005

	Calories from livestock products			Share of total calories from livestock products		
	(kcal/person/day)		(Annual % growth)	(Percentage)		(Annual % growth)
	1995	2005	1995–2005	1995	2005	1995–2005
WORLD	339.3	388.2	1.4	11.8	12.9	0.9
DEVELOPED COUNTRIES	670.8	694.6	0.3	20.7	20.3	–0.2
FORMER CENTRALLY PLANNED ECONOMIES	536.4	563.5	0.5	18.3	18.2	–0.1
Albania	705.8	758.5	0.7	25.1	26.5	0.6
Armenia	271.4	363.2	3.0	13.7	16.2	1.7
Azerbaijan	254.7	349.8	3.2	11.9	13.4	1.2
Belarus	747.4	618.8	–1.9	23.4	20.7	–1.2
Bosnia and Herzegovina	290.8	400.1	3.2	10.9	13.4	2.0
Bulgaria	553.1	495.3	–1.1	19.1	17.6	–0.8
Croatia	442.7	498.2	1.2	17.3	16.7	–0.4
Czech Republic	625.3	647.9	0.4	19.5	19.4	0.0
Estonia	708.8	672.7	–0.5	24.1	21.9	–1.0
Georgia	325.4	444.5	3.2	14.5	17.6	1.9
Hungary	611.7	591.4	–0.3	18.9	17.2	–1.0
Kazakhstan	617.4	731.8	1.7	18.9	22.7	1.8
Kyrgyzstan	513.1	552.2	0.7	21.6	17.7	–2.0
Latvia	728.9	718.7	–0.1	24.7	22.8	–0.8
Lithuania	481.7	676.5	3.5	16.9	19.8	1.6
Poland	638.6	631.6	–0.1	19.3	18.7	–0.3
Republic of Moldova	366.6	493.9	3.0	13.9	16.8	1.9
Romania	609.5	762.6	2.3	19.9	21.8	0.9
Russian Federation	518.6	565.0	0.9	18.0	17.9	–0.1
Serbia and Montenegro	724.0	721.6	0.0	25.4	26.8	0.5
Slovakia	489.1	446.0	–0.9	17.1	15.6	–0.9
Slovenia	682.1	729.1	0.7	23.0	21.7	–0.6
Tajikistan	182.3	219.3	1.9	9.1	9.7	0.7
The former Yugoslav Republic of Macedonia	373.7	368.6	–0.1	14.8	12.8	–1.5
Turkmenistan	412.0	535.9	2.7	16.1	19.4	1.8
Ukraine	524.1	492.9	–0.6	18.0	15.5	–1.5
Uzbekistan	465.9	436.0	–0.7	17.3	17.5	0.1
OTHER DEVELOPED COUNTRIES	738.1	753.8	0.2	21.9	21.2	–0.3
Australia	849.4	816.8	–0.4	27.5	26.5	–0.4
Austria	875.1	772.1	–1.2	24.6	21.0	–1.6
Belgium		687.4			18.7	
Canada	641.2	622.6	–0.3	20.0	17.5	–1.3
Denmark	803.7	806.4	0.0	23.7	23.8	0.1
Finland	950.7	969.4	0.2	31.4	29.9	–0.5

TABLE A4 *(cont.)*

	Calories from livestock products			Share of total calories from livestock products		
	(kcal/person/day)		*(Annual % growth)*	*(Percentage)*		*(Annual % growth)*
	1995	**2005**	**1995–2005**	**1995**	**2005**	**1995–2005**
France	981.5	878.3	–1.1	27.8	24.5	–1.2
Germany	682.0	707.1	0.4	20.3	20.0	–0.1
Greece	714.4	748.4	0.5	20.3	20.2	–0.1
Iceland	920.6	1 072.5	1.5	29.6	32.6	1.0
Ireland	800.4	864.5	0.8	22.8	23.6	0.3
Israel	562.2	646.8	1.4	16.5	17.9	0.8
Italy	672.3	733.2	0.9	19.3	19.9	0.3
Japan	353.2	353.6	0.0	12.5	12.9	0.3
Malta	650.7	671.7	0.3	18.9	18.9	0.0
Netherlands	960.6	837.8	–1.4	30.3	26.1	–1.5
New Zealand	721.3	630.4	–1.3	23.1	20.0	–1.4
Norway	761.5	755.1	–0.1	23.7	21.8	–0.8
Portugal	610.4	720.0	1.7	17.4	19.9	1.4
Spain	725.5	738.8	0.2	22.2	22.5	0.2
Sweden	741.5	815.9	1.0	24.0	26.0	0.8
Switzerland	907.2	878.2	–0.3	27.9	25.9	–0.7
United Kingdom	801.4	850.5	0.6	25.1	24.9	–0.1
United States of America	867.9	900.0	0.4	24.5	23.4	–0.5
DEVELOPING COUNTRIES	**247.0**	**311.8**	**2.4**	**9.3**	**11.1**	**1.8**
EAST AND SOUTHEAST ASIA	**314.4**	**476.7**	**4.2**	**11.3**	**16.1**	**3.5**
Brunei Darussalam	522.0	561.0	0.7	18.1	17.1	–0.6
Cambodia	112.0	141.7	2.4	5.7	6.4	1.1
China, mainland	385.3	610.0	4.7	13.6	20.1	4.0
China, Hong Kong Special Administrative Region	737.1	854.9	1.5	22.9	26.8	1.6
China, Macao Special Administrative Region	652.7	752.2	1.4	23.7	26.6	1.1
China, Taiwan Province of	592.5	539.6	–0.9	19.4	18.3	–0.6
Democratic People's Republic of Korea	83.4	129.6	4.5	3.8	6.0	4.7
Indonesia	78.3	82.4	0.5	3.1	3.4	0.9
Lao People's Democratic Republic	109.6	132.8	1.9	5.3	5.7	0.6
Malaysia	452.6	390.6	–1.5	15.5	13.6	–1.2
Mongolia	702.8	624.7	–1.2	35.9	28.2	–2.4
Myanmar	79.6	181.7	8.6	4.0	7.4	6.5
Republic of Korea	236.5	288.6	2.0	7.9	9.5	1.8
Singapore	223.7	256.9	1.4	9.6	10.3	0.7
Thailand	231.5	234.6	0.1	9.8	9.3	–0.5
Timor-Leste	251.5	248.8	–0.1	10.7	11.5	0.7
Viet Nam	168.0	324.0	6.8	7.1	12.0	5.4

TABLE A4 *(cont.)*

	Calories from livestock products			Share of total calories from livestock products		
	(kcal/person/day)		*(Annual % growth)*	*(Percentage)*		*(Annual % growth)*
	1995	2005	1995–2005	1995	2005	1995–2005
LATIN AMERICA AND THE CARIBBEAN	**455.5**	**496.5**	**0.9**	**16.2**	**16.7**	**0.3**
Antigua and Barbuda	586.3	597.5	0.2	26.8	26.7	−0.1
Argentina	845.2	793.0	−0.6	26.7	26.1	−0.2
Bahamas	572.1	618.4	0.8	22.6	23.0	0.2
Barbados	547.3	556.5	0.2	19.9	18.8	−0.6
Belize	401.7	409.3	0.2	14.6	14.5	−0.1
Bolivia, Plurinational State of	294.9	330.3	1.1	14.0	15.3	0.9
Brazil	567.0	603.2	0.6	19.8	19.3	−0.2
Chile	513.7	552.4	0.7	18.9	18.4	−0.3
Colombia	391.3	414.5	0.6	15.2	15.4	0.2
Costa Rica	454.0	439.4	−0.3	16.2	15.7	−0.4
Cuba	281.3	277.8	−0.1	12.1	8.5	−3.5
Dominica	572.1	602.0	0.5	19.1	19.5	0.3
Dominican Republic	268.7	341.9	2.4	11.9	14.8	2.2
Ecuador	335.5	396.3	1.7	15.5	16.7	0.8
El Salvador	201.6	287.2	3.6	8.2	11.4	3.3
Grenada	441.9	542.6	2.1	18.0	23.1	2.5
Guatemala	163.3	178.3	0.9	7.1	7.8	0.9
Guyana	231.4	374.8	4.9	9.0	13.2	3.8
Haiti	85.4	108.9	2.5	4.9	5.9	1.9
Honduras	259.6	339.2	2.7	10.8	13.1	1.9
Jamaica	362.0	428.6	1.7	13.5	15.2	1.2
Mexico	399.0	530.6	2.9	12.9	16.3	2.4
Netherlands Antilles	650.8	695.4	0.7	24.2	22.6	−0.7
Nicaragua	144.7	246.3	5.5	7.4	10.3	3.4
Panama	345.6	387.8	1.2	15.0	16.1	0.7
Paraguay	492.8	323.9	−4.1	19.4	12.5	−4.3
Peru	182.2	216.1	1.7	8.3	8.5	0.2
Saint Kitts and Nevis	553.3	598.1	0.8	22.4	24.1	0.7
Saint Lucia	621.5	656.5	0.6	23.7	23.8	0.1
Saint Vincent and the Grenadines	397.7	464.0	1.6	17.6	16.8	−0.4
Suriname	246.8	277.5	1.2	9.5	10.2	0.7
Trinidad and Tobago	295.9	345.9	1.6	11.6	12.5	0.7
Uruguay	915.1	636.4	−3.6	32.9	21.7	−4.1
Venezuela, Bolivarian Republic of	306.1	320.9	0.5	12.4	13.2	0.6
NEAR EAST AND NORTH AFRICA	**227.9**	**255.5**	**1.1**	**7.6**	**8.5**	**1.1**
Afghanistan	210.3	184.8	−1.3	12.1	9.6	−2.3
Algeria	253.1	303.1	1.8	8.8	9.8	1.1
Cyprus	806.7	792.9	−0.2	24.5	24.7	0.1
Egypt	149.8	173.3	1.5	4.4	5.2	1.6

TABLE A4 *(cont.)*

	Calories from livestock products			Share of total calories from livestock products		
	(kcal/person/day)		*(Annual % growth)*	*(Percentage)*		*(Annual % growth)*
	1995	**2005**	**1995–2005**	**1995**	**2005**	**1995–2005**
Iran, Islamic Republic of	212.4	280.5	2.8	7.0	9.0	2.6
Iraq	60.3	110.3	6.2	2.9	5.0	5.6
Jordan	283.5	295.1	0.4	10.5	10.1	–0.4
Kuwait	618.9	561.4	–1.0	20.7	18.1	–1.4
Lebanon	329.2	455.2	3.3	11.0	14.3	2.7
Libyan Arab Jamahiriya	339.4	344.2	0.1	10.6	11.4	0.7
Morocco	142.3	163.5	1.4	4.8	5.2	0.6
Occupied Palestinian Territory		263.2			12.1	
Saudi Arabia	346.3	383.8	1.0	11.9	12.5	0.5
Syrian Arab Republic	296.0	345.6	1.6	10.2	11.4	1.2
Tunisia	240.5	291.7	1.9	7.6	8.9	1.6
Turkey	335.3	321.8	–0.4	9.7	9.6	–0.1
United Arab Emirates	743.2	491.0	–4.1	22.1	16.9	–2.7
Yemen	83.3	140.5	5.4	4.2	7.0	5.3
SOUTH ASIA	**136.9**	**138.7**	**0.1**	**5.8**	**5.9**	**0.2**
Bangladesh	38.3	43.0	1.2	2.0	1.9	–0.4
India	131.7	125.3	–0.5	5.5	5.3	–0.4
Maldives	142.0	316.4	8.3	5.9	11.9	7.3
Nepal	112.8	123.3	0.9	5.1	5.1	0.0
Pakistan	284.8	335.5	1.7	12.0	14.5	1.9
Sri Lanka	86.4	87.9	0.2	3.9	3.7	–0.3
SUB-SAHARAN AFRICA	**120.2**	**128.8**	**0.7**	**5.6**	**5.7**	**0.1**
Angola	97.2	125.1	2.6	5.8	6.6	1.2
Benin	56.3	63.1	1.1	2.7	2.7	0.2
Botswana	325.6	231.1	–3.4	14.8	10.4	–3.4
Burkina Faso	108.5	120.4	1.0	4.3	4.5	0.4
Burundi	34.6	25.9	–2.8	2.1	1.6	–2.6
Cameroon	87.9	87.9	0.0	4.4	3.9	–1.1
Cape Verde	385.4	382.4	–0.1	15.7	15.7	0.0
Central African Republic	151.9	181.6	1.8	8.5	9.4	1.1
Chad	102.5	98.0	–0.4	5.8	4.9	–1.6
Comoros	58.3	60.6	0.4	3.2	3.3	0.5
Congo	93.4	116.4	2.2	4.8	4.9	0.3
Côte d'Ivoire	72.1	70.7	–0.2	3.0	2.8	–0.7
Democratic Republic of the Congo	23.7	21.1	–1.2	1.3	1.4	0.7
Djibouti	190.8	204.8	0.7	10.2	9.2	–1.0
Eritrea	75.0	63.6	–1.6	4.8	4.0	–1.7
Ethiopia	66.6	80.6	1.9	4.4	4.4	0.0
Gabon	265.6	321.7	1.9	10.1	11.5	1.3
Gambia	60.5	79.8	2.8	2.8	3.7	2.8

TABLE A4 *(cont.)*

	Calories from livestock products			Share of total calories from livestock products		
	(kcal/person/day)		(Annual % growth)	(Percentage)		(Annual % growth)
	1995	2005	1995–2005	1995	2005	1995–2005
Ghana	42.4	50.2	1.7	1.8	1.8	0.2
Guinea	57.9	64.7	1.1	2.3	2.5	1.0
Guinea–Bissau	127.3	113.7	−1.1	5.7	5.5	−0.3
Kenya	200.3	216.6	0.8	9.7	10.4	0.8
Lesotho	116.8	120.1	0.3	4.8	4.9	0.3
Liberia	54.3	57.9	0.6	2.8	2.8	−0.1
Madagascar	176.6	129.2	−3.1	8.9	6.3	−3.3
Malawi	42.5	43.2	0.2	2.2	2.0	−0.7
Mali	201.5	218.4	0.8	8.4	8.5	0.1
Mauritania	397.2	427.3	0.7	14.5	15.2	0.5
Mauritius	328.1	354.8	0.8	11.5	12.4	0.7
Mozambique	40.4	37.5	−0.7	2.3	1.8	−2.3
Namibia	135.4	277.0	7.4	6.7	11.9	5.9
Niger	92.1	90.1	−0.2	4.8	4.2	−1.4
Nigeria	65.3	55.6	−1.6	2.6	2.1	−1.9
Rwanda	52.0	54.4	0.4	3.0	2.8	−0.7
Sao Tome and Principe	56.5	123.0	8.1	2.5	4.7	6.4
Senegal	91.0	111.2	2.0	4.4	5.1	1.5
Seychelles	273.8	242.2	−1.2	11.7	10.1	−1.4
Sierra Leone	35.5	30.1	−1.6	1.8	1.6	−1.5
Somalia	598.2	509.8	−1.6	38.0	28.8	−2.7
South Africa	308.2	351.7	1.3	11.2	12.1	0.7
Sudan	387.1	535.9	3.3	17.6	23.2	2.8
Swaziland	204.3	324.0	4.7	9.4	13.9	4.0
Togo	42.0	42.2	0.0	2.2	2.1	−0.5
Uganda	107.8	112.0	0.4	4.8	4.7	−0.2
United Republic of Tanzania	99.0	91.0	−0.8	5.1	4.5	−1.3
Zambia	77.3	82.3	0.6	3.9	4.3	1.1
Zimbabwe	75.0	106.7	3.6	3.9	5.2	2.7

TABLE A5
Per capita protein intake from livestock products, 1995–2005

	Protein from livestock products			Share of total protein from livestock products		
	(g/person/day)		(Annual % growth)	(Percentage)		(Annual % growth)
	1995	2005	1995–2005	1995	2005	1995–2005
WORLD	21.1	23.9	1.3	25.8	27.9	0.8
DEVELOPED COUNTRIES	47.1	49.8	0.6	47.1	47.8	0.2
FORMER CENTRALLY PLANNED ECONOMIES	35.2	37.5	0.7	40.0	41.0	0.2
Albania	40.2	45.2	1.2	43.1	46.3	0.7
Armenia	16.4	22.9	3.4	28.5	33.3	1.6
Azerbaijan	15.4	21.9	3.6	24.6	29.4	1.8
Belarus	48.0	42.4	–1.2	50.0	47.2	–0.6
Bosnia and Herzegovina	17.6	24.0	3.1	22.0	26.9	2.0
Bulgaria	35.9	34.7	–0.4	41.4	44.4	0.7
Croatia	27.7	32.0	1.5	42.9	43.3	0.1
Czech Republic	48.3	49.0	0.1	51.7	50.4	–0.2
Estonia	47.1	46.5	–0.1	47.9	51.5	0.7
Georgia	19.4	26.7	3.3	28.2	34.1	1.9
Hungary	43.4	42.0	–0.3	50.9	48.2	–0.6
Kazakhstan	37.8	44.7	1.7	37.4	45.7	2.0
Kyrgyzstan	30.7	33.4	0.8	38.2	33.7	–1.3
Latvia	44.1	47.0	0.6	46.7	51.1	0.9
Lithuania	32.6	45.9	3.5	36.9	41.3	1.1
Poland	42.4	43.8	0.3	43.3	44.0	0.2
Republic of Moldova	21.4	30.2	3.5	32.4	38.7	1.8
Romania	39.8	50.0	2.3	41.9	44.9	0.7
Russian Federation	35.3	38.6	0.9	39.9	40.9	0.2
Serbia and Montenegro	44.5	41.4	–0.7	51.6	55.0	0.7
Slovakia	33.7	32.2	–0.5	45.2	45.3	0.0
Slovenia	50.4	54.3	0.7	51.3	52.2	0.2
Tajikistan	10.6	12.4	1.5	20.3	20.3	0.0
The former Yugoslav Republic of Macedonia	23.5	26.2	1.1	33.5	35.9	0.7
Turkmenistan	24.7	31.9	2.6	33.6	36.5	0.8
Ukraine	32.3	32.5	0.1	37.9	37.0	–0.3
Uzbekistan	28.4	26.2	–0.8	35.4	34.7	–0.2
OTHER DEVELOPED COUNTRIES	53.1	55.4	0.4	50.6	50.9	0.1
Australia	58.9	60.8	0.3	55.3	56.7	0.3
Austria	63.2	60.2	–0.5	60.5	56.2	–0.7
Belgium		51.2			52.7	
Canada	49.4	50.0	0.1	50.4	48.0	–0.5
Denmark	59.1	61.9	0.5	55.6	54.8	–0.2

TABLE A5 *(cont.)*

	Protein from livestock products			Share of total protein from livestock products		
	(g/person/day)		*(Annual % growth)*	*(Percentage)*		*(Annual % growth)*
	1995	2005	1995–2005	1995	2005	1995–2005
Finland	51.8	53.2	0.3	53.3	50.2	–0.6
France	64.0	59.7	–0.7	55.5	52.2	–0.6
Germany	50.0	52.8	0.6	53.1	53.7	0.1
Greece	53.0	54.7	0.3	46.7	46.7	0.0
Iceland	52.2	62.8	1.9	43.6	49.7	1.3
Ireland	52.4	59.4	1.3	49.2	53.5	0.8
Israel	50.5	60.1	1.8	44.6	47.3	0.6
Italy	48.7	52.2	0.7	45.6	46.2	0.1
Japan	27.1	27.1	0.0	28.3	30.0	0.6
Malta	49.4	50.1	0.2	45.2	43.5	–0.4
Netherlands	67.1	59.5	–1.2	64.8	56.7	–1.3
New Zealand	52.0	44.2	–1.6	51.3	48.3	–0.6
Norway	45.5	46.8	0.3	45.4	44.9	–0.1
Portugal	43.0	51.0	1.7	39.7	44.4	1.1
Spain	52.2	53.9	0.3	48.8	50.4	0.3
Sweden	53.9	62.1	1.4	56.1	57.6	0.3
Switzerland	50.6	50.0	–0.1	55.5	55.2	–0.1
United Kingdom	46.6	52.3	1.1	50.1	50.5	0.1
United States of America	65.8	69.0	0.5	59.5	59.5	0.0
DEVELOPING COUNTRIES	**13.9**	**17.4**	**2.3**	**19.9**	**22.9**	**1.5**
EAST AND SOUTHEAST ASIA	**14.5**	**22.3**	**4.4**	**19.3**	**25.6**	**2.9**
Brunei Darussalam	37.3	37.8	0.1	41.9	40.7	–0.3
Cambodia	5.2	6.3	1.9	11.7	11.4	–0.2
China, mainland	16.9	27.7	5.0	21.4	29.7	3.3
China, Hong Kong Special Administrative Region	47.5	50.5	0.6	45.8	46.3	0.1
China, Macao Special Administrative Region	33.5	39.9	1.8	43.3	46.4	0.7
China, Taiwan Province of	32.1	32.2	0.0	35.6	36.7	0.3
Democratic People's Republic of Korea	3.8	7.4	6.9	6.2	12.4	7.2
Indonesia	4.9	5.4	1.0	8.9	10.1	1.4
Lao People's Democratic Republic	5.3	6.7	2.3	10.4	10.5	0.1
Malaysia	25.6	23.6	–0.8	33.9	30.5	–1.1
Mongolia	41.4	38.3	–0.8	57.3	53.2	–0.7
Myanmar	4.7	11.2	9.1	9.2	16.4	5.9
Republic of Korea	17.0	20.6	1.9	19.7	24.0	2.0
Singapore	11.7	13.2	1.2	21.5	22.5	0.4
Thailand	15.2	13.9	–0.8	26.4	24.2	–0.9
Timor-Leste	16.1	15.8	–0.2	26.1	28.8	1.0
Viet Nam	6.7	12.6	6.4	12.1	18.3	4.2

TABLE A5 *(cont.)*

	Protein from livestock products			Share of total protein from livestock products		
	(g/person/day)		*(Annual % growth)*	*(Percentage)*		*(Annual % growth)*
	1995	**2005**	**1995–2005**	**1995**	**2005**	**1995–2005**
LATIN AMERICA AND THE CARIBBEAN	**30.5**	**33.6**	**1.0**	**40.8**	**41.7**	**0.2**
Antigua and Barbuda	38.2	41.3	0.8	51.1	51.8	0.1
Argentina	57.7	55.0	–0.5	58.4	57.7	–0.1
Bahamas	38.6	41.8	0.8	49.7	51.9	0.4
Barbados	35.4	38.9	1.0	44.2	43.0	–0.3
Belize	22.7	26.0	1.4	35.8	34.5	–0.4
Bolivia, Plurinational State of	20.0	22.1	1.0	37.1	38.7	0.4
Brazil	37.0	39.7	0.7	48.6	46.7	–0.4
Chile	31.3	35.0	1.1	40.4	40.5	0.0
Colombia	25.6	27.3	0.6	41.8	44.3	0.6
Costa Rica	32.9	30.8	–0.7	45.2	43.6	–0.3
Cuba	17.6	18.3	0.4	33.2	23.6	–3.4
Dominica	37.8	39.3	0.4	42.9	43.4	0.1
Dominican Republic	19.0	23.4	2.1	38.7	43.1	1.1
Ecuador	20.6	25.1	2.0	41.1	44.0	0.7
El Salvador	14.4	19.6	3.1	23.5	29.6	2.3
Grenada	30.4	38.6	2.4	45.4	50.4	1.0
Guatemala	12.0	13.5	1.2	20.9	24.0	1.4
Guyana	14.9	27.9	6.5	21.6	34.0	4.6
Haiti	5.0	6.3	2.4	12.5	15.3	2.0
Honduras	18.1	24.0	2.9	30.6	36.3	1.7
Jamaica	23.6	30.7	2.7	32.8	39.8	1.9
Mexico	26.9	35.5	2.8	32.3	38.4	1.7
Netherlands Antilles	46.0	46.0	0.0	54.4	50.6	–0.7
Nicaragua	10.1	15.8	4.5	23.6	26.4	1.1
Panama	27.3	31.6	1.4	44.1	45.5	0.3
Paraguay	37.4	21.2	–5.5	48.5	32.7	–3.9
Peru	14.7	18.4	2.3	24.0	25.5	0.6
Saint Kitts and Nevis	33.3	41.8	2.3	48.1	52.0	0.8
Saint Lucia	40.3	43.4	0.7	48.0	47.9	0.0
Saint Vincent and the Grenadines	27.8	34.2	2.1	45.9	45.9	0.0
Suriname	18.3	19.8	0.8	30.5	33.2	0.8
Trinidad and Tobago	21.3	24.1	1.2	35.0	34.8	–0.1
Uruguay	54.9	40.2	–3.1	61.3	47.5	–2.5
Venezuela, Bolivarian Republic of	24.8	28.1	1.3	38.4	42.2	1.0
NEAR EAST AND NORTH AFRICA	**16.0**	**18.3**	**1.3**	**19.6**	**22.0**	**1.1**
Afghanistan	13.2	11.8	–1.1	26.5	22.2	–1.7
Algeria	17.6	20.3	1.4	22.4	23.4	0.5
Cyprus	51.9	51.7	0.0	50.0	52.5	0.5
Egypt	11.5	13.6	1.7	12.6	14.3	1.3

TABLE A5 *(cont.)*

	Protein from livestock products			Share of total protein from livestock products		
	(g/person/day)		(Annual % growth)	(Percentage)		(Annual % growth)
	1995	2005	1995–2005	1995	2005	1995–2005
Iran, Islamic Republic of	15.3	20.7	3.0	19.4	23.7	2.0
Iraq	4.1	7.5	6.3	9.3	15.2	5.0
Jordan	21.1	21.4	0.1	29.1	29.0	0.0
Kuwait	43.4	43.5	0.0	46.4	47.1	0.2
Lebanon	22.1	32.5	3.9	28.9	37.9	2.7
Libyan Arab Jamahiriya	23.7	23.7	0.0	29.3	32.0	0.9
Morocco	11.8	13.6	1.5	15.2	15.6	0.3
Occupied Palestinian Territory		18.4			30.6	
Saudi Arabia	25.7	29.7	1.4	32.1	34.6	0.8
Syrian Arab Republic	17.4	20.3	1.5	24.3	25.6	0.5
Tunisia	16.5	20.2	2.1	19.1	22.1	1.5
Turkey	22.7	22.4	–0.2	22.3	23.3	0.4
United Arab Emirates	51.0	37.2	–3.1	46.2	39.2	–1.6
Yemen	6.2	10.3	5.2	11.5	19.6	5.5
SOUTH ASIA	**8.6**	**9.4**	**0.9**	**14.9**	**17.0**	**1.3**
Bangladesh	2.6	2.9	1.1	6.3	6.0	–0.4
India	8.1	8.7	0.7	13.9	15.9	1.3
Maldives	10.1	18.0	6.0	11.6	16.7	3.7
Nepal	7.2	7.7	0.7	12.8	12.7	–0.1
Pakistan	19.1	21.6	1.2	31.7	36.7	1.5
Sri Lanka	5.5	6.0	0.9	10.6	11.4	0.8
SUB-SAHARAN AFRICA	**8.1**	**8.6**	**0.6**	**14.7**	**14.6**	**–0.1**
Angola	6.0	8.5	3.5	17.2	20.0	1.5
Benin	4.6	5.6	1.9	9.3	10.3	1.1
Botswana	24.0	19.8	–1.9	34.5	30.1	–1.3
Burkina Faso	7.7	8.2	0.7	9.9	10.3	0.3
Burundi	2.3	1.7	–2.9	4.6	4.0	–1.4
Cameroon	6.9	6.9	0.1	14.2	12.0	–1.6
Cape Verde	19.6	20.8	0.6	32.1	32.4	0.1
Central African Republic	11.7	13.9	1.7	28.4	30.9	0.8
Chad	7.6	7.2	–0.5	14.5	11.8	–2.0
Comoros	4.4	5.1	1.5	10.1	11.7	1.4
Congo	8.2	10.6	2.5	20.5	21.1	0.3
Côte d'Ivoire	7.0	7.0	0.0	14.5	13.9	–0.4
Democratic Republic of the Congo	2.4	2.2	–1.2	8.9	9.3	0.5
Djibouti	11.5	12.7	1.0	28.5	25.6	–1.1
Eritrea	5.0	4.2	–1.8	10.0	9.0	–1.0
Ethiopia	4.9	5.6	1.5	11.2	10.7	–0.4
Gabon	25.9	29.3	1.2	33.2	34.1	0.2

TABLE A5 *(cont.)*

	Protein from livestock products			Share of total protein from livestock products		
	(g/person/day)		(Annual % growth)	(Percentage)		(Annual % growth)
	1995	2005	1995–2005	1995	2005	1995–2005
Gambia	3.9	5.6	3.6	8.7	11.3	2.7
Ghana	4.5	5.2	1.4	9.4	9.2	−0.3
Guinea	3.9	4.6	1.8	7.1	8.5	1.8
Guinea-Bissau	6.4	5.8	−1.0	14.5	14.4	−0.1
Kenya	12.0	13.0	0.9	20.0	22.6	1.2
Lesotho	8.8	8.5	−0.3	13.0	12.4	−0.4
Liberia	4.6	4.5	−0.2	12.3	13.2	0.7
Madagascar	10.4	7.9	−2.8	22.3	16.9	−2.7
Malawi	2.4	2.4	0.1	4.8	4.5	−0.6
Mali	14.2	15.1	0.6	19.9	20.7	0.4
Mauritania	24.8	28.7	1.5	31.5	34.5	0.9
Mauritius	22.6	27.6	2.0	31.3	34.4	0.9
Mozambique	2.7	2.5	−0.6	7.5	6.2	−1.9
Namibia	9.1	19.0	7.6	17.0	29.5	5.7
Niger	7.6	7.2	−0.5	14.6	11.6	−2.3
Nigeria	5.1	4.3	−1.7	9.1	7.2	−2.3
Rwanda	3.5	3.7	0.6	8.3	8.3	0.0
Sao Tome and Principe	4.5	8.7	6.7	8.9	15.0	5.3
Senegal	7.1	7.7	0.9	12.3	13.3	0.7
Seychelles	18.6	20.2	0.9	25.1	26.4	0.5
Sierra Leone	2.9	2.5	−1.4	6.9	5.2	−2.8
Somalia	32.7	27.8	−1.6	62.7	51.7	−1.9
South Africa	20.5	24.2	1.6	28.5	31.1	0.9
Sudan	22.4	29.7	2.9	32.1	39.9	2.2
Swaziland	14.5	21.6	4.0	25.7	33.5	2.7
Togo	3.2	3.0	−0.4	6.9	6.5	−0.7
Uganda	6.0	5.9	−0.2	11.9	10.4	−1.4
United Republic of Tanzania	6.8	6.1	−1.1	14.0	12.6	−1.0
Zambia	6.5	7.0	0.7	12.7	14.5	1.4
Zimbabwe	5.6	8.3	4.0	12.5	16.7	2.9

TABLE A6
Trade in livestock products, 1995–2006[1]

	Livestock imports			Livestock exports		
	(Million US$)		(Annual % growth)	(Million US$)		(Annual % growth)
	1995	2006	1995–2006	1995	2006	1995–2006
WORLD	73 972.5	117 599.4	4.3	74 264.9	120 258.7	4.5
DEVELOPED COUNTRIES	58 780.6	90 760.6	4.0	65 181.8	98 939.1	3.9
FORMER CENTRALLY PLANNED ECONOMIES	4 983.0	10 781.6	7.3	3 292.6	8 044.7	8.5
Albania	40.4	59.3	3.6	0.3	0.9	10.1
Armenia	58.0	38.7	–3.6	0.1	4.3	36.6
Azerbaijan	79.7	40.2	–6.0	0.0	1.9	53.8
Belarus	13.8	166.4	25.4	122.7	995.9	21.0
Bosnia and Herzegovina	102.1	143.7	3.2	0.0	27.7	
Bulgaria	50.5	203.5	13.5	86.8	148.7	5.0
Croatia	178.0	242.9	2.9	65.8	83.7	2.2
Czech Republic	96.0	901.7	22.6	273.7	738.9	9.4
Estonia	47.8	89.7	5.9	104.5	146.1	3.1
Georgia	34.8	86.5	8.6	18.0	1.5	–20.2
Hungary	96.9	499.8	16.1	681.7	824.9	1.7
Kazakhstan	26.4	307.9	25.0	87.4	14.2	–15.3
Kyrgyzstan	8.3	21.5	9.0	7.7	20.4	9.3
Latvia	8.2	173.0	32.0	20.8	161.4	20.5
Lithuania	6.8	204.5	36.3	198.5	496.3	8.7
Poland	174.4	701.6	13.5	562.1	2 954.8	16.3
Republic of Moldova	3.0	35.9	25.4	63.7	13.3	–13.3
Romania	100.6	683.3	19.0	76.1	85.4	1.1
Russian Federation	3 185.5	5 038.4	4.3	82.0	235.0	10.0
Serbia		25.7			108.1	
Serbia and Montenegro	41.3			0.0		
Slovakia	44.2	451.4	23.5	56.5	361.4	18.4
Slovenia	79.4	243.5	10.7	114.1	222.3	6.3
Tajikistan	45.4	27.7	–4.4	0.0	0.0	
The former Yugoslav Republic of Macedonia	76.7	110.0	3.3	11.7	25.0	7.1
Turkmenistan	39.5	5.8	–15.9			
Ukraine	78.7	257.6	11.4	657.4	372.4	–5.0
Uzbekistan	266.6	21.4	–20.5	0.9	0.0	–30.1
OTHER DEVELOPED COUNTRIES	53 784.9	79 958.2	3.7	61 889.2	90 894.4	3.6
Australia	153.9	589.7	13.0	3 610.4	6 760.4	5.9
Austria	553.1	1 385.9	8.7	562.7	2 103.8	12.7
Belgium		4 512.9			6 049.2	
Belgium-Luxembourg	3 807.0			5 226.3		

TABLE A6 *(cont.)*

	Livestock imports			Livestock exports		
	(Million US$)		(Annual % growth)	(Million US$)		(Annual % growth)
	1995	**2006**	**1995–2006**	**1995**	**2006**	**1995–2006**
Canada	998.4	1 913.4	6.1	1 381.7	3 680.7	9.3
Denmark	591.0	1 753.5	10.4	5 340.7	6 895.2	2.3
Finland	152.6	431.3	9.9	250.4	583.3	8.0
France	6 021.5	7 030.7	1.4	9 206.0	9 287.6	0.1
Germany	8 478.4	10 786.7	2.2	6 518.4	12 478.1	6.1
Greece	1 480.9	2 166.8	3.5	155.5	290.7	5.9
Iceland	0.8	9.5	25.2	5.4	7.7	3.3
Ireland	411.7	1 206.9	10.3	3 439.7	4 335.2	2.1
Israel	116.8	249.7	7.2	44.5	38.6	−1.3
Italy	6 136.5	8 890.0	3.4	1 638.2	3 580.8	7.4
Japan	9 814.4	9 048.5	−0.7	20.8	25.3	1.8
Luxembourg		451.4			302.5	
Malta	60.3	105.4	5.2	0.1	0.3	17.6
Netherlands	4 042.0	5 541.6	2.9	9 591.8	11 447.5	1.6
New Zealand	43.8	161.6	12.6	3 363.9	7 009.1	6.9
Norway	60.5	151.3	8.7	86.9	126.0	3.4
Portugal	536.4	1 340.9	8.7	158.1	322.8	6.7
Spain	1 652.9	3 091.8	5.9	1 013.8	3 627.8	12.3
Sweden	425.6	1 483.3	12.0	235.6	499.6	7.1
Switzerland	718.5	906.7	2.1	507.8	505.2	0.0
United Kingdom	4 619.0	10 164.7	7.4	3 076.8	2 585.4	−1.6
United States of America	2 909.0	6 584.0	7.7	6 454.0	8 351.6	2.4
DEVELOPING COUNTRIES	**15 191.8**	**26 838.7**	**5.3**	**9 083.1**	**21 319.6**	**8.1**
EAST AND SOUTHEAST ASIA	**5 726.6**	**9 561.1**	**4.8**	**4 634.6**	**4 517.5**	**−0.2**
Brunei Darussalam	57.8	35.5	−4.3	5.5	0.5	−19.8
Cambodia	15.2	24.3	4.3	0.0	0.0	
China, mainland	151.3	1 109.8	19.9	1 405.0	2 191.3	4.1
China, Hong Kong Special Administrative Region	1 683.6	1 813.9	0.7	574.8	412.9	−3.0
China, Macao Special Administrative Region	26.2	58.8	7.6	0.8	0.2	−11.9
China, Taiwan Province of	563.4	746.8	2.6	1 619.4	38.8	−28.8
Democratic People's Republic of Korea	4.7	4.9	0.5	0.0	0.0	
Indonesia	245.0	632.2	9.0	35.3	96.7	9.6
Lao People's Democratic Republic	10.6	8.1	−2.5	0.0	0.0	
Malaysia	514.3	709.1	3.0	123.5	202.9	4.6
Mongolia	2.5	7.1	9.9	2.9	15.6	16.5
Myanmar	41.9	38.1	−0.8	0.0	0.0	12.8
Philippines	512.3	696.1	2.8	1.1	59.0	43.5

TABLE A6 *(cont.)*

	Livestock imports			Livestock exports		
	(Million US$)		(Annual % growth)	(Million US$)		(Annual % growth)
	1995	2006	1995–2006	1995	2006	1995–2006
Republic of Korea	870.9	1 998.1	7.8	110.7	47.8	–7.3
Singapore	601.8	1 019.8	4.9	137.4	277.4	6.6
Thailand	338.4	359.1	0.5	589.6	1 145.3	6.2
Timor-Leste	8.5	0.8	–19.2			
Viet Nam	78.3	298.5	12.9	28.5	29.1	0.2
LATIN AMERICA AND THE CARIBBEAN	3 372.9	6 456.3	6.1	3 537.0	14 219.5	13.5
Antigua and Barbuda	11.7	15.9	2.8	0.3	0.1	–11.7
Argentina	176.4	68.0	–8.3	1 440.3	2 309.8	4.4
Bahamas	60.0	132.7	7.5	1.1	0.2	–15.2
Barbados	29.0	42.3	3.5	2.2	4.2	5.8
Belize	13.8	15.9	1.3	0.3	0.0	–20.1
Bolivia, Plurinational State of	13.9	13.5	–0.2	4.9	14.5	10.3
Brazil	857.8	261.4	–10.2	1 293.1	8 572.7	18.8
Chile	180.9	414.2	7.8	61.5	663.9	24.1
Colombia	58.1	39.5	–3.4	21.2	133.7	18.2
Costa Rica	10.5	39.3	12.8	56.9	86.4	3.9
Cuba	136.9	383.0	9.8	0.0	0.8	
Dominica	8.6	9.4	0.8	0.0	0.0	15.3
Dominican Republic	79.5	42.0	–5.6	5.7	0.4	–22.3
Ecuador	10.6	24.9	8.1	5.9	1.3	–13.0
El Salvador	73.2	196.5	9.4	5.1	13.1	9.0
Grenada	15.9	14.6	–0.8	0.0	0.0	7.7
Guatemala	44.4	166.9	12.8	8.9	25.2	9.9
Guyana	23.0	28.9	2.1	0.0	0.1	
Haiti	38.3	78.4	6.7	0.0	0.3	
Honduras	26.0	91.3	12.1	14.3	14.3	0.0
Jamaica	83.1	105.4	2.2	6.4	6.0	–0.6
Mexico	855.9	3 403.1	13.4	75.1	462.3	18.0
Netherlands Antilles	60.9	43.4	–3.0	1.4	0.2	–18.1
Nicaragua	20.5	30.8	3.8	62.5	88.5	3.2
Panama	15.3	56.8	12.6	13.5	33.3	8.5
Paraguay	26.9	12.9	–6.5	42.9	418.7	23.0
Peru	134.0	96.7	–2.9	2.0	61.5	36.7
Saint Kitts and Nevis	7.7	6.2	–1.9	0.0	0.0	
Saint Lucia	26.9	31.5	1.4	0.0	0.0	
Saint Vincent and the Grenadines	9.9	17.5	5.3	0.0	0.0	
Suriname	11.8	20.7	5.3	0.0	0.0	
Trinidad and Tobago	60.2	95.5	4.3	7.5	5.8	–2.3
Uruguay	9.9	28.5	10.1	375.5	1 300.9	12.0
Venezuela, Bolivarian Republic of	181.3	428.4	8.1	28.4	1.3	–24.3

TABLE A6 *(cont.)*

	Livestock imports			Livestock exports		
	(Million US$)		(Annual % growth)	(Million US$)		(Annual % growth)
	1995	2006	1995–2006	1995	2006	1995–2006
NEAR EAST AND NORTH AFRICA	**4 206.6**	**7 600.9**	**5.5**	**300.5**	**1 321.0**	**14.4**
Afghanistan	1.7	23.9	27.4			
Algeria	541.4	873.2	4.4	1.8	4.2	8.1
Bahrain	82.5	137.8	4.8	0.2	6.6	40.3
Cyprus	44.0	103.6	8.1	15.5	42.9	9.7
Egypt	352.4	558.3	4.3	6.4	36.2	17.0
Iran, Islamic Republic of	210.1	203.6	−0.3	0.4	99.6	64.1
Iraq	38.5	245.7	18.4			
Jordan	144.3	241.4	4.8	17.5	86.9	15.7
Kuwait	278.4	395.0	3.2	3.8	6.9	5.6
Lebanon	223.2	278.5	2.0	0.4	11.7	34.7
Libyan Arab Jamahiriya	117.8	223.8	6.0	0.0	0.2	
Morocco	117.0	141.7	1.8	3.4	99.8	35.8
Occupied Palestinian Territory		55.0			2.6	
Oman	184.1	325.6	5.3	15.9	86.7	16.7
Qatar	87.9	238.8	9.5	6.4	4.3	−3.5
Saudi Arabia	978.1	1 971.0	6.6	117.0	548.2	15.1
Syrian Arab Republic	36.7	106.6	10.2	5.8	114.4	31.1
Tunisia	69.7	52.3	−2.6	8.7	7.3	−1.5
Turkey	111.9	154.7	3.0	38.3	44.0	1.3
United Arab Emirates	474.5	1 037.4	7.4	56.1	107.8	6.1
Yemen	112.5	233.0	6.8	2.9	10.6	12.6
SOUTH ASIA	**186.0**	**428.4**	**7.9**	**209.5**	**943.1**	**14.7**
Bangladesh	46.8	98.4	7.0	0.1	0.2	1.0
India	19.5	25.2	2.4	205.9	895.0	14.3
Maldives	14.2	34.0	8.3			
Nepal	0.9	6.4	19.6	0.3	2.0	18.7
Pakistan	18.4	54.0	10.3	1.3	41.9	37.4
Sri Lanka	86.2	210.3	8.5	1.8	4.0	7.6
SUB-SAHARAN AFRICA	**1 329.4**	**2 299.0**	**5.1**	**395.4**	**306.9**	**−2.3**
Angola	88.6	234.9	9.3	0.0	0.1	
Benin	21.6	62.8	10.2	0.0	0.6	40.7
Botswana	49.4	24.1	−6.3	83.5	37.7	−7.0
Burkina Faso	28.1	25.0	−1.1	0.1	0.0	−2.2
Burundi	2.9	3.9	2.8	0.0	0.0	
Cameroon	13.4	39.5	10.3	0.4	0.4	−1.5
Cape Verde	13.2	37.0	9.8	0.0	0.2	
Central African Republic	1.8	0.9	−5.8	0.0	0.0	
Chad	3.5	6.6	5.8	0.5	0.8	5.7

TABLE A6 *(cont.)*

	Livestock imports			Livestock exports		
	(Million US$)		(Annual % growth)	(Million US$)		(Annual % growth)
	1995	2006	1995–2006	1995	2006	1995–2006
Comoros	5.8	9.7	4.7	0.0	0.0	
Congo	42.5	67.0	4.2	0.2	0.2	−1.5
Côte d'Ivoire	51.5	81.5	4.3	0.4	17.7	42.7
Democratic Republic of the Congo	53.8	102.6	6.0	0.0	0.0	
Djibouti	15.0	33.9	7.7	0.0	0.5	
Eritrea	2.9	0.2	−21.0	0.1	0.1	0.0
Ethiopia	2.0	8.4	14.0	1.2	16.7	26.6
Gabon	51.5	85.4	4.7	0.0	0.0	18.4
Gambia	7.4	21.4	10.2	0.0	0.0	
Ghana	30.9	124.6	13.5	0.0	4.8	
Guinea	18.0	21.7	1.7	0.0	0.0	
Guinea-Bissau	2.1	3.0	3.2	0.0	0.0	
Kenya	2.4	5.7	8.4	4.8	15.5	11.2
Lesotho	15.4	15.4	0.0	0.0	0.0	
Liberia	7.0	15.0	7.1	0.0	0.1	
Madagascar	5.2	9.1	5.3	8.7	0.4	−24.4
Malawi	4.3	8.6	6.4	0.1	0.0	−11.2
Mali	15.6	30.2	6.2	0.0	0.1	
Mauritania	16.9	45.7	9.5	0.0	0.0	
Mauritius	78.1	94.0	1.7	14.6	1.3	−19.8
Mozambique	23.6	29.5	2.1	0.0	0.3	
Namibia	8.4	9.1	0.8	107.5	42.3	−8.1
Niger	13.8	25.1	5.6	1.1	0.1	−23.9
Nigeria	277.2	323.0	1.4	0.1	0.0	−19.2
Rwanda	4.0	1.1	−11.2	0.0	0.3	
Sao Tome and Principe	1.7	3.4	6.4	0.0	0.0	
Senegal	37.3	118.4	11.1	0.1	12.2	61.4
Seychelles	9.0	24.4	9.5	0.0	0.2	45.5
Sierra Leone	5.6	9.7	5.1	0.0	0.0	
Somalia	4.0	1.7	−7.7	0.0	0.1	
South Africa	241.6	358.4	3.7	109.3	109.2	0.0
Sudan	10.5	85.4	21.0	18.3	9.2	−6.0
Swaziland	21.9	45.8	6.9	4.2	3.4	−1.9
Togo	9.1	26.1	10.0	0.5	0.3	−5.4
Uganda	3.8	3.9	0.2	0.6	0.8	2.8
United Republic of Tanzania	3.2	5.1	4.3	0.0	3.4	
Zambia	2.2	8.3	12.6	0.3	1.9	20.0
Zimbabwe	1.9	3.1	4.6	38.9	26.1	−3.5

[1] Livestock products include meat, dairy and eggs.

Notes: Data values rounded to nearest whole number. Totals for developing countries and the world include a few countries not included in the regional aggregates.

- References

- Special chapters of
  The State of Food and Agriculture

References

Abe, K., Yamamoto, S. & Shinagawa, K. 2002. Economic impact of an *Escherichia coli* O157:H7 outbreak in Japan. *Journal of Food Protection,* 65(1): 66–72.

AHA (Animal Health Australia). 2009. *Corporate information* (available at www. animalhealthaustralia.com.au/corporate/ corporate_home.cfm).

Ahuja, V., ed. 2004. *Livestock and livelihoods: challenges and opportunities for Asia in the emerging market environment.* Anand, India, National Dairy Development Board, and Rome, FAO, Pro-Poor Livestock Policy Facility (South Asia Hub).

Ahuja, V. & Sen, A. 2008. Scope and space for small-scale poultry production in developing countries. *In: Poultry in the 21st century: avian influenza and beyond. Proceedings of the International Poultry Conference, Bangkok, November 2007,* pp. 61–62. FAO Animal Production and Health Proceedings No. 9. Rome, FAO.

Ahuja, V., Dhawan, M., Punjabi, M. & Maarse, L. 2008. *Poultry based livelihoods of the rural poor: case of Kuroiler in West Bengal.* Study Report. Doc 012. South Asia Pro-Poor Livestock Policy Programme (available at sapplpp.org/ informationhub/files/doc012-PoultryBasedLRP-Kuroiler-updated09Mar31.pdf).

Alders, R.G., Azhar, M., Brum, E., Lubis, A.S., McGrane, J., Morgan, I., Roeder, P. & Sawitri Siregar, E. In press. Participatory disease surveillance and response in Indonesia: strengthening veterinary services and empowering communities to prevent and control highly pathogenic avian influenza. *Avian Diseases.*

Alston, J.M., Marra, M.C., Pardey, P.G. & Wyatt, T.J. 2000. Research returns redux: a meta-analysis of the returns to agricultural R&D. *Australian Journal of Agricultural and Resource Economics,* 44(2): 185–215.

Anriquez, G. Forthcoming. *Rural feminization and the gender burden: a cross-country examination.* Rome, FAO.

Archer, D.L. & Kvenberg, J.E. 1985. Incidence and cost of foodborne diarrheal disease in the United States. *Journal of Food Protection,* 48(10): 882–894.

Ashdown, S. 1992. Adat and the buffalo in South Sulawesi. *In* P.W. Daniels, S. Holden, E. Lewin & S. Dadi, eds. *Livestock services for smallholders: a critical evaluation. Proceedings of a seminar held in Yogyakarta, Indonesia, 15–21 November 1992,* pp. 240–242. Indonesia, Indonesian International Animal Science Research and Development Foundation.

Ayele, Z. & Peacock, C. 2003. Improving access to and consumption of animal source foods in rural households: the experiences of a women-focused goat development program in the highlands of Ethiopia. *Journal of Nutrition,* 133: 3981S–3986S.

Barker, T., Bashmakov, I., Bernstein, L., Bogner, J.E., Bosch, P.R., Dave, R., Davidson, O.R., Fisher, B.S., Gupta, S., Halsnæs, K., Heij, G.J., Kahn Ribeiro, S., Kobayashi, S., Levine, M.D., Martino, D., Masera, L.O., Metz, B., Meyer, L.A., Nabuurs, G.-J., Najam, A., Nakicenovic, N., Rogner, H.-H., Roy, J., Sathaye, J., Schock, R., Shukla, P., Sims, R. E. H., Smith, P.D., Tirpak, A., Urge-Vorsatz, D. & Zhou, D. 2007: Technical Summary. *In* B. Metz, O.R. Davidson, P.R. Bosch, R. Dave & L.A. Meyer, eds. *Climate Change 2007: Mitigation. Contribution of Working Group III to the Fourth Assessment. Report of the Intergovernmental Panel on Climate Change.* Cambridge, UK and New York, USA, Cambridge University Press.

Bingsheng, K. & Yijun, H. 2008. Poultry sector in China: structural changes during the past decade and future trends. *In: Poultry in the 21st century: avian influenza and beyond. Proceedings of the International Poultry Conference, Bangkok, November 2007,* pp. 25–26. FAO Animal Production and Health Proceedings No. 9. Rome, FAO.

Bio-Era. 2005. *Economic risks associated with an influenza pandemic.* Prepared testimony of James Newcomb, Managing Director for Research, Bio Economic Research Associates, before the United States Senate Committee on Foreign Relations, November 9, 2005.

Birner, R. 1999. *The role of livestock in agricultural development. Theoretical approaches and their application in the case of Sri Lanka.* Aldershot, UK, Ashgate.

Brown, C.G. & Waldron, S.A. 2003. Case study: beef industry in China. *In* L.J. Unnevehr, ed. *Food safety in food security and food trade.*

Brief 13 of 17. 2020 Focus 10. Washington, DC, International Food Policy Research Institute (available at www.ifpri.org/2020/focus/focus10/focus10.pdf).

Bruinsma, J., ed. 2003. *World agriculture: towards 2015/2030. An FAO perspective*. London, Earthscan Publications.

CAST (Council for Agricultural Science and Technology). 2001. *Role of animal agriculture in the human food supply*. Ames, USA.

Clarke, D. & McKenzie, T. 2007. *Legislative interventions to prevent and decrease obesity in Pacific Island countries*. Report to WHO. WPRO (available at www.wpro.who.int/internet/resources.ashx/NUT/Final+obesity+report.pdf).

Costales, A. & Catelo, M.A.O. 2008. *Contract farming as an institution for integrating rural smallholders in markets for livestock products in developing countries: (I) Framework and applications*. PPLPI Research Report No. 08-12 (available at www.fao.org/ag/againfo/programmes/en/pplpi/docarc/rep-0812_contractfarming.pdf).

Costales, A.C., Pica-Ciamarra, U. & Otte, J. 2007. *Livestock in a changing landscape: Social consequences for mixed crop–livestock production systems in developing countries*. PPLPI Research Report No. 07-05 (available at www.fao.org/ag/againfo/programmes/en/pplpi/docarc/rep-0705_lstklandscape.pdf).

Cunningham, E.P., ed. 2003. *After BSE – a future for the European livestock sector*. EAAP Publication No. 108. Wageningen, The Netherlands, Academic Publishers.

Dalgaard, T., Børgesen, C.D., Hansen, J.F., Hutchings, N.J., Jørgensen, U. & Kyllingsbæk, A. 2004. How to halve N-losses, improve N-efficiencies and maintain yields? The Danish case. *In* Z. Zhu, K. Minami & G. Xing, eds. *3rd International Nitrogen Conference. Contributed Papers*, pp. 291–296. Monmouth Junction, USA, Science Press.

Datt, G. & Ravallion, M. 1998. *Farm productivity and rural poverty in India*. FCND Discussion Papers No. 42. Washington, DC, International Food Policy Research Institute.

de Castro, J.J. 1997. Sustainable tick and tickborne disease control in livestock improvement in developing countries. *Veterinary Parasitology*, 71(2–3): 77–97.

de Wit, J., van de Meer, H.G. & Nell, A.J. 1997. Animal manure: asset or liability? *World Animal Review*, 88 (available at www.fao.org/ag/AGA/AGAP/FRG/FEEDback/War/W5256t/W5256t05.htm#TopOfPage).

Delgado, C., Narrod, C. & Tiongco, M. 2008. *Determinants and implications of the growing scale of livestock farms in four fast-growing developing countries*. Research Report No. 157. Washington, DC, International Food Policy Research Institute.

Delgado, C., Rosegrant, M., Steinfeld, H., Ehui, S. & Courbois, C. 1999. *Livestock to 2020. The next food revolution*. Food, Agriculture and the Environment Discussion Paper No. 28. Washington, DC, International Food Policy Research Institute, Rome, FAO, and Nairobi, International Livestock Research Intitute.

Demment, M.W., Young, M.M. & Sensenig, R.L. 2003. Providing micronutrients through food-based solutions: a key to human and national development. *Journal of Nutrition*, 133: 3879S–3885S.

Dolberg, F. 2004. Review of household poultry production as a tool in poverty reduction with focus on Bangladesh and India. *In* V. Ahuja, ed. *Livestock and livelihoods: challenges and opportunities for Asia in the emerging market environment*. India, National Dairy Development Board, and Rome, FAO, Pro-Poor Livestock Policy Facility (South Asia Hub).

Dourmad, J., Rigolot, C., & van der Werf, H. 2008. Emission of greenhouse gas: developing management and animal farming systems to assist mitigation. *In* P. Rowlinson, M. Steele & A. Nefzaoui, eds. *Livestock and global change*. Proceedings of an international conference, Hammamet, Tunisia, 17–20 May 2008. Cambridge, UK, Cambridge University Press.

EEA (European Environment Agency). 2003. *Europe's environment: the third assessment*. Copenhagen.

Fafchamps, M. & Gavian, S. 1997. The determinants of livestock prices in Niger. *Journal of African Economies*, 6(2): 255–295.

Fang, C. 2009. *How China stabilized grain prices during global price crisis: lessons learned*. Paper presented for the workshop Rice Policies in Asia, Chiang Mai, Thailand, 10–12 February 2009.

FAO. 2004a. *The State of Food Insecurity in the World 2004*. Rome.

FAO. 2004b. *Building on gender, agrobiodiversity and local knowledge, a training manual* (available at ftp.fao.org/docrep/fao/009/y5956e/y5956e00.pdf).

FAO. 2005. The *dynamics of sanitary and technical requirements: assisting the poor to cope*. Expert Consultation, 22–24 June 2004. FAO Animal

Production and Health Proceedings No. 4. Rome.

FAO. 2006. *Livestock Report 2006*. Rome.

FAO. 2007a. *The State of Food and Agriculture 2007: paying farmers for environmental services*. FAO Agriculture Series No. 38. Rome.

FAO. 2007b. *Global plan of action for animal genetic resources and the Interlaken Declaration*. Adopted by the International Technical Conference on Animal Genetic Resources for Food and Agriculture, Interlaken, Switzerland, 3–7 September 2007. Rome.

FAO. 2007c. *The State of the World's Animal Genetic Resources for Food and Agriculture*, by B. Rischkowsky & D. Pilling, eds. Rome.

FAO. 2008a. *Capacity building to implement good animal welfare practices*. Report of the FAO Expert Meeting, 30 September–3 October 2008. Rome.

FAO. 2008b. *The State of Food and Agriculture 2008*. Rome.

FAO. 2008c. *The State of Food Insecurity in the World 2008*. Rome.

FAO. 2009a. Rural Income Generating Activities database (available at www.fao.org/es/ESA/riga/english/index_en.htm).

FAO. 2009b. FAOSTAT statistical database. Rome (available at faostat.fao.org).

FAO. 2009c. *The State of Food Insecurity in the World 2009*. Rome.

FAO. 2009d. *Crop Prospects and Food Situation*. No. 2, April 2009. Rome.

FAO. 2009e. *Policy responses to higher food prices*. Committee on Commodity Problems, Sixty-seventh Session, CCP 09/8. Rome.

FAO. 2009f. *Country responses to the food security crisis: nature and preliminary implications of the policies pursued*, by M. Demeke, G. Pangrazio & M. Maetz. FAO Initiative on Soaring Food Prices. Rome.

FAO, IIED (International Institute for Environment and Development) & IFAD (International Fund for Agricultural Development). 2009. *Land grab or development opportunity? Agricultural investment and international land deals in Africa*, by L. Cotula, S. Vermeulen, R. Leonard & J. Keeley. Rome, FAO and IFAD. London, IIED (available at www.fao.org/docrep/011/ak241e/ak241e00.htm).

FAO, World Bank & OIE (World Organisation for Animal Health). 2008. *Biosecurity for highly pathogenic avian influenza: issues and options*. FAO Animal Production and Health Paper No. 165. Rome, FAO.

FAO, OIE (World Organisation for Animal Health), WHO (World Health Organization), UN System Influenza Coordination, UNICEF (United Nations Children's Fund) and The World Bank. 2008. *Contributing to One World, One Health. A strategic framework for reducing risks of infectious diseases at the animal–human–ecosystems interface* (available at ftp.fao.org/docrep/fao/011/aj137e/aj137e00.pdf).

Frenzen, P.D., Drake, A. & Angulo, F.J. 2005. Economic cost of illness due to *Escherichia coli* O157 infections in the United States. *Journal of Food Protection*, 68(12): 2623–2630.

Frohberg, K. 2009. *Trends in vertical integration and vertically coordinated processing in livestock supply chains*. SOFA 2009 background paper. Unpublished. Rome, FAO.

Gallup, J., Radelet, S. & Warner, A. 1997. *Economic growth and the income of the poor*. CAER II Discussion Paper No. 36. Boston, USA, Harvard Institute for International Development.

Gardner, G. & Halwell, B. 2000. *Underfed and overfed: the global epidemic of malnutrition*. Worldwatch Paper No. 150. Washington, DC, Worldwatch Institute.

Gellynck, X., Messens, W., Halet, D., Grijspeerdt, K., Hartnett, E. & Viaene, J. 2008. Economics of reducing *Campylobacter* at different levels within the Belgian poultry meat chain. *Journal of Food Protection*, 71(3): 479–485.

Gulati, A. & Dutta, M. 2009. *Rice policies in India in the context of global rice price spike*. Paper presented for the workshop Rice Policies in Asia, Chiang Mai, Thailand, 10–12 February 2009.

Hall, A. & Dijkman, J. 2008. *New global alliances: the end of development assistance?* LINK News bulletin, August 2008 (available at innovationstudies.org/index.php?option=com_docman&task=doc_download&gid=2&Itemid=9 9999999).

Hamilton, K., Sjardin, M., Marcello, T. & Xu, G. 2008. *Forging a frontier: state of the voluntary carbon markets 2008*. New York, USA, and Washington, DC, Ecosystem Market Place and New Carbon Finance.

Harkin, T. 2004. *Economic concentration and structural change in the food and agriculture sector*. Washington, DC, United States Senate.

Harris, M. 1978. *Cows, pigs, wars and witches: the riddles of culture*. New York, USA, Vintage Books.

Hartono, D. 2004. *Economic impact of AI on price and supply of poultry product*. Paper presented at the National Workshop on Post Avian Influenza Recovery, Jakarta, Indonesia, 4–5 October 2004.

Hoffman, M.T. & Vogel, C. 2008. Climate change impacts on African rangelands. *Rangelands*, 30: 12–17.

Horowitz, M. 2001. *The culture role of agriculture: scope documentation and measurement.* Paper presented at the First Expert Meeting on the Documentation and Measurement of Roles in Agriculture in Developing Countries. Rome, FAO.

Hunton, P. 1990. Industrial breeding and selection. *In* R.D. Crawford, ed. *Poultry breeding and genetics*, pp. 985–1028. Amsterdam, The Netherlands, Elsevier.

ICASEPS (Indonesian Center for Agro-socioeconomic and Policy Studies). 2008. *Livelihood and gender impact of rapid changes to bio-security policy in the Jakarta area and lessons learned for future approaches in urban areas.* Rome, ICASEPS in collaboration with FAO.

IFPRI (International Food Policy Research Institute). 2004. The changing face of malnutrition. *IFPRI FORUM, October 2004*: 1, 9–10. Washington, DC.

IFPRI. 2008. *High food prices: the what, who, and how of proposed policy actions.* Policy Brief, May 2008. Washington, DC.

IMF (International Monetary Fund). 2009. *World economic outlook. Crisis and recovery.* Washington, DC.

International Obesity Taskforce. 2009. *Global prevalence of adult obesity* (available at www.iotf.org/database/documents/ GlobalPrevalenceofAdultObesityJune2009 updateonweb.pdf).

IPCC (Intergovernmental Panel on Climate Change). 2007. *Climate change 2007: the physical science basis.* Contribution of Working Group I to the Fourth Assessment Report of the Intergovernmental Panel on Climate Change [S. Solomon, D. Qin, M. Manning, Z. Chen, M. Marquis, K.B. Averyt, M. Tignor & H.L. Miller, eds.]. Cambridge, UK, Cambridge University Press.

Johnson, J., McCabe, J., White, D., Johnston, B., Kuskowski, M. & McDermott, P. 2009. Molecular analysis of *Escherichia coli* from retail meats (2002–2004) from the United States National Antimicrobial Resistance Monitoring System. *Clinical Infectious Diseases*, 49: 195–201.

Ke, B. 1998. Area-wide integration of crop and livestock: case study – Beijing. *In* Y. Ho & Y. Chan, eds. *Proceedings of the Regional Workshop on Area-wide integration of Crop–Livestock Activities.* Bangkok, FAO.

Kennedy, G., Nantel, G. & Shetty, P. 2004. Globalization of food systems in developing countries: a synthesis of country case studies. *In* FAO. *Globalization of food systems in developing countries: impact on food security and nutrition.* FAO Food and Nutrition Paper No. 83. Rome, FAO.

King, B.S., Tietyen, J.L. & Vickner, S.S. 2000. *Consumer trends and opportunities.* Lexington, USA, University of Kentucky.

Kotter, J. 2005. *Our iceberg is melting.* London, Macmillan.

Leslie, J., Barozzi, J. & Otte, M.J. 1997. The economic implications of a change in FMD policy: a case study in Uruguay. *Épidémiologie et Santé Animale*, 31/32: 10.21.1–10.21.3.

Livestock in Development. 1999. *Livestock in poverty-focused development.* Somerset, UK, Crewkerne.

Lovett, D.K., Stack, L.J., Lovell, S., Callan, J., Flynn, B., Hawkins, M. & O'Mara, F.P. 2005. Manipulating enteric methane emissions and animal performance of late-lactation dairy cows through concentrate supplementation at pasture. *Journal of Dairy Science*, 88: 2836–2842.

Maes, E., Lecomte, P. & Ray, N. 1998. A cost-of-illness study of Lyme disease in the United States. *Clinical Therapeutics*, 20: 993–1008.

Mariner, J.C. & Roeder, P.L. 2003. Use of participatory epidemiology in studies of the persistence of lineage 2 rinderpest virus in East Africa. *The Veterinary Record*, 152(21): 641–647.

Maxwell, S. & Slater, R. 2003. Food policy old and new. *Development Policy Review*, 21(5–6): 531–553.

McKay, J.C. 2008. The genetics of modern commercial poultry. *In: Proceedings of the 23rd World's Poultry Congress, Brisbane, Australia, 30 June to 4 July 2008.* (CD-ROM). Beekbergen, The Netherlands, World's Poultry Science Association.

McMichael, A.J., Powles, J.W., Butler, C.D. & Uauy, R. 2007. Food, livestock production, energy, climate change and health. *The Lancet*, 370: 1253–1263.

MEA (Millennium Ecosystem Assessment). 2005. *Ecosystems and human well-being: synthesis.* Washington, DC, Island Press.

Mellor, P.S. & Boorman, J. 1995. The transmission and geographical spread of African horse sickness and bluetongue viruses. *Annals of*

Tropical Medicine and Parasitology, 89: 1–15.

Menzi, H., Oenema, O., Burton, C., Shipin, O., Gerber, P., Robinson, T. & Franceschini, G. 2009. Impacts of intensive livestock production and manure management on ecosystems. *In* H. Steinfeld, H. Mooney, F. Schneider & L. Neville, eds. *Livestock in a changing landscape, Vol. 1: Drivers, consequences, and responses.* Washington, DC, Island Press.

Meuwissen, M.P.M., Horst, S.H., Huirne, R.B.M. & Dijkhuizen, A.A. 1999. A model to estimate the financial consequences of classical swine fever outbreaks: principles and outcomes. *Preventive Veterinary Medicine*, 42(3–4): 249–270.

Mikkelsen, S.A, Iversen, T.M., Jacobsen, B.H. & Kjær, S.S. 2009. EU: reducing nutrient losses from intensive livestock operations. *In* P. Gerber, H. Mooney, J. Dijkman, S. Tarawali & C. de Haan, eds. *Livestock in a changing landscape, Vol. 2: Experiences and regional perspectives.* Washington, DC, Island Press.

Minjauw, B. & McLeod, A. 2003. *Tick-borne diseases and poverty. The impact of ticks and tick-borne diseases on the livelihoods of small-scale and marginal livestock owners in India and eastern and southern Africa.* Research report. Roslin, UK, DFID Animal Health Programme, Centre for Tropical Veterinary Medicine, University of Edinburgh.

NAO (National Audit Office of the UK Government). 2002. *The 2001 outbreak of foot and mouth disease. Report by the comptroller and auditor general.* HC 939 Session 2001–2002: 21 June 2002. London, The Stationery Office.

Neumann, C.G., Bwibo, N.O., Murphy, S.P., Sigman, M., Whaley, S., Allen, L.H., Guthrie, D., Weiss, R.E. & Demment, M.W. 2003. Animal source foods improve dietary quality, micronutrient status, growth and cognitive function in Kenyan school children: background, study design and baseline findings. *Journal of Nutrition*, 133: 3941S–3949S.

Nugent, R. & Knaul, F. 2006. Fiscal policies for health promotion and disease prevention. *In* D. Jamison, J. Breman, A. Measham, G. Alleyne, M. Claeson, D. Evans, P. Jha, A. Mills & P. Musgrove, eds. *Disease control priorities in developing countries*, pp. 211–223. New York, USA, Oxford University Press.

OECD–FAO (Organisation for Economic Co-operation and Development–Food and Agriculture Organization of the United Nations). 2008. *OECD–FAO Agricultural Outlook: 2008–2017.* Paris.

OECD–FAO. 2009. *OECD–FAO Agricultural Outlook: 2009–2018.* Paris.

OIE (World Organisation for Animal Health). 2008a. Zoning and compartmentalisation. *In: Terrestrial Animal Health Code 2008.* Paris.

OIE. 2008b. Animal welfare. *In: Terrestrial Animal Health Code 2008.* Paris.

PAHO (Pan American Health Organization). 2006. *Assessing the economic impact of obesity and associated chronic diseases: Latin America and the Caribbean.* Fact Sheet, April 2006. Washington, DC.

Peden, D., Tadesse, G. & Misra, A.K. 2007. Water and livestock for human development. *In* D. Molden, ed. *Water for food, water for life: a comprehensive assessment of water management in agriculture*, pp. 485–514. London, Earthscan, and Colombo, International Water Management Institute.

Pelant, R., Chandra, B., Pu, J., Lohani, N., Suknaphasawat, N. & Xu, G. 1999. Small ruminants in development: the Heifer Project International experience in Asia. *Small Ruminant Research*, 34(3): 249–257.

Pica, G., Pica-Ciamarra, U. & Otte, J. 2008. *The livestock sector in the World Development Report 2008: re-assessing the policy priorities.* PPLPI Research Report No. 08-07. Rome, Pro-Poor Livestock Policy Initiative, FAO.

Popkin, B.M. 1994. The nutrition transition in low-income countries: an emerging crisis. *Nutritional Review*, 52: 285–298.

Popkin, B.M. & Du, S. 2003. Dynamics of the nutrition transition toward the animal foods sector in China and its implications: a worried perspective. *The American Society for Nutritional Sciences*, 133: 3898S–3906S.

PPLPI (Pro-poor Livestock Policy Initiative). 2008. *Pro-poor livestock policy and institutional change: case studies from South Asia, the Andean region and West Africa.* Rome, FAO.

Pym, R.A.E. 1993. Meat genetics: conventional approaches. *In* J.S. Gavora, ed. *Proceedings of the 10th International Symposium on Current Problems of Avian Genetics*, pp. 3–16. Bratislava, Publishing House of the Slovak Technical University.

Pym, R.A.E., Farrell, D.J., Jackson, C.A.W. & Mulder, R.W.A.W. 2008. *Technological change and its impact on poultry development. A review.* SOFA 2009 background paper. Unpublished. Rome, FAO.

Quisumbing, A.R., Brown, L.R., Feldstein, H.S., Haddad, L. & Peña, C. 1995. *Women: the key* *to food security*. Food Policy Statement No. 21. Washington, DC, International Food Policy Research Institute.

Rae, A. 1998. The effects of expenditure growth and urbanisation on food consumption in East Asia: a note on animal products. *Agricultural Economics*, 18(3): 291–299.

Randolph, T.F., Schelling, E., Grace, D., Nicholson, C.F., Leroy, J.L., Cole, D.C., Demment, M.W., Omore, A., Zinsstag, J. & Ruel, M. 2007. Role of livestock in human nutrition and health for poverty reduction in developing countries. *Journal of Animal Science*, 85: 2788–2800.

Reid, R.S., Bedelian, C., Said, M.Y., Kruska, R.L., Mauricio, R.M., Vincent Castel, V., Olson, J. & Thornton, P.K. 2009. Global livestock impacts on biodiversity. *In* H. Steinfeld, H. Mooney, F. Schneider & L. Neville, eds. *Livestock in a changing landscape, Vol. 1: Drivers, consequences, and responses*. Washington, DC, Island Press.

Rosegrant, M.W. & Thornton, P.K. 2008. *Do higher meat and milk prices adversely affect poor people?* id21 insights, issue No. 72, February 2008 (available at www.id21.org/insights/insights72/art04.html).

Rowlinson, P. 2008. *Adapting livestock production systems to climate change – temperate zones*. Paper presented at Livestock and Global Climate Change conference, 17–20 May. Hammamet, Tunisia (available at www.bsas.org.uk/downloads/pp/LGCC_08_18_Rowlinson.pdf).

Royal Society of Edinburgh. 2002. *Inquiry into Foot and Mouth Disease in Scotland, July 2002* (available at www.royalsoced.org.uk/enquiries/footandmouth/fm_mw.pdf).

Sansoucy, R. 1995. Livestock – a driving force for food security and sustainable development. *World Animal Review*, 84/85 (available at www.fao.org/docrep/V8180T/v8180T07.htm#livestock%20%20%20a%20driving%20force%20for%20food%20security%20and%20sustainable%20development).

Scharff, R.L., McDowell, J. & Medeiros, L. 2009. Economic cost of foodborne illness in Ohio. *Journal of Food Protection*, 72(1): 128–136.

Schmidhuber, J. 2007. *The EU diet – evolution, evaluation and impacts of the CAP*. Paper presented at the WHO Forum on Trade and Healthy Food and Diets, Montreal, 7–13 November, 2007.

Schmidhuber, J. & Shetty, P. 2005. The nutrition transition to 2030. Why developing countries are likely to bear the major burden. *Acta Agriculturae Scandinavica, Section C Economy*, 2(3–4): 150–166.

SCN (UN Standing Committee on Nutrition). 2004. *5th report on the world nutrition situation. Nutrition for improved development outcomes*. Geneva, Switzerland.

Sidahmed, A. 2008. Livestock and climate change: coping and risk management strategies for a sustainable future. *In* P. Rowlinson, M. Steele & A. Nefzaoui, eds. *Livestock and global change*. Proceedings of an international conference, Hammamet, Tunisia, 17–20 May 2008. Cambridge, UK, Cambridge University Press.

Sones, K. & Dijkman, J. 2008. *The livestock revolution – revisited*. SOFA 2008 background paper. Unpublished. Rome, FAO.

Staal, S.J., Pratt, A.N. & Jabbar, M., eds. 2008a. *Dairy development for the resource poor. Part 1: Pakistan and India dairy development case studies*. Nairobi, International Livestock Research Institute.

Staal, S.J., Pratt, A.N. & Jabbar, M., eds. 2008b. *Dairy development for the resource poor. Part 2: Kenya and Ethiopia dairy development case studies*. Nairobi, International Livestock Research Institute.

Steinfeld, H. 1998. Livestock production in Asia and the Pacific region: current status, issues and trends. *World Animal Review*, 90 (available at www.fao.org/docrep/w8600t/w8600t04.htm#TopOfPage).

Steinfeld, H. & Opio, C. 2009. *Measuring productivity growth in the livestock sector*. SOFA 2009 background paper. Unpublished. Rome.

Steinfeld, H., de Haan, C. & Blackburn, H. 1998. Livestock and the environment, issues and options. *In* E. Lutz, ed. *Agriculture and the environment. Perspectives on sustainable development*, pp. 283–301. Washington, DC, World Bank.

Steinfeld, H., Gerber, P., Wassenaar, T., Castel, V, Rosales, M. & de Haan, C. 2006. *Livestock's long shadow. Environmental issues and options*. Rome, FAO.

Taheripour, F., Hertel, T.W. & Tyner, W.E. 2008a. *Biofuels and their by-products: global economic and environmental implications*. West Lafayette, USA, Department of Agricultural Economics, Purdue University.

Taheripour, F., Hertel, T.W. & Tyner, W.E. 2008b. *Implications of the biofuels boom for the global livestock industry: a computable general* *equilibrium analysis.* SOFA 2009 background paper. Unpublished. West Lafayette, USA, Center for Global Trade Analysis, Purdue University.

Tambi, N.E., Maina, W.O. & Ndi, C. 2006. An estimation of the economic impact of contagious bovine pleuropneumonia in Africa. *Revue Scientifique et Technique De l'Office International des Epizooties,* 25(3): 999–1012.

Tamminga, S. 2003. Pollution due to nutrient losses and its control in European animal production. *Livestock Production Science,* 84: 101–111.

The Times of India. 2005. The flesh-eater of India – a recent trend. Editorial, 25 October 2005 (available at timesofindia.indiatimes.com/ articleshow/1273309.cms).

Thirtle, C., Irz, X., Lin, L., McKenzie-Hill, V. & Wiggins, S. 2001. *Relationship between changes in agricultural productivity and the incidence of poverty in developing countries.* Report commissioned by Department for International Development. London.

Thornton, P.K., Kruska, R.L., Henninger, N., Kristjanson, P.M., Reid, R.S., Atieno, F., Odero, A.N. & Ndegwa, T. 2002. *Mapping poverty and livestock in the developing world.* A report commissioned by the UK Department for International Development, on behalf of the Inter-Agency Group of Donors Supporting Research on Livestock Production and Health in the Developing World. Nairobi, International Livestock Research Institute.

Thuy, N. 2001. *Epidemiology and economics of foot and mouth disease at the small holder level in Vietnam.* Reading, UK, Department of Agriculture, University of Reading. (MSc thesis)

Timmer, P. 1988. The agricultural transformation. *In* H. Chenery & T.N. Srinivasan, eds. *Handbook of development economics, Volume 1.* Handbooks in Economics No. 9. Amsterdam, The Netherlands, North-Holland.

Umali-Deininger, D. & Sur, M. 2007. Food safety in a globalizing world: opportunities and challenges for India. *Agricultural Economics,* 37(Suppl. 1): 135–147.

UN. 2007. World urbanization prospects. The 2007 revision population database (available at esa. un.org/unup/).

UN. 2008. World population prospects. The 2008 revision population database (available at esa. un.org/unpp/).

UNEP (United Nations Environment Programme). 2004. *Land degradation in drylands (LADA): GEF grant request.* Nairobi.

UNFCCC (United Nations Framework Convention on Climate Change). 2008. *Challenges and opportunities for mitigation in the agricultural sector.* FCC/TP/2008/8. Bonn, Germany.

UN Millennium Project. 2004. *Halving hunger by 2015: a framework for action.* Interim Report. Task Force on Hunger. New York, USA, Millennium Project.

USDA (United States Department of Agriculture). 2005. *High-pathogenicity avian influenza: a threat to U.S. poultry.* Program Aid No. 1836. Riverdale, USA, Animal and Plant Health Inspection Service (available at www.aphis. usda.gov/publications/animal_health/content/ printable_version/USA_AvianInFluenzanewweb. pdf).

USITC (United States International Trade Commission). 2008. *Global beef trade: effects of animal health, sanitary, food safety, and other measures on US beef exports.* USITC Investigation No. 332-488. Publication 4033. Washington, DC.

VCS (Voluntary Carbon Standard). 2008. *VCS guidance for agriculture, forestry and other land use projects.* Washington, DC, Voluntary Carbon Standard.

Wassenaar, T., Gerber, P., Verburg, P.H., Rosales, M., Ibrahim, M. & Steinfeld, H. 2006. Projecting land use changes in the neotropics. The geography of pasture expansion into forest. *Global Environmental Change,* 17(1): 86–104.

Waters-Bayer, A. 1995. *Living with livestock in town: urban animal husbandry and human welfare.* Leusden, The Netherlands, ETC International.

WCRF/AICR (World Cancer Research Fund / American Institute for Cancer Research). 2007. *Food, nutrition, physical activity, and the prevention of cancer: a global perspective.* Washington, DC, AICR.

White, R.P., Murray, S. & Rohweder, M. 2000. *Pilot analysis of global ecosystems: grassland ecosystems.* Washington, DC, World Resources Institute.

WHO (World Health Organization). 2005. *International Health Regulations (2005).* Second edition. Geneva. Switzerland.

WHO. 2006. *Obesity swallows rising share of GDP in Europe: up to 1% and counting* (available at www.euro.who.int/mediacentre/ PR/2006/20061101_5).

WHO/FAO. 2003. *Diet, nutrition, and the prevention of chronic disease.* Report of a joint WHO/FAO Expert Consultation. WHO Technical Report Series 916. Geneva, Switzerland, World Health Organization.

World Bank. 2006a. *Repositioning nutrition as central to development: a strategy for large-scale action*. Directions for Development. Washington, DC.

World Bank. 2006b. *Enhancing agricultural innovation: how to go beyond the strengthening of research systems*. Economic Sector Work Report. Washington, DC.

World Bank. 2007. *World Development Report 2008*. Washington, DC.

World Bank. 2008a. *Rising food prices: policy options and World Bank response*. Washington, DC.

World Bank. 2008b. *Implementation completion results report for the Regional Integrated Silvopastoral Ecosystem Management Project*. Washington, DC.

Yalcin, C. 2006. *The Turkish situation*. Paper presented at the Symposium on Market and Trade Dimensions of Avian Influenza Prevention and Control, held in conjunction with the 21st Session of the Intergovernmental Group on Meat and Dairy Products, Rome, Italy, 14 November 2006 (available at www.fao.org/es/ESC/en/20953/21014/21574/event_109566en.htm).

Zhang, C. *et al*. 2004. *China's livestock industry in transition: trends and policy adjustment*. Report prepared as part of the ACIAR/MLA Project: Analysis of Socio-economic and Agribusiness Developments in the Chinese Cattle and Beef Industry. Brisbane, Australia, University of Queensland.

Special chapters of
The State of Food and Agriculture

In addition to the usual review of the recent world food and agricultural situation, each issue of this report since 1957 has included one or more special studies on problems of longer-term interest. Special chapters in earlier issues have covered the following subjects:

1957 Factors influencing the trend of food consumption
Postwar changes in some institutional factors affecting agriculture

1958 Food and agricultural developments in Africa south of the Sahara
The growth of forest industries and their impact on the world's forests

1959 Agricultural incomes and levels of living in countries at different stages of economic development
Some general problems of agricultural development in less-developed countries in the light of postwar experience

1960 Programming for agricultural development

1961 Land reform and institutional change
Agricultural extension, education and research in Africa, Asia and Latin America

1962 The role of forest industries in the attack on economic underdevelopment
The livestock industry in less-developed countries

1963 Basic factors affecting the growth of productivity in agriculture
Fertilizer use: spearhead of agricultural development

1964 Protein nutrition: needs and prospects
Synthetics and their effects on agricultural trade

1966 Agriculture and industrialization
Rice in the world food economy

1967 Incentives and disincentives for farmers in developing countries
The management of fishery resources

1968 Raising agricultural productivity in developing countries through technological improvement
Improved storage and its contribution to world food supplies

1969 Agricultural marketing improvement programmes: some lessons from recent experience
Modernizing institutions to promote forestry development

1970 Agriculture at the threshold of the Second Development Decade

1971 Water pollution and its effects on living aquatic resources and fisheries

1972 Education and training for development
Accelerating agricultural research in the developing countries

1973 Agricultural employment in developing countries

1974 Population, food supply and agricultural development

1975 The Second United Nations Development Decade: mid-term review and appraisal

1976 Energy and agriculture

1977 The state of natural resources and the human environment for food and agriculture

1978 Problems and strategies in developing regions

1979 Forestry and rural development

1980 Marine fisheries in the new era of national jurisdiction

1981 Rural poverty in developing countries and means of poverty alleviation

1982 Livestock production: a world perspective

1983 Women in developing agriculture

1984 Urbanization, agriculture and food systems

166

1985 Energy use in agricultural production
Environmental trends in food and agriculture
Agricultural marketing and development

1986 Financing agricultural development

1987–88 Changing priorities for agricultural science and technology
in developing countries

1989 Sustainable development and natural resource management

1990 Structural adjustment and agriculture

1991 Agricultural policies and issues: lessons from the 1980s and prospects
for the 1990s

1992 Marine fisheries and the law of the sea: a decade of change

1993 Water policies and agriculture

1994 Forest development and policy dilemmas

1995 Agricultural trade: entering a new era?

1996 Food security: some macroeconomic dimensions

1997 The agroprocessing industry and economic development

1998 Rural non-farm income in developing countries

2000 World food and agriculture: lessons from the past 50 years

2001 Economic impacts of transboundary plant pests and animal diseases

2002 Agriculture and global public goods ten years after the Earth Summit

2003–04 Agricultural biotechnology: meeting the needs of the poor?

2005 Agriculture trade and poverty: can trade work for the poor?

2006 Food aid for food security?

2007 Paying farmers for environmental services

2008 Biofuels: prospects, risks and opportunities